A
TREASURY
of
AMERICAN-
JEWISH
FOLKLORE

A
TREASURY
of
AMERICAN-
JEWISH
FOLKLORE

LION KOPPMAN
STEVE KOPPMAN

JASON ARONSON INC.
Northvale, New Jersey
Jerusalem

First Jason Aronson Inc. softcover edition—1998

This book was set in 10 pt. Stempel Schneidler by Alabama Book Compositon Deatsville, AL.

Library of Congress Cataloging-in-Publication Data

Koppman, Steve.
    A treasury of American-Jewish folklore / Steve Koppman, Lion Koppman.
        p. cm.
    Includes bibliographical references.
    ISBN 1-56821-620-3 (hardcover)
    ISBN 0-7657-6024-x (softcover)
    1. Jews—United States—Anecdotes. 2. Jews—United States—Folklore. 3. Jewish wit and humor. 4. United States—Ethnic relations I. Koppman, Lionel. II. Title.
E184.J5K774 1996
305.892'4073—dc20

96-941

Manufactured in the United States of America. Jason Aronson Inc. offers books and cassettes. For information and catalog write to Jason Aronson Inc., 230 Livingston Street, Northvale, New Jersey 07647.

To Mae,
Hana,
and
Sharon

Contents

Acknowledgments

Special thanks for their aid in the preparation of this book are due to the Memorial Foundation for Jewish Culture, for a research grant; the late Dr. Jacob R. Marcus, eminent historian and former director of the American Jewish Archives, for his generosity in allowing us to draw freely from his books, essays, monographs and other works; anthropologist and folklorist Nathan Hurvitz for his material on the street rhymes of Jewish children and the relationship between black and Jewish folklore; the late Samuel Asofsky for his collection of Yiddish folk expressions and to the YIVO Institute for Scientific Research; the Yeshiva University Museum; the San Francisco Jewish Community Library and Joey Liebman, formerly of that library; Dr. Ellen Frankel; the American Jewish Historical Society, *Jewish Currents*, Moses Rischin, Atheneum Publishers, *Western States Jewish Historical Quarterly*, and the Jewish Publication Society, for permissions to reprint; Mae Koppman for her valuable suggestions for improving the manuscript and for her encouragement; and Brenda Blau and Jean Cullen for typing portions of the manuscript.

INTRODUCTION

B. A. Botkin, one of America's most eminent folklorists and author of *A Treasury of American Folklore*, said, "When one thinks of American folklore, one thinks not only of the folklore of American life—the traditions that have sprung up on American soil—but also of the literature of folklore—the migratory traditions that have found a home here." The very same can be said about American-Jewish folklore. There are Jewish tales, anecdotes, jokes and customs that could have developed only in America. At the same time, there are traditions that have traveled here from other places and been transformed in their American environment.

Folklore is made up of the stories, anecdotes, recollections, sayings, jokes, beliefs, superstitions, customs and songs of a people that have been handed down so long they have a life of their own. They travel from person to person and region to region and become "classic." They are patterned by common experience, varied by individual repetition, and cherished because they are somehow characteristic or expressive. Folklore is not history and it is not biography, although some of it is about people who lived and what others remember or heard about them.

In its purest form, folklore is associated with the "grapevine." Virtually every story, every folk belief, every song has variations, since it has been passed orally from person to person and, in the retelling, inevitably changed and embellished.

Folklore includes the archetypal and the atypical, the character who is strikingly different and therefore legendary, and the character so representative of his community at that time and place that he epitomizes it and becomes legendary.

American-Jewish folklore is an expression of the land, the people, and their experiences. Since 1654—more than 340 years ago—when a handful of refugees found a grudging haven in New Amsterdam, American Jews as a community have undergone many profound changes. Since they started coming from Eastern Europe by the hundreds of thousands in the late nineteenth century, they have evolved from an immigrant, generally low-income and embattled group to an overwhelmingly native-born, educated, predominantly middle-class community, accepted as an inseparable part of the nation's fabric.

As Botkin says, we become estranged from the folklore of the past, which we cannot help feeling a little self-conscious about, without yet being able to fully appreciate folklore in the making. Yet each period has developed a literature about the folk, ranging from anecdotes, old-timers' reminiscences and homespun humor to local color and sketches.

In some respects, American-Jewish folklore is singular and unlike other peoples' folklore. There are no folk tales about animals, witches, ghosts or devils. There are few tall yarns. There are no mythical folk heroes, although there are folk heroes who once lived. On the other hand, American-Jewish folklore has its share of boosters and knockers, trailblazers and eccentrics, rogues and fighters, wise men and fools, folk beliefs and superstitions, riddles and rhymes, customs and sayings, folk humor, anecdotes, ballads and folk songs reflecting the American-Jewish experience.

Botkin noted too how folklore perpetuates ignorance as well as wisdom. For example, negative attitudes that some Christians held about Jews in earlier times were unwittingly repeated and spread by Jews themselves. Nowhere is this more evident than in street rhymes making fun of Jews, chanted by Jewish children, who typically didn't have the faintest notion of their original meaning.

This book includes anecdotes, jokes, sketches of legendary figures—the bits and pieces of American-Jewish life that are "classic" in the folkloristic sense—that provide a characteristic glimpse, that capture something significant or memorable of the development and experience of the Jewish community in America over the past 340 years.

Any work of this kind is inherently selective, both the boundaries and selection of folklore of necessity subjective. Our view is that folklore by its nature is not new or recent; folklore does not become folklore until long after the events referred to first occur. It has to become part of legend, tradition, collective memory beyond the individual memories of those who directly experience it, and to mutate into different versions over time, told not only from person to person but generation to generation. For this reason, relatively little material from recent decades has been included here.

Much of the material will be familiar to readers old enough to have heard it from their parents or grandparents; for others, it will be quite new. In either case, it is an attempt to capture and preserve the wisdom, insights, laughter, tears and daily living of those who have gone before us.

1

JEWS AMONG THE INDIANS

Some of the earliest American-Jewish folklore reflects the relatively little-known saga of Jews among the American Indians. There were Jewish peddlers who took part in the opening of the West and assimilated with Indian communities, living out their lives on reservations. Some of them took up with Indian women and were absorbed into Indian tribes. It is still possible to find Jewish names on Indian reservations in the Southwest.

There were Jews who made their living trading with the Indians, establishing trading posts and traveling great distances to sell or exchange their wares. Many Christian Americans, on the other hand, were convinced that the American Indians were descendants of the Ten Lost Tribes of Israel and went to great lengths to prove their thesis. One of the most famous believers in this theory was William Penn, who visited the Quaker colony in West Jersey in 1681 and described the Indians there as closely resembling Jews.

Scrupulous honesty and friendship in trading with Indians made Morris Simpson, pioneer Jewish settler in Oklahoma, a widely popular figure. Quanah Parker, last chief of the Comanches, who lived on the outskirts of what became Lawton, Oklahoma, named one of his sons for Simpson "in honor of my good white friend."

Lewis Gomez and his son Daniel built a stone house near Newburgh, New York, between 1717 and 1720 as a combined Indian trading post, fortress and home. The Gomez House stands in a hollow of the famous Devil's Dance Chamber, where Indians used to gather for ceremonial rites.

The Jew, as trader or peddler, was typically the Indians' peaceful link to the white settlers. Some Jews became Indian scouts. Like other pioneers, Jews were also in militias that fought the Indians. There were individual Jews who were captured; some were freed, others tortured and killed. Francis Salvador, then fighting in the new American army against Britain, was found in the bushes of the South Carolina countryside by Indians and scalped, ironically the first Jewish casualty of the American Revolution.

The following is a more elaborate sampling of stories of individual Jews among the Indians.

'Navajo Sam' and Billy the Kid

One of the first white men to learn the Navajo language was Sam Dittenhoefer, who came to New Mexico in the 1860s. He was known as 'Navajo Sam' because he lived for a time on a Navajo reservation. While Indians were being cheated and robbed by many whites, 'Navajo Sam' earned their friendship by fair dealing.

In Santa Fe, Sam found a job as clerk for Spiegelberg Brothers. In the summer of 1877, he went to Chihuahua to pick up 25,000 Mexican silver dollars owed the Spiegelbergs. He knew he would have to cross territory where Billy the Kid operated. Sam had known Billy before the latter became a highway bandit, and he wasn't about to take more chances than he had to.

Sam packed the silver into six large flour barrels, each with double heads and bottoms. The spaces were filled with flour and the coins wrapped in paper to keep them from jingling. Each barrel was then prominently labeled "Mexican Flour" and loaded on a wagon beside which 'Navajo Sam' rode on horseback.

Passing through a narrow canyon, Sam ran into the dreaded outlaw. As Billy came closer, he recognized Sam.

"Hi, Sam. What in hell are you doing so far from Santa Fe?"

"Just taking some Mexican flour back there for the wives of my employers, the Spiegelberg Brothers."

The cowboy-turned-bandit struck one of the barrels with his gun butt.

"I've a good mind to help myself to a few pounds of this flour. I haven't had a slice of real homemade bread since I was a boy."

Navajo Sam thought fast.

"Aw, Billy, you wouldn't break open the ladies' flour just for a few pounds for yourself?"

Billy glared at Sam, then smiled.

"Okay, kid, you win, this time," he said, and rode off.

Sam's favorite pastime from them on was regaling his friends with the tale of his face-to-face encounter with Billy the Kid and how he managed to outwit the notorious outlaw.

Immigrant to Indian Chief

Solomon Bibo, an immigrant from Prussia, married an Indian squaw and learned to speak the Queres dialect, a feat achieved by few white men.

He came to New Mexico to work for his brothers at a trading post. Solomon became deeply involved in the affairs of the Indians, particularly the Acomans, a remarkable accomplishment as this tribe was known for its suspicion of whites.

The Acomans had been fighting for years to regain lands taken from them. The government had given the Acomans 95,000 acres for a reservation, but the tribe was not satisfied. Using his ability to speak Queres, Bibo helped the Acomans fight their case in court, and they were able to get the government to investigate their grievance.

Bibo was granted a license to open his own trading post among the Indians. In an Indian ceremony, he married Juana Valle, the granddaughter of the pueblo's chief and became a member of the pueblo. Later, the Acoma tribe named Bibo its chief. An editor wrote that Bibo "has done more for his pueblo than all the Indian agents in a lump."

In 1885, Bibo moved his trading post to the village of Cubero, just outside the Acoma reservation. Here four of his six children were born. All were raised as Jews. Later the Bibos moved to California, where they lived out their lives.

"Box-Ka-Re-Sha-Hash-Ta-Ka"

Fourteen-year-old Julius Meyer came to the frontier town of Omaha to join his brothers Max and Moritz. With trinkets from Max's store and cigars rolled by Moritz, Julius traded with the Indians and became a close friend of many tribal chiefs. He learned several Indian languages—the Omaha, Ponca, Sioux, Winnebago, Pawnee and Ogallala—served as a government interpreter, and was adopted by the Pawnees.

On his long trading trips—sometimes on foot, sometimes on horseback—Julius lived with Indians in their tepees and wigwams. He traded what he had for furs, beads, moccasins and wampum pouches.

Julius narrowly escaped with his life on more than one occasion. Once he was returning from a trading trip with a lot of merchandise when he came upon a band of drunken Indians. A huge Indian approached the youthful trader, grabbed his pack, and started pushing him around. Julius leaped into the air and landed a right on the big Indian's chin, sending him to the ground. The other Indians were so amazed they let Julius go free.

Another time, Julius found himself surrounded by another band of unfriendly Indians. The Indians seized his pack, bound him, and were about to scalp him when Pawnee chief Standing Bear stepped in to save the young trader's life. His friendship with this Indian chief lasted a lifetime.

To the Indians, Julius was known as "Box-ka-re-sha-hash-ta-ka," which means "curly-haired white chief with one tongue." The Indians believed that Julius was honest and meant what he said. His business cards listed his specialties as "tomahawks, bows, and arrows, petrifications, beadwork and photographs of buffalo robes."

As an indication of the Indians' high regard and trust for Julius, he was often guest of honor at Sioux dog feasts. Because Julius kept kosher, he had to decline the dog. The Indians offered him hard-boiled eggs instead.

The magician Herman the Great went with Julius on one trading trip. Around a campfire, Herman entertained the Indians by drawing gold pieces from a silk hat. After the magician had gone to bed, the Indians crept into his tent to steal what they thought was a magic hat. Herman might have been scalped. But Julius, a light sleeper, awakened just in the nick of time. The Indians didn't get the hat, but they forced Herman to show them exactly how the trick was done.

"The Indian Wigwam" was the name of the curio shop Julius operated in Omaha. The Wigwam was the headquarters for his Indian friends. Julius lived alone above the Wigwam for more than forty years.

One time Julius brought four Indian chiefs together to pose for a picture. When the Indians saw a photographer with a black cloth over his head fingering a box on a three-legged stand, they were frightened and insisted Julius stand by their side to protect them from the "magic box."

One day, Julius was found in a public park with a bullet in his heart. The mystery of his death is still unsolved.

Ute with a Yiddish Accent

Lithuanian-born Otto Mears served under Kit Carson in the Civil War. After being mustered out in 1864, he settled at Conejos in Colorado's San Luis Valley, where he became friendly with Indians, including Chief Ouray of the Utes.

Mears was a plug-hatted, bewhiskered character who spoke the Ute Indian language with a Yiddish accent. His friendship with the Utes helped him to persuade them, with the aid of gold, to move peaceably from Colorado to Utah.

Trailblazer and pioneer road builder, Mears hacked out one of Colorado's first toll roads at Poncha Pass in 1875. The road became part of a 300-mile network of highways Mears built to open southwest Colorado to miners, ranchers and settlers.

When Mears was past 70, he saved the residents of Silverton from starvation by organizing a group to repair a washed-out roadbed before the onset of winter blizzards. He died in California in 1931.

"Old Mordecai"

Abraham Mordecai was known as the most colorful character of the early days of Alabama Jewry. Much of his life was spent among the Indians, who he was convinced were descended from the Ten Lost Tribes of Israel. He attended an Indian ceremony where the Indians chanted "Yavohoya, Yavohoya." To Mordecai's ears, it sounded like "Jehovah, Jehovah." The Indians told him it meant the Great Spirit and that they were giving thanks for the harvest with which they were blessed. Mordecai never gave up hope that one day an Indian would give a Hebrew answer to his Hebrew questions and prove his theory.

Using pack ponies, 'Old Mordecai' penetrated the wilderness and traded with the Indians. Once he visited the Creek tribal chiefs to arrange for the ransom of captive settlers. For twenty years, he dealt in skins, hickory-nut oil, pink root and furs. He would ship these in canoes to New Orleans, Mobile and other places. The hickory-nut oil was considered a special delicacy by the Spaniards, and the Spanish governor of New Orleans bought huge supplies.

Not all the Indians were Mordecai's friends, and once some cut off his ear. Some say it happened this way:

Two of Mordecai's horses strolled into the low grounds, opposite Coosawda, and ate some corn belonging to the Indians of that town. Chief Towerculla of Coosawda never had liked Mordecai living so close to him. The white man's corn-eating horses gave the Indian the excuse to drive Mordecai off. Together with sixteen of his warriors, each armed with a long hickory pole, Towerculla surrounded Mordecai's house.

Mordecai offered to pay for his horses' sins. The chief wouldn't listen. Instead, he struck Mordecai. Mordecai grabbed Towerculla around the waist and tried to throw him over the bluff. The other warriors ran to the chief's rescue and threw Mordecai to the ground. They thrashed him with their poles and cut off his ear.

Another version of the story is that Towerculla learned Mordecai had been fooling around with a married Indian squaw. The chief led twelve warriors to Mordecai's house, pinned him down, and thrashed him until he was unconscious. Then they cut off his ear.

Mordecai married an Indian woman after the American Revolution, in which he fought as a soldier in General Floyd's militia. He was forced to separate from his wife when the government ordered the Creek Indians westward.

'Old Mordecai' died in his late nineties, in a lonely hut in Dudleyville, beside a coffin that had served as his eating table most of his life.

The Magic Name of Franks

In the village of Wagontown, Pennsylvania, on the Old King's Highway, is a spot where, according to folklore, the name of Franks saved the lives of young people of the elite families of Lancaster in 1757. En route to a high society affair—a dance of the Assembly at the State House in Philadelphia—the group was ambushed by Canadian Mohawks at the ford of the Brandywine River. While asking the names of those being taken captive,

> the magic name of Franks was uttered. . . . . A gleam of human kindness came into the eyes of Le Loup Blanc, the hardened war chief. "If this party is composed of people of the blood of the Franks and Gratzes . . . you are paroled and may return to Hickory Town," the chief told the scared youngsters.

Hickory Town was the name the Indians had given to Lancaster, Pennsylvania. The mention of the name Franks, who had dealt fairly with the Indians, stopped what might have been an Indian raid on Philadelphia and saved from capture a substantial number of the younger set of Lancaster society.

Wild Man of the Frontier

At the start of the Indian War of 1763, Chapman Abraham, a Jewish trader, was captured by Chippewa Indians on the Detroit River and marked for death. A Frenchman who was his friend spirited Abraham away from the Indians and hid him. But Abraham's hiding place was revealed, and the Indians took him across the river to be tortured and burned.

Abraham was tied to the stake. A fire was kindled at his side. He grew so thirsty from the heat that he begged the Indians to give him something to drink. Instead, the Indians gave their prisoner a bowl of pottage as his "last meal."

Eager to quench his thirst, Abraham put the bowl to his lips. The pottage was so hot it scalded his mouth. In a reflex motion, Abraham threw the bowl back full in the face of the man who had given it to him.

"He is mad! He is mad!" the Indians shouted. They untied the ropes that bound him and set him free.

"Jacob and the Indians," by Stephen Vincent Benét, was based on this incident.

He Got the Grand Canyon in a Trade

An early Arizona prospector, Solomon Barth was an Indian trader, Pony Express rider, miner and gambler. He worked for Michael Goldwater in La Paz, Arizona in 1862. Later, he won a contract to carry mail between Prescott and Albuquerque, New Mexico. He was captured by the Apaches, stripped, and threatened with torture. When he was set free, he walked barefoot to a friendly nearby Zuni village. Folklore has it that Barth entered into an agreement with Indian chiefs for the transfer of ownership of the Grand Canyon.

The town of St. Johns on the Coronado Trail was founded by Barth in 1874, when he won several thousand sheep and a large sum of money in a card game. Barth named the town for its first woman resident, Señora Maria San Juan de Padilla de Baca.

He served in two state legislatures and was a county treasurer. When he died in 1928, flags were flown at half-mast throughout the state. His brother Nathan was the first sheriff of Apache County.

"Bosh-Bish-Gay-Bish-Gonsen"

Edward Kanter was penniless and friendless when he arrived in New Orleans from his native Germany and nearly died of the yellow fever. Nursed back to health, he made his way by peddling cigars and clerking in a drugstore. He had to leave town in a hurry when he accidentally blew up the shop in a chemical experiment.

Kanter shipped out as a waiter on a Red River steamboat and survived an explosion that sank the vessel. After swimming ashore, he reached St. Louis and got another job on a boat to Pekin, Illinois, and from there, walked to Chicago. Shipping out on a steamer on the Great Lakes, he reached Detroit in 1844 and headed for Mackinac. After working as a clerk and interpreter, Kanter went into business for himself.

Quick at languages, he mastered the Huron, Chippewa and Pottawat-omie tongues and became good friends with the Indians. Because of Kanter's hustling and bustling, the Indians called him "Bosh-bish-gay-bish-gonsen," which means "firecracker."

Powwow at Levy's

Four years after the village of La Crosse, Wisconsin, was first occupied by whites in 1841, John and Augusta Levy arrived on the Mississippi River steamboat *Berlin* with a horse, dog, two cats, a family of hogs and a raccoon. There were then only a few rough shanties huddling on the riverfront, and the total white population consisted of nine men and four women. Levy became a close friend of the local Indians, who once held a powwow in his house. When the federal government sought in 1848 to move the Winnebagos west of the Mississippi, they engaged Levy as their agent in fighting the edict.

A powwow at Levy's house was called by the Indians to resist the removal order. Winnebago chiefs, dressed and painted, feathers on their heads and tomahawks in their hands, arrived in about fifty canoes.

Mrs. Levy didn't know about the powwow and was frightened half to death. The Indians knocked and knocked but she would not open the door. She shut the windows, locked the doors, and hid her son and herself in a dark room. Then she heard someone pounding and kicking the door, trying to break it in. Levy came around to the kitchen window and called Augusta's name.

"Open the doors quickly, in Heaven's name!" said Levy. "What did you lock yourself in for?"

"Didn't you see the Indians at the front door to kill us?" Augusta asked.

"If you don't open the doors quick, I'll kick them in!"

The Indian chiefs then came into the dining room, sat down on the floor, had a smoke, and proceeded with their powwow. They got Levy to write to Washington to ask the government to withdraw the order.

But the request was refused, and the Winnebago had to leave the country.

Until they moved from around La Crosse to Minnesota, Levy was a successful trader. Although the Indians and merchants sought to prevail upon him to follow them to Minnesota, Levy cast his lot with La Crosse.

Levy built La Crosse's first hotel, wharf boat and dock and speculated in real estate. The panic of 1857 bankrupted him, but he remained one of the town's leading citizens, serving eight terms as alderman, one as tax assessor, and three as mayor.

A.K.A. Señor Nogales

San Francisco merchant Jacob Isaacson had reached Arizona's "last frontier." He went deep into the interior of the Santa Cruz Valley and traded with the Indians. They never harmed him although it was during the height of Indian warfare, and the white man was the intruder. Years later, he said:

> Always there existed the awful dread that [the Apaches] would come in the dead of the night, or with the rising of the sun, and find me unprepared to fight for my life. More than one visit did I receive from them, but I always managed to get away with my life. . . . It was lonely in those times—yes, very, very lonely. On some days there would be little or no travel, and at night I had only the stars to keep me company.

The little settlement that had grown up around his training post was named for him. In 1883, during President Garfield's administration, Isaacson was appointed postmaster of the town of Isaacson. Later, the town was renamed Nogales for the *nogales*, or wild walnut trees, that grew on the original site, and Isaacson, presumably because of his toughness, was also known as "Señor Nogales."

2

PIONEERS AND TRAILBLAZERS

Many contemporary American Jews, descendants of immigrants from the Great Migration from Eastern Europe, don't realize that the first significant community of Jews in the United States were Sephardim—many of them 'Marranos' (secret Jews), refugees from Inquisition persecution in Spain and Portugal. So deeply ingrained, it is said, were Marrano customs in the Newport, Rhode Island, Sephardic community of the eighteenth century that it was normal to see Jewish women on the street counting their Jewish daily prayers on necklaces of rosary beads.

The first synagogue building in the United States was the Sephardic Touro Synagogue in Newport, built by this early group of Sephardim in the 1760s. Aaron 'Duarte' Lopez was one of the prominent members of this community, and probably the wealthiest Jew in the American colonies at this time, having lived in Portugal with his family as an apparent Christian (as had his family before him for centuries) before fleeing in 1752 to Newport, where a half brother had settled.

On arriving in the New World, Duarte took the name Aaron; he was circumcised, and he and his wife remarried in a Jewish ceremony. He tried to make a living through maritime commerce, as did many Newport Jews, dealing at first mainly with whale spermaceti for candles, whaling and fishery.

At first he had little luck, but over the years he grew very wealthy; by the 1770s he owned thirty ships. He met with heavy losses during the American Revolution, when part of his fleet was captured and taken to Britain.

When he tried to become a citizen of Rhode Island in 1761, his petition was denied, a court ruling that only Christians could become full citizens of the colony. Massachusetts, however, accepted Lopez, although he continued living in Newport until the Revolution, when he was forced by a British advance to flee to Leicester, Massachusetts.

When the Revolutionary War had ended and Lopez was returning to Newport from Leicester, he drowned en route. Folklore has it that about five miles outside Providence, he stopped to water his horse. Suddenly the animal stepped out of its depth and plunged into the pond. Lopez was flung forward. He could not swim and drowned.

Cohen and Isaacs and
Daniel Boone

Daniel Boone, the pioneer who blazed the Wilderness Trail, was commissioned by Isaiah Isaacs and Jacob I. Cohen in the 1780s to locate some land for them; they gave him six pounds gold specie as an advance payment.

After Boone signed the receipt for the land warrants and cash, a brief description of the contents was scrawled on the back of the document in American Yiddish: "Resit fun Kornel Bon for 10,000 agir lanit" ("Receipt of Colonel Boone for 10,000 acres land").

Cohen and Isaacs later commissioned Boone to survey other lands for them, this time on the Licking River in Kentucky.

Boone did his job and presented his bill for a little more than twenty-two pounds specie. "Send the money by the first opertunety," the frontiersman wrote. "Mr. Samuel Grant, my sister's sun, will lykly hand you this letter. If so, he will be a good hand to send by, and I will be accountable for any money put into his hands inless kild by the Indins."

❁

People who had never before seen a Jew came as far as a hundred miles to look at Joseph Jonas when he reached Cincinnati in March 1817, after journeying by wagon over the mountains to Pittsburgh and then by flatboat down the ice-flecked Ohio River.

"Art thou a Jew?" an old Quaker woman asked him.

"Yes," Jonas answered.

"Thou art one of God's chosen people," she said. "Wilt thou let me examine thee?"

Jonas consented. After turning him around and around, she exclaimed in disappointment, "Thou are no different to other people!"

Jonas was the first professing Jew to settle in Ohio.

Mr. Texas

Jacob De Cordova was a descendant of Spanish knights. He followed the Texas Revolution with keen interest and rejoiced when he learned the new republic welcomed Jews as well as Christians. He saw the recently-written Texas Declaration of Independence and was moved to read the Texans were rebelling against "the combined despotism of the sword and the priesthood."

He arrived in Galveston in 1837, and within a few weeks became a naturalized citizen of Texas. He engaged in a variety of business ventures and officiated as *hazzan* (reader) for Jewish religious services held in various homes. (He moved to Houston, where he became a leading merchant and helped that city become the main trading center for the half of Texas east of the Brazos River. But the tubercular De Cordova's health deteriorated, and a doctor warned him his only chance for life was a long stay in the high, dry, almost uninhabited areas west of the Brazos.

De Cordova set out toward the wilderness, traveling beyond Austin to where the last faint traces of white civilization gradually faded into unmapped Indian hunting grounds. As he rode seemingly endless miles, De Cordova understood the shape of his future career; he would bring people to Texas.

In 1846, Texas gave up its independence to become the twenty-eighth state of the Union. The new state, twice the size of Germany, had far fewer people than tiny Rhode Island. De Cordova opened a land and emigration agency that concentrated on bringing families to the vast spaces of the new state. He published the first descriptive map of Texas.

On a platform of "More Families for Texas," he was elected in 1847 to the second state Legislature convening in Austin. Governor Peter Bell invited De Cordova to move his agency to the state capital. Within a few months, it became the largest land agency that ever operated in the American Southwest.

De Cordova embarked on an extensive program of advertising, marketing and publicity to persuade people to "Come to Texas." A prime selling point: "Come where your children can get a start on rich land that can be bought at a poor man's price." Throughout Texas, thriving settlements rose on once desolate sites.

De Cordova founded the town of Waco, which became a trading center of both the cotton and cattle belts. To each Christian denomination in Waco, he deeded a free lot for a church. He helped organize the state's first synagogue in Houston and was called to read the Torah wherever he visited his former community. A number of Jews followed De Cordova to Waco and helped him develop it commercially and culturally.

De Cordova invested his money in bringing Texas its first railroads after prophesying the ox-drawn wagons would vanish entirely "when the snort of the iron horse shall awaken the solitude of the prairies."

Until the Civil War, De Cordova was the acknowledged "Mr. Texas"— his state's leading land developer and its unofficial ambassador to the outside world. After Texas seceded from the Union, settlers stopped coming. Those who had settled couldn't ship their cotton to Europe or make their installment payments on land purchases.

De Cordova could have foreclosed on many of them: he said instead, "If I share good times with them, I have to share the hard times, too."

He went bankrupt. His health collapsed. He died in 1868 on a little ranch west of Waco. Jacob De Cordova had explored more Texas territory than its first European discoverer, Cabeza de Vaca; he brought more settlers into Texas than did Stephen F. Austin, its first American colonizer.

God-Fearing Guards

Long ago a High Holiday service was scheduled in the Brownsville, Texas, Masonic Hall, and a Mr. Marx north of the border asked his brother-in-law, a Mr. Cain, who lived in the Mexican border town of Matamoros, to bring Torah scrolls. It was about a mile between the two communities on opposite sides of the Rio Grande River. When Mr. Cain came to the customs house on his side of the river, he wanted to register the scrolls so there would be no question that he would be allowed to return with them when he returned to Matamoros. But the Mexican border guards wouldn't approach the scrolls and moved away from Cain in fear, saying they were afraid to touch the Jewish God.

Pioneer Advertiser

Isaac A. Isaacs was an early Cleveland haberdasher who went into business in 1845, ·claiming "the largest and most magnificent clothing wear house in the western country." He also acquired exclusive local rights to sell Singer's Sewing Machines, "Strong's Patent Army Trunk and Bed Combined," and other products. One announcement stated modestly in 1855:

> On entering the tenth year of our establishment in Cleveland, we have many causes for congratulation. We congratulate the public on the perfection which we have attained in the manufacture of ready made clothing . . . and in confirmation of our assertion you have merely to contrast the appearance of the people of the present day with the dress of the same community ten years ago on the advent of Isaac A. Isaacs in Cleveland.

One of Isaacs' poetic ads reads:

I have only one objection,
  Said a maiden to her lover;
I have only one objection
  To the matters you propose;
I would no longer tarry,.
  I am ready now to marry;
But I cannot wed a lover
  In those unwelcome clothes. . . .
He went back unto his charmer,
  With a suit of Isaacs' latest,
And the maiden, filled with rapture,
  In his open arms did fall. . . .

Another, which appeared during the panic of 1857, took a different tack:

Give the producing classes help;
  Sustain the men of toil;

Avoiding those who rob the till,
   Aid those who till the soil. . . .
You have no cause to be alarmed,
   Except about your diet,
If you should want a suit of Clothes,
   A little cash will buy it. . . .

Family Tragedy

When Benjamin II of Tudela, noted Jewish world traveler and adventurer, visited the Mother Lode country of California in the 1850s, he picked up this then-current and foreboding story of two brothers who refused to contribute toward a Jewish cemetery:

In the town of Mokelumne Hill, the Mayer brothers were the wealthiest of the community's thirty Jews, but they refused to pay their share for a communal burial ground, caustically saying they had no intention of staying there. No sooner did the rest of the community buy the cemetery than two-year-old Emma, daughter of Fredrick Mayer, one of the brothers, died.

Fredrick asked permission to bury the child in the Jewish cemetery and was turned down. He then arranged for her burial in the nearby Protestant cemetery and voiced public satisfaction in doing so. On returning home from the interment, Fredrick's remaining child, one-year-old Luisa, suddenly took sick and died the next day. Distraught, Fredrick offered the Jewish community a large sum if he could bury his second child in its cemetery. His request was again refused, and he buried Luisa next to her sister in the Christian graveyard. Immediately after this, his brother's only child collapsed and died.

Miner Problem

One of the many problems faced by men in the mining towns of 1850s California was the dearth of women. This problem seemed particularly acute for Jewish men. One Jewish resident of the Mother Lode reported that if one could not gain the honor of accompanying a "grown lady" (meaning a girl more than twelve years old) to a ball, he might succeed only in arranging for the escort of a "young lady" (age six to twelve) by inviting her at least a week in advance. Another recalled that "it was a proud privilege to be introduced to a Jewish girl in this country, particularly in California, where the Jewish girls in short dresses were addressed as ladies."

Dutch John's

"His stock of goods [was] two boxes of crackers, a few boxes of sardines, a few knives, and two barrels of the youngest whiskey I had ever tasted. The counter was the head of an empty barrel, set off with a broken tumbler, tin cup, and a junk bottle of the ardent [sic]. . . . A drink was paid for by his taking a pinch of gold dust with his thumb and forefinger from the miner's bag, or sorting out a lump the size and value of a dollar according to the Jewish ideas of such things. Before taking the pinch from the bag, John's fingers could be seen sliding down his throat (as far as the balance of the hand would permit) for the purpose of covering them with saliva to make the gold stick, and he then thrust it into the miner's pile—The amount of such a pinch was from 4 to 8 dollars! 'Gott und Himmel,' John, if we have an account to settle in the next world, won't the clerks have a time of it with yours! This mode of settling was looked upon as a source of fun for the miners, [rather] than an imposition."

> —Description by miner James H. Carson of business
> at a store in a mining camp on the road to
> Wearverville, California, in the 1850s.

Bulls and Bears

One of the few diversions in the violent, virtually all-male Mother Lode gold mining towns were "bull and bear" fights. Grizzly bears were matched against bulls, whose horns were normally sawed off before the contest.

These were cruel, though often thrilling, fights, and the highly valued grizzlies had an unfair advantage. After the fight, "the ugly mood of the brooding, beastly spectators was dissipated in a shoot-out and a drunken binge," reports historian I. Harold Sharfman. Jews generally condemned the whole practice, but their disapproval didn't exempt them from its consequences.

In a particularly memorable fight in the town of Jackson, California, a grizzly was mauling a bull. The bull had been lassoed, his horns sawed off, and the fight apparently taken out of him before he even got into the ring. The miners, angry at the unfairness of the contest, demanded that a new untamed bull, horns and all, be let in to take over and give the grizzly a real battle.

More prone to direct action than contemporary sports fans, some hundred spectators reportedly drew their pistols and threatened to shoot the grizzly if their request was not granted promptly. The cowboys who kept the animals complied, and an energetic new bull charged in. The grizzly, however, was undisturbed; he stripped off one of the new bull's ears and methodically tore at the animal's trunk. After five minutes the bull was howling so loudly he was heard a mile away.

The grizzly, a spectator said, "entertaining no malice," let the bull loose; the crazed animal charged at the picket fence that separated the crowd from the arena and ripped through it, scattering spectators in all directions.

The enraged bull charged through town, down Main Street, and came to a halt at the Jewish-owned clothing shops. Apparently attracted to the prominently displayed bright red flannel shirts, the wounded bull charged through the shops, destroying one after the other. Cowboys finally lassoed the bull. As the Jewish merchants denounced the animal, the crowd expressed its admiration for the powerful grizzly, the verdict being, "That thar bar's some, you bet."

Forty-niner

Five-foot, one-eyed Morris Shloss rode shotgun on a California stage-coach carrying gold dust for an express company. He arrived in San

Francisco in 1849 after being narrowly missed by a monster shark when he jumped overboard into the Pacific Ocean for a swim.

Shloss brought with him a wagon packed in a large shipping container. At the landing, a man asked him what was in the big box.

"A wagon," Shloss answered.

"How much do you want for it?" Shloss had paid $15 for the wagon and $3 more for the container.

"One hundred twenty-five dollars."

"I'll give you a hundred dollars."

Shloss agreed. The man paid him in gold dust, without even asking to see the wagon first.

In opening the box the man took great care not to break the lid. Taking out the wagon, he said to Shloss, "Stranger, you can keep the wagon. I only want the box. I am a cobbler, and in the daytime it will be my shop, and at night, my residence." The box measured seven by four feet.

Shloss got a job playing piano at the El Dorado gambling house every evening from seven to ten o'clock for $16 plus a "grab," a handful of silver from the monte table, for an additional hour of overtime.

Shloss opened a store, buying trunks from passengers who were "wild to go to the mines" and reselling them. In seven or eight weeks, he made more than $5,000. But just as fortunes were quickly made in the Old West, it seemed they could be lost even quicker. A fire broke out in back of Shloss's store. He recalled, "As I had (accidentally) scattered gunpowder all over my store, I had to run for my life, and lost all I had made."

Reports that gold nuggets had been found all along the bay shore led Shloss to board a ship bound for Trinidad Bay, California.

"When I landed, I found Digger Indians, but no signs of gold and no ship to return on; so I had to remain there four months, living on beans, crackers and clams."

After returning to San Francisco, Shloss opened another store. A customer by the name of Joaquin Murrieta visited him every day and read the newspaper. When Murrieta became sick, Shloss saw that he got food and medical care. When he recovered, he offered to repay Shloss, but Shloss refused.

"Consider me your everlasting friend," Murrieta said. A monte gambler, Murrieta became a notorious bandit; there was a $10,000 reward for his head.

Later, Shloss joined the Vigilante Committee. He was on guard when Yankee Sullivan, a ballot box stuffer, committed suicide by cutting off his arm. In 1856, more than 5,000 Vigilantes marched and demonstrated.

"We dispersed the thieves. Then we elected honest judges, banished all ballot box stuffers, and San Francisco was saved," Shloss concluded his memoirs.

Levi Strauss: Blue Gold

Levi Strauss, a young Jewish immigrant from Bavaria, came to California in 1850 and struck gold—with a pair of pants.

Levi had peddled for a couple of years back East. When he got to San Francisco, demand for his goods was strong; in those days, materials couldn't get out West fast enough to meet the needs of the new settlers.

One story of what happened next goes like this:

All Levi had left of the supplies he'd brought from New York was canvas he planned to sell for tents. He'd set himself up selling on San Francisco's Montgomery Street. A prospector happened by and asked what Levi was selling; when told tenting, the man was uninterested. What he needed were pants. Pants weren't made that fit the rough work of a miner; they were always coming apart, the knees and seat wore out, and soon they'd be in tatters.

"Pants don't wear worth a damn in the diggings," the miner said. "Can't get a pair strong enough to last."

Levi thought fast and brought the man and the canvas to a tailor and asked him to cut a pair of pants from it. The bemused tailor set to work and soon there was a new kind of pants in San Francisco. The miner was happy. He hit his usual bars, boasting, "Doggone it, if a man ever had a pair of pants as strong as Levi's before!"

The Levi's name stuck. Other miners began looking for the fellow with the Levi's. Levi Strauss pioneered a new kind of durable pants that suited the rough-and-tumble Western life—out of canvas, 'duck,' a similar but lighter material—and later, denim. Word-of-mouth advertising deluged Levi with orders. Soon he was sending to his brothers back East for more material and starting the huge company that still bears his name.

The next big step forward for blue jeans came twenty years later from another Western Jewish immigrant clothier meeting the needs of his hard-wearing customers. Jacob Davis was a Russian-born tailor in

Virginia City in the Comstock mining country of Nevada. One particularly tough customer, an irritable and irritating prospector known as "Alkali Ike," stopped by every time he came into town to berate Davis because his pants pockets had torn again.

Ike, like many miners, stuffed his pockets with ore, tools, and all the other things a miner needed, and the pockets were giving way all the time. Every time they ripped, Ike complained bitterly and drunkenly to the tailor, demanding he fix them right this time.

On one of Ike's visits, he gave Davis so much trouble that the tailor, as a joke, sneaked out his back door, took Ike's pants to a local harness-maker, and had the pockets reinforced with copper harness rivets. The pockets held, and on Ike's next trip to town he was a happy, satisfied customer for a change and told everybody he knew. Soon Davis couldn't keep up with the demand for riveted pockets. He feared his competitors would swoop in and take advantage of his idea. With the help of the town druggist, who wrote the letter, he contacted Levi Strauss in San Francisco, suggesting they go into partnership and get a patent for riveted pants, offering the company half the rights for $68—the cost of a patent application. Levi agreed and Davis went to San Francisco to manage the Strauss overall factory.

Soon the company was advertising its riveted pants as "so tough a team of plow horses could not tear them apart"; a corresponding two-horse logo became a Strauss trademark. Denim, dyed blue, replaced the then-popular 'duck' material, and the virtually indestructible work pants spread to cowboys, lumberjacks, construction men, farmers and factory workers—and, in the Twentieth Century, to college students and everyone else. The jeans were 'guaranteed to shrink, wrinkle and fade'; according to tradition, miners, farmers and cowboys made their jeans fit by putting them on new and jumping straight into a watering trough. When the pants dried, the story goes, they fit.

Levi jeans are basically unchanged to this day. One of the few changes was made after a 1933 camping trip taken by Walter Haas, Sr., President of the company and husband of a Strauss great-niece. At that time, one reinforcing copper rivet was used on the crotch of the pants. One problem was that if the wearer crouched for a while too near a campfire, this rivet could suddenly grow painfully hot. After Haas reportedly learned first-hand of this "hot rivet" problem during the trip, that rivet was removed.

By the 1970s, the company used enough material each year, as Ed

Cray put it in his book *Levi's*, "to wrap a cummerbund of cloth six times around the Equator."

Strauss was the first American clothing company to offer year-round jobs to its employees. When the Great Earthquake of 1906 hit San Francisco and destroyed Strauss factories, the company took out newspaper ads to advise employees their pay would be continued and retail dealers they could see the company for inexpensive loans to rebuild. Strauss integrated its Southern plants before the law required, adopted a policy of aggressively hiring blacks and other minorities and built a reputation for promoting the welfare of communities where its plants were located. Strauss remained something of a family business, owned largely by the Haases of San Francisco, Strauss' indirect descendants (a bachelor, Strauss left most of his estate to his four nephews). In 1985, apparently to maintain the firm's distinctive character and prevent future takeover bids, the family engineered a buyout of the company's publicly traded shares, 'going private' only 14 years after first going public.

The "Menken"

Adah Isaacs Menken, probably the highest paid and most gossiped-about actress of her day, leaped into international stardom before audiences from Vienna to San Francisco in the early 1860s as, clad only in flesh-colored tights, she climaxed the melodrama *Mazeppa* by riding an unsaddled horse tortuously up a papier-mâché mountain.

Menken's performance scandalized prevalent Victorian sensibilities but her popularity was enormous. Nowhere was she greeted with wilder enthusiasm than in the American West, at performances in San Francisco and Virginia City, Nevada, in the heart of the Comstock Lode mining country. For a sixty-day run in San Francisco she was paid $500 a performance, reportedly the highest pay ever received by a stage performer until that time.

"A magnificent spectacle dazzled my vision," Mark Twain wrote in Virginia City's *Territorial Enterprise* (March 8, 1864), "the whole constellation of the Great Menken came flaming out of the heavens like a vast spray of gas-jets, and shed a glory abroad over the universe as it fell!"

Miners threw thousands of dollars worth of gold dust at her feet after performances. A newly organized mining company named itself the Menken Shaft and Tunnel Company and printed her likeness on its stock certificates. A mine was renamed Mazeppa Mountain Lodge in her honor and a mining region dubbed "the Menken." In Virginia City, miners presented her with a solid silver brick and made her an honorary member of the local fire brigade.

Menken combined her sensational stage career and personal life (she married and divorced four times in ten years, interspersed with numerous well-publicized affairs) with a reputation as a poet of some note, largely for Jewish publications and on Jewish subjects.

In response to questions about her background, she affirmed in a letter to the *New York Illustrated News* that she had been born a Jew, and that she had "adhered to it through all my erratic career. Through that pure and simple religion, I have found greatest comfort and blessing."

Menken's theatrical success came suddenly, after only a few years of acting experience, starting with a New Orleans amateur society. Her time in the spotlight was also brief; she died in London at the age of thirty-three after a short illness.

Bank in the Back

Banking in Southern California got started in a men's clothing store. When Isaias Wolf Hellman came to Los Angeles in 1859 at the age of sixteen, he went to work in the business of his cousin, I. M. Hellman, but within six years, Isaias Wolf bought his own haberdashery. Hellman was to become known as the founder of banking in Los Angeles and the top financier on the West Coast until his death in 1920. He headed up Los Angeles's Farmers and Merchants Bank, at the same time running the San Francisco–based Wells-Fargo Nevada Bank. But it all started in that clothing store.

In those days, merchants were often asked to care for others' gold dust and valuables, which, it was felt, were not safe in private homes. Miners, particularly, would ask a trusted storekeeper to take care of their gold while they went "on the town." Isaias Hellman even had a safe, which increased his attractiveness for such missions. This informal method of storing large quantities of wealth sometimes caused harrowing incidents, one of which prodded Hellman into banking.

The miners would typically drink heavily and gamble. Once out of money, they would return to the store where they'd left their gold, take more gold dust out of their purses, tie the purse back up again, and return it to the storekeeper.

One huge Irish miner, who'd drunk and spent generously, came back to Hellman's to find his purse practically empty.

"You dirty Jew," he accused Hellman, "you've stolen my gold." Fortunately for the storekeeper, a friend was with the Irishman and calmed him down, saying, "You took this gold out yourself, and you must apologize to Mr. Hellman."

Hellman told friends later that it had always been against his business judgment to have so much gold sitting idle. He realized there was nothing to keep an overwrought miner from drunkenly stabbing or shooting him. So he went to a friend who ran a newspaper; they printed up passbooks and deposit slips reading "I. W. Hellman, Banker." He had a carpenter fence off a corner of the clothing store, put the safe there, and hung up a sign: "I. W. Hellman, Banker."

The next miner who came with gold dust learned he couldn't just leave it there any more. But, Hellman told him, he was now a banker. He would buy the gold dust at current rates. The miner could deposit his money, which would be recorded in a book. He could even write checks against it. The idea caught on and the miners spent noticeably less of their money than they had before. This stood them in good stead in later years after the mines gave out when the men had thousands of dollars stored up with which to buy land and homes. Hellman was to become director or stockholder of a dozen other Los Angeles banks as well as head of two of the state's major banks, and he held vast other interests in real estate, public utilities, and other businesses.

Jackson A. Graves, an attorney and longtime associate of Hellman, felt the banker was at times excessively easy on debtors—for example, refusing to foreclose on mortgages until a statute of limitations was about to run out. Graves reported one of Hellman's replies in Ira Cross's book *Financing an Empire*: "Graves, I have to be a better man than you are, because I am a Jew. You can do things that I cannot do. If I did them, I would be criticized, while you will not be. . . . I have to keep that steadily in mind in all my dealings."

"Sadie" Earp— Adventure in the Blood

I don't know where I got the adventure in my blood. Certainly not from my parents, who were the soul of middle-class solid respectability. My upbringing was all directed toward taking my place some day as a proper matron in a middle-class setting.

So wrote Josephine Sarah "Sadie" Marcus Earp, who left her parents' well-off German-Jewish home in San Francisco in 1879 at the age of eighteen to perform with a traveling dance troupe in the Arizona Territory and soon marry famed lawman, entrepreneur, gambler and sharpshooter Wyatt Earp. "The thought of hurting my family was not as compelling as the thought of missing out on a chance for adventure and applause," she continued in her memoirs.

On the way to Arizona she met lawman Johnny Behan, who helped the troupe avoid an ambush by Indians, and to whom Josephine became engaged. Later she became ill and went home to San Francisco. When she returned to Arizona, originally with the intention of marrying Behan, he introduced her to Earp, and the two soon became constant companions.

"I liked the traveling sort of man better than the kind that sat back in one town all his life and wrote down little rows of figures all day or hustled dry goods or groceries and that sort of thing," she wrote. "I can see the need for solid citizens such as those, but they were never my type for a husband. My blood demanded excitement, variety and change."

Wyatt and Sadie, as he called her, lived together for nearly fifty years until Earp's death in 1929, traveling and working in Mexico, Texas, Colorado, Idaho, and Alaska. Later they returned to California and built a home in Los Angeles, though they continued their lifelong pastimes of hiking and gambling.

"Get the Hell Off the Wire!"

Morris Goldwater, one of the sons of Arizona pioneer "Big Mike" Goldwater and uncle of 1964 Republican presidential candidate Barry Goldwater, served as mayor of Prescott, Arizona, for more than twenty years. In 1964, Prescott named him "Man of the Century." He was founder of the city's volunteer fire department, secretary of the Prescott Rifles, member of both houses of the Territorial Legislature, a prominent banker, and a "booster" of roads and railroads.

A pioneer telegraph operator, Morris was instrumental in bringing the first telegraph line into Prescott. The town was to be bypassed but Morris persuaded officials to change their route and bring the line into town through what came to be known as Telegraph Pass.

Folklore has it that Morris was able to persuade the authorities because he had a set of telegraph instruments that he offered to give them. He also offered to operate the telegraph himself without pay. The men in charge thought they had a bargain, but found out soon that Morris didn't know as much about the telegraph as he let on he did. When the wire was installed and Morris began fiddling with the key, back along the line from the other end came an abrupt message—the first signal to travel along the brand new Prescott telegraph line: "Get the hell off the wire!"

Morris was soon replaced by an official representative of the U.S. Army Signal Corps.

Baseball's Forgotten Hero

No longer a household word to baseball fans, in fact known to some as "Baseball's Forgotten Hero," Johnny Kling became the first Jew to play in the major leagues when he broke in with the Chicago Cubs in 1901. That first season, he alternated as a catcher with Frank Chance, who switched to first base to become the last part of the famed "Tinker to Evers to Chance" double play combo.

When Kling was first announced as the Cubs' catcher, the opposing New York Giants wasted no time letting the rookie know he was in for it. Giant Wil Mercer had the job of seeing whether the young ballplayer could take it. Mercer slid into home plate with his spikes aimed at the new catcher's face. Kling held his ground and tagged Mercer out with room to spare; Kling didn't have a scratch but Mercer was so roughed up in the play he had to leave the game. No one bothered Kling after that.

Born Jonah Kline in Kansas City in 1875, he changed his name before starting in the majors. Due to an unusually strong throwing arm, he was known for being the first catcher in the majors to throw runners out from a crouching position. At this time, also, catchers usually stood at a distance behind the batter unless he had two strikes on him; Kling was the first to stand directly behind the batter at all times. Through his courage at the start and his solid reputation over a thirteen-year career in the majors, Kling was credited for smoothing the way for other Jewish ballplayers.

Kling became nationally known during the 1906–1908 period as the Cubs won three straight National League pennants. In 1907, as catcher, he held Tiger great Ty Cobb without a stolen base through the entire World Series. In 1908, after two straight Cub World Championships, Kling's picture adorned national magazines and posters in saloons across Chicago. He was called the "guiding spirit" of the Cub championship teams. In 1909, he refused to play with the Cubs, and instead won the world's pro pocket billiard championship. Chicago lost the pennant for the first time in four years. He rejoined the Cubs the next year and they again won the pennant.

In 1912, Kling became playing manager of the Boston Braves and the next year ended his playing days with Cincinnati. He returned to pro ball in the 1930s as owner of the minor league Kansas City Blues.

3

FIGHTERS AND FREELANCERS

No Loyalty Oath

When the Newport, Rhode Island, shipbuilding and freighting business suffered severe losses, Moses Michael Hays and his partner, Myer Pollock, were forced into bankruptcy and thrown into prison as debtors. Released in December 1771, penniless, young Hays determined to stick it out in Newport. He engaged in general merchandising and was working hard when the Revolution broke out. Then a new difficulty confronted him. The Rhode Island Assembly passed a number of acts demanding an oath of loyalty from suspected Tories. Hays turned out to be one of them.

Hays, a patriot, was furious that his loyalty was questioned. He refused to take the oath, denouncing the whole procedure as an unjust imputation of disloyalty. If an oath of loyalty was demanded of any, it should be demanded of all, he argued. To the Assembly he wrote:

> Moses M. Hays of New Port begs leave humbly to represent to your honors that he hath ever been warmly and zealously attacht to the rights and liberties of the colonies . . . and allways despised inimicall principles. . . . Yet I was informed that an information had been lodged against me of being inimicall to the country. I denied, and do still deny holding or entertaining such principles, and desired to know my accusers and accusations.
>
> I ask your Honors the rights and priviledges due other free citizens when I conform to everything generally done and acted, and again implore that the justice of your Honors may interfer in my behalf, and will give me leave again to call for the cause and my accusation of inimcality, that I may have an opper[tunit]'y of vindication before your Honors. I am, with great respect,

> Your Honors most ob. and most hb'e serv't,
> M. M. Hays.

Hays told the authorities the fact that he was a Jew made it all the more unjust because he didn't even have the rights and opportunities of citizenship, including the right to vote. "I am an Israelite and am not allowed the liberty of a vote or a voice in common with the rest of the voters though consistent with the Constitution of the other Colonies," he wrote. Hays' argument finally prevailed; he did not have to sign the oath.

Jewish Paul Revere

Francis Salvador, known both as "The Jewish Paul Revere" and "The Southern Paul Revere," enlisted in the cause of colonial independence shortly after his arrival in 1773 from Britain. The nephew of a prominent British financier, Salvador came to South Carolina to manage his family's plantations. He was elected to the colony's Second Provincial Congress, becoming probably the first Jewish elected official in the modern world.

In 1776 the British fleet docked at Charleston and encouraged the Cherokee Indians to attack outlying colonial settlements. The twenty-nine-year-old Jew sped through the countryside on his horse, the story goes, rousing plantation men to action, shouting, "Let's go, men, and fight for our independence."

Starting with a group of only forty men, by July there were more than a thousand ready to fight. On July 21, Salvador and a detachment of 330 men under Continental Army Major Andrew Williamson launched an expedition against Cherokees and Tories.

Salvador was ambushed and scalped. Williamson found Salvador on the verge of death. "Did we win, sir?" Francis asked the major. When the major answered "yes," Salvador responded, "I'm glad," and then died. Salvador is believed to have been the first Jew to die for the American Revolution.

A bronze marker in his honor in Charleston's City Hall Park reads:

Born an aristocrat, he became a democrat—
An Englishman, he cast his lot with America;
True to his ancient faith, he gave his life
For new hopes of human liberty and understanding.

Belle of Philadelphia

Using a pseudonym, Rebecca Franks attacked George Washington with verses such as:

Was it ambition, vanity or spite
That prompted thee with Congress to unite?
Or did all three within thy bosom roll?
Thou heart of hero, with a traitor's soul.

Born in Philadelphia around 1757, Rebecca Franks was the daughter of the distinguished colonial merchant and ardent anglophile David Franks. She too was a Tory sympathizer. Her reputation as "Belle of the City" made her the toast of General Sir William Howe, the British commander, and her home was his social headquarters in the city. At her soirees she would entertain the British officers and dandies with the wit and doggerel for which she became known:

From garrets, cellars, rushing through the street
The newborn statesmen in committees meet
Legions of senators infest the land
And mushroom generals thick as mushrooms stand.

The Revolutionary general Charles Lee nursed no grudge against the female Tories of Philadelphia. While in temporary retirement in the Pennsylvania capital during the winter of 1778, he carried on a spirited correspondence with Rebecca, whom he greatly admired. In a mock-heroic letter, studded with double entendre, he reproached her for attacking him. He wrote that he could have borne the accusations of treasonable correspondence with the enemy, of drunkenness and theft, of never parting with his shirt until his shirt parted with him—all these calumnies he could endure, but she had diabolically slandered him by reporting that he wore green breeches *patched* with leather, rather than genuine riding breeches *reinforced* with leather! "You have already injured me in the tenderest part," he cried out grandiloquently, "and I demand satisfaction."

When the British fled Philadelphia, David Franks and his family obtained permission to reside in New York, the last Tory stronghold. In 1782, Rebecca married Colonel Henry Johnson, a British officer, and lived in England as Lady Rebecca Johnson.

Later she had a change of mind. General Winfield Scott met Lady Johnson in London. In advanced age, Rebecca reminisced about the American Revolution and said, "I ought to have been a patriot—would to God I too had been a patriot."

The Truth about Haym Salomon

Probably in few places is the gap between American Jewish folklore and American Jewish history as wide as in the case of Haym Salomon. While Salomon was indeed an ardent patriot, an able financier, and a generous supporter of the American Revolution, Salomon's story has grown like a traditional "tall tale."

According to folklore, Salomon financed the American Revolution with huge sums of his own money. Salomon never made any such claim. His youngest son, several decades after his father's death, provided much of the grist for the legend by claiming the U.S. government owed Salomon's estate some $658,000 in "loans" made to the Continental treasury and never repaid. Congressional committees in the nineteenth century even reported favorably on these claims, but Congress never went along and actually paid anything to the Salomon family. Disagreements continued into the twentieth century.

The weight of historical opinion, is that Salomon never had the kind of money he would have needed to do what he is supposed to have done. Salomon would have had to be the richest man in America to provide the monies out of his own pocket that had been claimed, and the evidence doesn't support this. It appears that the huge amounts of money he provided to the Continental Treasury were funds raised from selling French bills of exchange and Continental securities, and not personal donations.

The story of Salomon has made such an impression on both Jewish and general American folklore that "Financial Hero" is what the U.S. postage stamp dedicated to Haym Salomon in 1975 calls him. A monument of Salomon, George Washington and Robert Morris stands tall on East Wacker Drive in Chicago. The Haym Salomon Memorial Park is one of the historic sites in Frazer, Pennsylvania. There is an organization called the American Jewish Patriots and Friends of Haym Salomon in Beverly Hills, California. The basic facts of what we know about Saloman's life are these:

Born in Lissa, Poland, about 1740, Salomon was quick to pick up languages. At an early age he knew at least six—German, French, Italian, Russian, Polish, and English. With that ability and with his understanding of finance, he was able to make friends among bankers of the major European commercial centers. He left Poland in 1775, which may have been forced by his connections with the unsuccessful Polish revolutionary movement.

Salomon became known for his warm attachment to the cause of Colonial independence shortly after his arrival, and he associated himself with the Sons of Liberty. He was twice arrested and jailed by the British. He propagandized among pro-British Hessian mercenaries in New York and helped American and French prisoners of war to escape. He was betrayed to the British, however, and fled for his life in 1778, barely managing to reach Philadelphia, where he set himself up as a financier.

Salomon was engaged by the French armed forces in America to sell their bills of exchange. When Robert Morris accepted the post of Continental superintendent of finance in 1781, he needed an able, honest broker to help sell the financial instruments that were coming in from France, Holland and Spain and engaged Salomon as his chief agent.

When the drive to stop Cornwallis in Virginia was mapped, Morris was called upon to raise the necessary funds, and Salomon pitched in to help him. He sold bills of exchange, negotiated drafts and floated securities. In July 1782, Salomon, with Morris' permission, advertised himself as "Broker to the Office of Finance."

Salomon made great contributions to the cause of independence. His role in selling bills of exchange and securities of various kinds was a vital one and played a central role in putting the new government on a more stable financial footing. France, for example, would not risk sending the continentals gold because it might be intercepted on the seas by the British Navy. Instead, they sent notes, whose value was not so easily determined and from which the raising of money was not assured. The Continental Congress was impotent to raise taxes and depended on these foreign loans. Continental currency was trusted so little in 1781, when Salomon began working with Morris, that one dollar in coin could buy between 500 and 1,000 paper Continental dollars. Under such circumstances, credible financing was not easy. And Salomon worked for the Revolution for little recompense.

"The great thing about Haym Salomon," writes historian Bertram Korn, "was that he charged only one half of 1 percent interest [fees on transactions], while other brokers charged 5 or 6 percent."

Salomon also lent and gave money to colonial officials whom the depleted Continental treasury could not pay, so they could continue their work.

In August 1782, James Madison wrote to Edmond Randolph, ". . . I have for some time past been a pensioner on the favor of Haym Salomon, a Jew broker." At another time he wrote to Randolph, "The kindness of our little friend in Front Street, near the coffee-house, is a fund which will preserve me from extremities, but I never resort to it without great mortification, as he obstinately rejects all recompense."

Salomon also gave $2,000 to relieve suffering among the poor in Philadelphia. He probably invested much of his own money in Continental securities of dubious financial value, for patriotic reasons. His generosity to the American cause eroded his personal finances: when he died in 1785, he owed more than he had.

Perhaps thinking Salomon was richer than he was, relatives sought his help. As Salomon wrote one uncle in London who had asked persistently for money, "Your bias of my riches is too extensive. Rich I am not, but the little I have I think it my duty to share with my poor father and mother."

Gracious Seixas

During the American Revolution, Abraham M. Seixas (pronounced Say-chus) served as a Continental Army officer in Georgia and South Carolina. He ran for office in the 1790s and was defeated. Undaunted, he resorted to his favorite weapon—verse.

In the newspapers he asked voters where they stood:

The man I love, who will avow
He is my friend or is my foe;
But he who comes with double face,
I do despise as being base.

The people did commit themselves. In the next election, he ended up at the very bottom of the list.

As a merchant and slave dealer, Seixas also used poetry to advertise. Here are a few of his verses taken from the *South-Carolina State-Gazette* of September 6, 1794:

ABRAHAM SEIXAS,

All so gracious,
Once again does offer
His service pure,
For to secure
Money in the coffer.

He has for sale
Some negroes, male,
Will suit full well grooms.
He has likewise
Some of their wives,
Can make clean, dirty rooms.

He surely will
Try all his skill
To sell, for more or less,
The articles
Of beaux and belles,
That they do him address.

At War with the Navy

After a promising start, Uriah P. Levy had a hard life on the high seas. Born in 1792, he ran away to sea at the age of ten; by the time he was twenty, he'd already become master and part owner of his own ship and lost it in a mutiny. When he was seventeen, he was shanghaied by the British, who offered him a commission in their navy.

As a teenage merchant seaman, he once drifted for five days in an open boat after it foundered. He barely escaped with his life in the mutiny, when his crew seized a cargo of $2,500 in gold and fourteen cases of Tartuffe wine; he chased the ringleaders through the Caribbean, finally getting one of them hanged and another sentenced to life in prison.

Things didn't get much calmer when he joined the U.S. Navy during the War of 1812. He was captured and spent sixteen months as a prisoner of war in a British prison. After the war ended, it seemed he and the Navy were still at war. Although he rose to Commodore, the first Jew to achieve that rank, he also, from 1818 to 1857, faced six court-martials and two courts of inquiry and was twice "cashiered" out of the Navy (though reinstated both times).

Levy had a combative personality and the environment wasn't friendly; one historian described his problem as "responding violently to extreme provocation." He wasn't a regular Navy man and the brass never took to him; he had risen through the ranks and he was a Jew, one of very few in the Navy in his day. He also got something of a reputation as an eccentric in an institution not known for its tolerance, as when he ordered all the guns on one of his ships painted blue.

His 1839 court-martial for having one of his sailors let down his pants to be tarred and feathered became a *cause celebre*. Levy was a staunch opponent of the then-accepted practice of flogging sailors with cat-o'-nine-tails, which was greatly reduced aboard his ships. Yet the naval court found that for using this embarrassing but considerably less painful punishment—imposed, as Levy put it, as a "badge of disgrace" to punish the sailor for mimicking officers—he should be dismissed from the Navy.

"I was unwilling to flog the boy upon his naked back with a cat [o'-nine-tails], for what might possibly be termed a trivial offense," Levy argued, "but . . . I deemed it right by exposing *him* to ridicule, to satisfy him of the impropriety of ridiculing others. I called the boys together to witness the example to be made of juvenile offenders of this class, had his trowsers taken down, a little tar, on a piece of oakum, dabbed on his bottum, and a few colored feathers from a dead parrot stuck on him to ridicule his mocking propensities, and the whole affair ended in a few minutes."

President John Tyler, on review, referred the case back twice to the naval court, which twice refused to mitigate Levy's punishment. Finally Tyler, acting on his own and finding Levy's punishment "exceedingly severe and disproportionate," reduced it to a one-year suspension without pay. He was the second president to reverse a Levy dismissal from the Navy; James Monroe had done similarly years before.

In later years Levy agitated in writings in the newspapers and public statements for the abolition of flogging and the development of apprenticeship programs in the Navy. In Levy's time, flogging with the lash or worse was considered, by conventional wisdom, the only way to keep order in the navies of the world. The usual argument, as one historian put it, was that "only the scum of the underworld manned the Navy and only the lash could keep these men subdued." Even in the United States, which legally prohibited application of more than twelve lashes, a New Hampshire senator reported a case where a seaman received four hundred lashes in twelve-lash installments. Levy argued that only abolition of the lash would attract men who would not need such restraint. He tried to set an example on his own ships; various newspapers commented on his success with the crew of the Vandalia in 1839:

> We observe that Commander Levy, of the *Vandalia* managed matters so well, that he kept his ship always in prime order, and yet seldom had occasion to use either the cat or the colt. If this is true . . . we would call upon the officer to impart his mystery. He owes it to the service . . . no less than to the advancement of his own fame.

> —*New York Evening Post*, January 18, 1840

On the side, Levy bought Thomas Jefferson's Monticello mansion after Jefferson's death, lived there, rebuilt and restored it, and left it to the United States on his death, although the mansion actually remained in private hands into the twentieth century due to conflict between his heirs.

Over his grave in Cypress Hills Cemetery in Brooklyn is the statue of a uniformed naval captain, which Levy ordered in his will, giving specific instructions as to its dimensions. He also left instructions for the following words to be inscribed on his gravestone:

> Father of the law for the abolition
> of the barbarous practice of corporal
> punishment in the Unites States Navy.

John Brown's Bondi

Anshel Bondi itched for a part in history long before he joined up with John Brown's antislavery fight for "bleeding Kansas." As a Vienna teenager in 1848, he was the youngest member of Company Five of the Philosophy Battalion of the Academic Legion, dedicated to overthrowing Prince Metternich's autocratic regime. Before that autumn's revolt, though, his family had left for America and later settled in St. Louis. Anshel became August.

In 1851 he joined a brief abortive effort to free Cuba from Spain. Later that year, Bondi tried to join Commodore Matthew Perry's history-making expedition to Japan, but got to the port of New Orleans too late. In 1855, he arrived in Kansas City and settled on the Mosquite branch of Pottawomi Creek near the village of Osawatomie.

Bondi and another Jewish immigrant named Jacob Benjamin had come to homestead, run a store, and support the "free-soil" movement against proslavery forces. Since Kansas had been opened the year before to white settlement, it had become the focus of a conflict over whether the territory would enter the Union as a free or slave state.

Bondi had seen slavery firsthand in New Orleans, and in his words, "fairly fanaticized with sympathy for the down-trodden of the globe." He'd broken up with a woman he'd planned to marry because her family owned slaves—"My father's son was not meant to be a slave-driver," he said. Bondi credited his mother for his antislavery zeal. "My mother said that, as a Jehudi, I had a duty to perform, to defend the institutions that give equal rights to all beliefs."

John Brown's sons had a ranch four miles from Bondi's claim, and they became acquainted. Late that year, Bondi was sick with fever but, the story has it, so anxious was he to vote in state elections that he had himself put in a cart and carried to the polls; there he met John Brown, recently arrived in Kansas. When virtual war broke out between proslavers and free-soilers, Bondi joined forces with Brown's contingent. Shortly after proslavers had burned Bondi's own cabin and plundered his new partner Theadore Wiener's storehouse, Brown's force engaged the "border ruffians" in the Battle of Black Jack.

Bondi told this anecdote of the fight:

"When we followed Captain Brown up the hill toward the Border Ruffians' camp, I next to Brown and in advance of Wiener, we walked with bent backs, nearly crawled, that the tall dead grass of the year before might somewhat hide us from the Border Ruffians' marksmen, yet the bullets kept whistling.

"Wiener was 37 and weighed 250 pounds, I, 22 and lithe. Wiener puffed like a steamboat, hurrying behind me. I called out to him. 'Nu, was meinen sie jetst?' (Well, what do you think of it now?) His answer, 'Was soll Ich meinen?' (What should I think of it?) I quoted a Hebrew saying, 'Sof odom muves' (Hebrew for the 'end of man is death').

"In spite of the whistling of the bullets, I laughed when he said, 'Machen wir den alten mann sonst broges.' (Look out, or we'll make the old man angry.) We started and came up with Captain Brown and we finished the job."

Later in 1856, Bondi and Wiener helped found the town of Greeley, Kansas, and Bondi was named postmaster. He lost that post the following year after helping push a band of proslavery Missourians back across their state border. A U.S. marshal was part of the Missouri mob, and the political situation at that time was such that Bondi lost the job for the offense of firing at a U.S. marshal. Later Bondi fought in the Civil War, was badly wounded in 1864 in Arkansas, and received a disability discharge.

Bondi's family name was originally Yomtov (Hebrew for "good day" or "holiday"). A Bohemian ancestor of August, on a trip to Italy, changed it to Bondi (Italian for "good day").

In the days of "bleeding Kansas," Bondi and Benjamin, both observant Jews, were known for giving away their share of bacon seized in raids on the supplies of the proslavers.

Chaplain without Leave

At the Civil War battle of Gettysburg, Rabbi Ferdinand Leopold Sarner's horse was killed under him. Sarner, the first American Jewish chaplain to serve in combat and one of the first three rabbis permitted to serve as U.S. Army chaplains, was severely wounded during the battle.

The German-born Sarner was elected chaplain of the 54th New York Volunteer Regiment, known as the Schwarze Jaeger (Black Hunters) because it was made up mainly of German-speaking soldiers and regiment members wore black hunting caps. Although Sarner returned to duty and took part in the Union's invasion of South Carolina, he never fully recovered his health. He was hospitalized again in July 1864; he was told he would be discharged from the Army for disability. But, for some unknown reason, Sarner wouldn't wait. He left the hospital without permission. As a result, his proposed honorable discharge was changed to a discharge for absence without leave.

This made Sarner not only the first American Jewish chaplain to be wounded in battle, but also the first Jewish chaplain to go AWOL.

No Furlough

Jews served, of course, on both sides during the Civil War. Although many more fought as soldiers for the Union than the Confederacy (7,000 to 3,000, according to historian Bertram Korn), a study by historian Simon Wolf in his *The American Jew as Patriot, Soldier and Citizen* indicates there may have been more Jews who were actually officers serving the Confederacy (thirty-five, according to Wolf's exhaustive but admittedly incomplete count, as compared with only sixteen as Northern officers).

There were apparently too many Jews in the Confederate Army for them to be permitted a furlough for the High Holidays, at least according to Commander Robert E. Lee, who in 1861 wrote M. J. Michelbacher of Richmond, Virginia: "I feel assured that neither you or any other member of the Jewish Congregation would wish to jeopardize a cause you have so much at heart by the withdrawal even for a season of a portion of its defenders."

Lincoln's Corn Doctor

Abraham Lincoln's friendship with his English-Jewish chiropodist, dubbed by the press the president's "corn doctor" and "bunionist," led to a satiric field day when Lincoln permitted the doctor, Issachar Zacharie, to meet with Confederate president Jefferson Davis on a "semiofficial" peace mission in 1863.

The *New York Herald*, in an editorial titled "The Head and Feet of the Nation," lampooned Lincoln and his "corn doctor," whom the paper described as "a wit, gourmet and eccentric with a splendid Roman nose, fashionable whiskers, a dazzling diamond breastpin, great skill in his profession, and an ingratiating address." The editorial ended: "What is needed is someone to operate on the head and remove the corns from the brain of Dr. Zacharie."

The *New York World* declared Dr. Zacharie "has enjoyed Mr. Lincoln's confidence perhaps more than any other private individual. He has visited the cotton states, armed with letters from the President. He was courted, feted, flattered by high officials because he was regarded as standing so high in the graces of the President, who has often left his business apartment to spend his evenings in the parlor of the famous bunionist."

Lincoln met Zacharie in 1861 and was impressed with his intelligence as well as his healing abilities. Lincoln had sent him to New Orleans secretly earlier in 1863 to evaluate conditions there under Union military occupation. The president had questions about Zacharie's proposed "peace" mission and the Cabinet opposed it. When reports hit the papers after the October 1863 meeting in Richmond, the doctor assured Lincoln he had not "lisped a word" about it.

Lincoln was once quoted as saying, regarding the idea of helping restore a Jewish state in Palestine:

> I myself have a regard for the Jews. My chiropodist is a Jew and he has so many times put me upon my feet that I would have no objection to giving his countrymen a leg up.

Order Number 11

When, as part of an effort to cut off the South's cotton trade, General U. S. Grant issued his infamous Order #11, expelling Jews from areas of Tennessee and Kentucky occupied by the Union Army, Cesar J. Kaskel of Paducah, Kentucky, managed to meet with Rabbi Isaac Mayer Wise and his congressman in Cincinnati and organize a campaign against the order. This led to an audience with President Lincoln, who claimed to be unaware of the order and agreed to revoke it. The following dialogue between Kaskel and Lincoln was reported:

> *Lincoln*: And so the children of Israel are driven from the happy land of Canaan?
> *Kaskel*: Yes, and that is why we have come into Father Abraham's bosom, asking protection.
> *Lincoln*: And this protection they shall have at once.

Lincoln ordered his then General-in-Chief of the Army, Henry W. Halleck, to revoke the order. Halleck communicated diplomatically with Grant, noting that "a paper purporting to be General Order #11 . . . has been issued by you. . . . If such an order has been issued, it will be immediately revoked." Halleck told Grant that Lincoln

> has no objection to your expelling traitors and Jew peddlers, which, I suppose, was the object of your order; but as it in terms proscribed an entire religious class, some of whom are fighting in our ranks, the President deemed it necessary to revoke it.

During Grant's 1868 campaign for president, with charges of anti-Semitism from the Order #11 controversy still dogging him, Grant wrote a congressman: "I have no prejudice against sect or race, but want each individual to be judged on his own merit. Order No. 11 does not sustain this statement, I admit, but I do not sustain the order. It would never have been issued if it had not been telegraphed the moment it was penned and without reflection."

'Pass Over' Story

David Mayer was a prominent member of the early Atlanta Jewish community and became known as "the father of public education in Atlanta," serving on the city's school board from its inception in 1870 until his death twenty years later. This bit of historical folklore relates less to the fact that Mayer was a Jew than that he was a devoted Shriner. As General W. T. ("War is Hell") Sherman's army approached Atlanta, Mayer apparently learned that Sherman, who had a reputation as an anti-Semite, was also a Shriner. Mayer hung his Shriner's apron on the doorpost of his house and the Northern army "passed over" it, leaving Mayer's residence, the story has it, the only thing standing for miles around.

"A Regular Fronthall"

A German-Jewish immigrant by the name of Max Frauenthal became a legendary hero of the Confederate Army. Frauenthal joined the Confederates as a private and was assigned as a drummer but shouldered a gun at his own request. As a member of Company A, 16th Mississippi Infantry, Frauenthal distinguished himself during the Battle of Spottsylvania Court House, Virginia, on May 12, 1864.

Judge A. T. Watts of Dallas, a member of Frauenthal's company, singled Frauenthal out in a description of the battle as "a little Jew who, though insignificant, in battle had the heart of a lion. For several hours he stood at the immediate point of contact amid the most terrific hail of lead and coolly and deliberately loaded and fired without cringing."

Watts wrote later, "I now understand how it was that a handful of Jews could drive before them the hundred kings—they were all Fronthals." Frauenthal's name was variously misspelled as Frankenthal, Fahrenthold, Fronthal, and Fronthall. In Texas and Mississippi, Confederate veterans after this frequently referred to a brave man as "a regular Fronthall," in admiration of Frauenthal's heroism.

Israelites with Egyptian Hearts?

The "brains of the Confederacy," Judah P. Benjamin, was the second Jew elected to the U.S. Senate. Northerners called him an "Israelite with an Egyptian heart."

Twice elected to the Senate from Louisiana, he defended slavery in debates with Daniel Webster. He served successively as the Confederacy's attorney general, secretary of war, and secretary of state.

After the Confederate surrender, the Union offered a $50,000 reward for his capture. Benjamin fled to Florida, where he hid in the mansion of Major Robert Gamble on the Manatee River while arrangements were made for his escape from the country. Disguised first as a Frenchman and later as a farmer, he spent most of his time on the mansion's upstairs veranda, scanning the Manatee with a spyglass for Union gunboats that were hunting for him.

When Union troops raided the Gamble estate, Benjamin barely had time to escape through the kitchen into a thicket of scrub palmetto in the rear of the house. After this close call, Benjamin moved to the secluded home of another Confederate sympathizer and stayed there until he was taken overland to Sarasota, Florida. There he boarded a sloop for Cuba and, from there, sailed to England. He started anew in Britain, becoming a noted lawyer.

Benjamin was not the only Jew in the top ranks of the Confederacy; another was "Florida Fire-Eater" David Yulee, the first Jew elected to the U.S. Senate. Yulee was born with the family name Levy but created a legend that his father was a Moroccan prince named Yulee who had taken his wife's Jewish name for business purposes. Five years before his 1845 election to the Senate when Florida was admitted to the Union, he had already begun urging secession. Ex-president John Quincy Adams called Yulee "the alien Jew delegate" although he had renounced Judaism. Yulee served five years in federal prison after the Civil War; when he died, the *Washington Post* called him the senator who "was better known than the State he represented."

When Salomon Rothschild of the House of Rothschild met with several Jewish Confederate leaders, he commented in a letter to Europe, "What is extraordinary is how all these men have a Jewish heart and show an interest in me because I represent the greatest Jewish house in the world."

All He Could Fit on His Chest

Philo Jacoby, cofounder of San Francisco's weekly *Hebrew*, was not your typical English-Jewish newspaper editor. Among other things, he was champion rifle shot of the world. He appeared in public wearing only a third of the medals he had won in national and international competitions, this being, according to a contemporary, "all he could place on his chest."

Jacoby won the champion rifle shot title at the U.S. Centennial Exposition in Philadelphia in 1876. Two hundred finalists gathered there, winnowed down from 20,000 original contestants throughout the world. As a novice at a local San Francisco rifle club, he had amazed everyone by making 101 bull's-eyes at 150 yards. During a triumphal tour of central Europe in 1890, Jacoby competed against the best shots of that region of the world. The Austro-Hungarian emperor Franz Joseph joined virtually everyone else that year in presenting Jacoby with a gold medal.

An amateur strongman, Jacoby was known as a fellow who could take care of himself. An ardent Union supporter, he helped found *The Hebrew* during the Civil War. In *The Hebrew*'s early years, Jacoby denounced a country editor who had assailed President Lincoln. The editor, a Confederate sympathizer, was incensed and spread the word that the next time he came to San Francisco, he'd find that "bullet-headed little Jew" and "horsewhip" him. On the editor's next trip to the big city, he was taken by a friend, the story goes, to an exhibition by a San Francisco athletic club.

A heavy-set black-bearded little man on the platform twisted horseshoes, bent a crowbar and broke cobblestones with his hand. Then he acted as the apex of a pyramid, fanning out six men. "I never thought one man could possess such strength," remarked the editor. "Who is that little man?"

The friend replied, "That's the bullet-headed little Jew you're intending to horsewhip."

Born in Poland in 1837, Jacoby studied in a naval academy and sailed with merchant marine ships in England and Prussia. In 1859, he arrived in San Francisco as third mate of a clipper ship.

Physical prowess alone didn't protect Jacoby, though, from the harshest sort of newspaper competition. Jacoby's arch-rival, Rabbi Julius Eckmann of *The Gleaner*, once told the Catholic ministry that Jacoby was trying to convert *The Hebrew*'s Gentile printer. While Jacoby was incensed, he prudently decided the rabbi was "too contemptible" to receive "just punishment."

Slinger the Slugger

One of the heroes of the bloody Battle of Beecher Island, Colorado, fought from September 17 to 20, 1868, was Sigmund Shlesinger, a Hungarian immigrant who had come to New York at the age of fifteen.

He was characterized by one of his officers as "in all respects unfit for the service. A Jew, small with narrow shoulders, sunken in chest, quiet manner and piping voice, but little knowledge of firearms and horse-manship; he was indeed unpromising as a son of Mars."

Shlesinger arrived in Leavenworth, Kansas, in 1865, at the time construction of the Union Pacific Railroad across the plains had aroused the Indians. After years of clerking, "Slinger," as he was known, moved west with the railroad workers, earning his keep as a bartender in a tent saloon, cook, mule driver, baker, laborer and peddler among the soldiers guarding the railroad men. Among his customers were General George Custer, Wild Bill Hickok and Buffalo Bill.

The summer of 1868 found "Slinger" without a job and broke. It was then that he signed up with Colonel George A. Forsyth's Scouts, a volunteer company formed to supplement the thinly-stretched Regular Army units on the Western frontier. Shlesinger was accepted only because he was the fiftieth man available among the frontiersmen, discharged soldiers and hunters.

His little company ran into an Indian ambush near the town of St. Francis, Colorado. Setting up camp on a sandy island in the middle of a stream, the scouts evaded the ambush party but then had to stand off a frontal attack by 600 Cheyenne Indians. At the end of the first day, every one of the company's horses and mules had been killed, six men were dead, and seventeen were wounded.

Scouts were sent out to bring reinforcements. Those who stayed faced not only more Indians but also hunger, thirst and cold. After four days, the Indians withdrew with heavy losses; among the dead were three who had been scalped by Shlesinger. Shlesinger also shot a coyote, which, according to Colonel Forsyth, "was boiled three successive times to extract the last shred of nutrient it contained."

Forsyth paid tribute to Shlesinger in a poem that appeared in the colonel's memoir, *Frontier Fights and Thrilling Days of Army Life*:

When the fore charged on the breastworks
With the madness of despair,
And the bravest of souls were tested,
The little Jew was there.

When the weary dozed on duty,
Or the wounded needed care,
When another shot was called for,
The little Jew was there.

With the festering dead around them,
Shedding poison in the air,
When the crippled chieftain ordered
The little Jew was there.

Sensationalism Sells

That sensationalism sells was quickly grasped by Western immigrant businessmen who had neither ad agencies nor sophisticated knowledge of English, as illustrated by this ad for Lewis Brothers' Boot and Shoe Store in the July 3, 1880 (Los Angeles) *Herald*:

HORRIBLE

INDIANS

A WOMAN
man or child in Los Angeles could hardly be
found that has not traded in the great half
price boot and shoe store opposite the post
office. And why? Because they have
FOUND
out that we are not only the cheapest but we
have the largest stock and best variety in Los
Angeles County. Credit has long been
DEAD
and as we buy only for cash, we are enabled

to undersell any house in the boot and shoe
line in Los Angeles. Try us and you will be
convinced that we have
                    MURDERED
the high prices charged elsewhere.

4

REBELS AND ECCENTRICS

"Rabbi" Monis

Judah Monis, a Jewish merchant who had come to Boston with some rabbinical training, was named instructor of Hebrew at Harvard College in 1722. Not until, however, he had publicly converted to Christianity, a necessary precondition for the post. Monis continued to observe Saturday as his Sabbath; in other respects, he was a Christian.

His Hebrew grammar, printed with the aid of Harvard in 1735, was the first Hebrew book published in North America. In contrast to the brief book titles fashionable in the late twentieth century, the book was described on its cover this way in English, the Hebrew lines being excluded:

A Grammar of the Hebrew Tongue, being an Essay to bring the Hebrew Grammar into English, to Facilitate the Instruction of all those who are desirous of acquiring a clear Idea of this Primitive Tongue by their own Studies; in order to [further] their more distinct Acquaintance with the Sacred Oracles of the Old Testament, according to the Original. And Published more especially for the Use of the Students of Harvard College at Cambridge, in New England. Composed and accurately Corrected by Judah Monis, M.A. Boston, N.E. Printed by Jonas Green, and are Sold by the Author at his House in Cambridge. MDCCXXXV

Monis ran a store to supplement his insufficient income from teaching. Harvard College bought hardware from him and was one of his best customers. He also sold tobacco and served as an interpreter. The royal governor of Massachusetts appointed him a justice of the peace for Middlesex County in 1740.

Monis died in 1764. On his grave in Northborough, Massachusetts, he is identified, albeit incorrectly, as a rabbi.

Buried Standing Up

Abraham Simons, a Georgian Jew who served as a captain in the American Revolution, is remembered for his request that he be buried standing up, musket at his side, so he could shoot the devil. The wish was honored on his death in 1824; Simons' coffin was placed on end and the grave dug twice the usual depth. He was buried vertically, dressed in his Revolutionary regimental brass-buttoned blue uniform, gripping his long-barreled gun.

Despite this unusual request, Simons was known as a very solid citizen. He conducted his extensive business affairs from a stately home built six miles east of Washington, Georgia, and was elected to Georgia's Legislature.

Three years after his death, Simons' widow remarried. Her second husband was the Reverend Jesse Mercer, a prominent Baptist minister, who used the fortune Simons built to establish Mercer University, a Baptist institution in Macon, Georgia. "Mercer University is largely indebted to the skill and enterprise of a Jewish financier," noted an official of the Georgia Baptist Church, Dr. H. R. Bernard, who added philosophically, "A copious Providence this which founds a Christian college on Jewish cornerstones."

Levi Solomon's Women

Levi Solomon, an English-American Jewish peddler of the eighteenth century, did not follow the peddler's traditional path of intermarriage and assimilation. Solomon, who lived near Freehold, New Jersey, married not one, not two, but three Jewish women in succession and arranged for his wives to be buried next to him, one on each side of his grave and one at his feet.

Noah's Hark

Mordecai Manuel Noah learned that service to one's country is no bed of roses. Appointed consul to Tunis during the War of 1812, Noah ransomed a group of Americans held captive by Barbary pirates. But the State Department, headed by James Monroe, felt he had spent too much money and freed the wrong men, so it refused to honor his drafts, and he was almost imprisoned for debt in a Tunisian jail.

Adding insult to injury, Noah received sealed orders in 1815, conveyed by U.S. Navy Commodore Stephen Decatur, to give up his post and return home due to his identity as a Jew, which Monroe said he hadn't known when he appointed him, and "confusion in his accounts."

Undeterred from public service by these experiences, Noah accepted appointment as New York County's first Jewish sheriff in 1822. Opponents protested that a Jewish sheriff might have to hang Christians. Noah's reply became legendary: "Pretty Christians to require hanging."

Fortunately Noah, the descendant of Sephardic Marranos ("secret Jews") who settled in Georgia, could fall back on careers as a journalist, lawyer and playwright. He was also appointed to a judgeship and served at one point as head of New York's Tammany Hall Democratic Party organization.

But Noah is best known in Jewish-American folklore for his 1825 attempt to found a Jewish agricultural colony in upstate New York, named Ararat—after the legendary mountain on which the biblical Noah's Ark came to rest after the Flood. After organizing a primarily non-Jewish syndicate to buy 2,500 acres of Grand Island, New York, for the colony, Noah issued a "manifesto" to Jews worldwide, inviting them to come to Ararat to relearn farming in preparation for a return to Palestine. (Noah also included American Indians in his invitation, as he believed them descendants of the "Ten Lost Tribes" of Israel.)

Then Noah went further in his manifesto, ordering a worldwide census of Jews and a return to the exclusive use of Hebrew for prayers, and "levying" a three-shekel tax on every Jew in the world to finance the colony. A booming cannon and a procession through the streets of Buffalo, New York, preceded dedication rites. City officials, army officers, Masonic dignitaries, and stewards carrying wine, oil, and corn paraded toward Buffalo's St. Paul's Episcopal Church, viewed by the city's populace and thousands of visitors. At the head of the procession strode Noah, garbed in his conception of the robes of a judge of Israel.

Ararat, of course, remained just a conception; this celebration was the beginning and end of its existence. While tempted to write Noah off as a crackpot, looking just a bit more than a century into the future from his time and seeing the huge movements both back to the land of Israel and up to the summer resorts and camps of upstate New York, we might also say he was just ahead of his time.

Difficult Conversion

One well-told story from pre-Civil War America told of the Jew who converted to Christianity, was baptized, actually became a Protestant clergyman, and also accumulated a fair bit of wealth along his way. Family and friends, naturally, expected to inherit it when he died but, when his will was read, it was found he had given the bulk of his estate to be divided among his city's poor. Family, friends, and the cook were to receive a large chest in his basement. The chest was hurriedly located and opened. It held a number of valuable black stones. It also contained full-scale models of a cat and a mouse, next to which a note read,

> As this cat is too large for a mouse to eat,
> So Christian from Jew's an impossible feat.

Emperor Norton

"Emperor" Joshua Norton, who proclaimed himself ruler of the United States and Protector of Mexico, was probably the best known of the eccentrics of California's Gold Rush era and possibly the best known Jew in the Western United States of his day.

Norton was born in Britain in 1819 and his family moved to South Africa during his infancy. In 1844, his family's store went bankrupt and, in the succeeding four years, both of Joshua's parents and his brother died. In 1849, the year of the Gold Rush, Norton left to start a new life in California. A handsome, muscular, well-to-do bachelor with a shrewd business sense, he seemed well fitted to the "rough and ready" life of the American West. He came to California with $40,000 and opened what was called a "mercantile shop" in San Francisco, engaging in various importing and real estate dealings, and in three years, had increased his capital by five times. Norton also joined the Vigilantes who were trying to control violence in lawless San Francisco.

He speculated in commodities and in 1853 lost heavily in an abortive attempt to corner the local rice market that failed when unexpected cargoes arrived in port. The price of rice fell drastically; partners bailed out fast and Norton was ruined. Court suits followed, his mercantile shop caught fire, and Norton's real estate holdings were sold to satisfy creditors. In 1856, he went into bankruptcy and then into seclusion for years.

Norton emerged from obscurity in 1859 an obviously changed man. The formerly hard-headed businessman sent a printed notice to the *San Francisco Bulletin* on September 17 of that year, declaring himself "Norton the First," Emperor of the United States. He appeared to believe that the California Legislature had made him Emperor of California, but this, he noted, was ridiculous, since California was only one state of a larger nation and couldn't have its own emperor. (He was reported variously as having described himself as the scion of English and French royalty.) One of his admirers suggested he also be Protector of Mexico, and this was added to his title though later, during the tempestuous period of Maximilian, he dropped it, saying, "It is impossible to protect such an unsettled nation."

In the heady, "anything-goes" atmosphere of old San Francisco, Norton's apparent delusion caught the popular imagination. Soon he was being treated as a city institution. The City Council voted to make him a "free citizen" and urged merchants to give him anything he wanted free of charge. He had the run of virtually all the city's restaurants, taverns, theaters, and clothing and cigar stores, and enjoyed free rides on trolley cars, railroads, and steamers.

He monitored construction sites, markets, and docks, and went to the state capital at Sacramento to observe the Legislature in session, where a special seat was reserved for him in the Senate gallery. He frequented libraries to stay well-informed and regularly attended religious services of various denominations, including, on Saturday, Temple Emanu-el, the city's large Reform temple, where he occupied a front pew, folklore has it, with his legendary dogs, Bummer and Lazarus. He traveled to the University of California in Berkeley and took part in debates at San Francisco's Lyceum of Free Culture.

Norton was allowed to draw "checks" for up to 50 cents at San Francisco banks. He also sold 50-cent "bonds," levied modest "taxes" to raise funds, and gave away much of the money so raised to those needier than himself. Once, when his clothing was getting visibly ragged, the City Council bought the emperor a new uniform.

Norton's insanity, if that was truly what it was, had clear limits. He was known for generally perceptive comments on public affairs and similarly shrewd business advice he continued to give friends and acquaintances. When he did visit "men of affairs," Robert Cowan, author of *Forgotten Characters of Old San Francisco*, notes: "The Emperor had the rare discretion that never permitted himself to be regarded as a nuisance. His own business training had taught him to appear at a suitable time and retire at a proper moment."

In physical appearance, Norton was said to bear a resemblance to then-reigning Napoleon III of France. A heavy-set man of medium height, Norton had slightly curly brown hair and heavy eyebrows under a massive forehead. He wore a mustache and beard and had clear, penetrating eyes. He dressed in an often-faded military-style navy blue uniform profusely adorned with brass buttons. His shoulders were decorated with massive gold epaulettes, often tarnished from exposure. He wore a red rose in his coat lapel and carried a brightly colored silk kerchief.

In his early years as "Emperor," he wore a military cap embellished with red trimming. In 1865, a follower gave him a tall beaver hat and this, replaced from time to time, became his headgear. His shoes were cut out in front to relieve discomfort from corns.

Though Norton's reign was generally calm, it had its turbulent moments. On July 12, 1860, he declared the Union dissolved. Also that year, he ordered a blockade of the Sacramento River to bring to terms a local shipping line that had refused him free transport. In 1862, he asked all Christian denominations to publicly and formally ordain him as emperor so he might "bring order out of chaos into which the country has been plunged. . . ." Another proclamation dissolved the Democratic and Republican parties in the interest of peace. Norton was infuriated in 1865 by one D. Stellifer Moulton of New York and Boston, who had proclaimed himself king and "reigning prince of the House of David." In a proclamation beginning, "Down with usurpers and imposters!" he ordered that Moulton be seized and brought in chains to San Francisco for trial.

In contrast to the general humorous support given Norton by San Franciscans, he was once and only once arrested, in 1867, by a new deputy who brought him before the Commissioner of Lunacy. He was promptly dismissed with an apology and a verdict that "he had shed no blood, robbed no one and despoiled no country, which is more than can be said of his fellows in that line." The imperial funds of $4.75 and the key to his "palace" were returned to him.

On only one occasion was violence of any kind attributed to the emperor. Ed Jump, a prominent San Francisco cartoonist, had drawn Norton eating a free lunch with his two dogs beside him waiting for crumbs. When Norton saw the caricature displayed in a store window, he reportedly growled, "It's an insult to the dignity of an emperor!" and crashed his walking stick through the window to demolish the offending print.

Probably his most famous and prophetic proclamation came in 1869, when he commanded that bridges be built across San Francisco Bay, connecting both with Marin to the north and with Alameda County, Oakland and Berkeley to the east. Though at the time the proposal was considered wildly impractical, Norton was remembered fondly sixty-five years later when both bridges were in fact built (the one to the north being the world-famous Golden Gate). Norton was so enthusiastic about this idea that he didn't stop with a proclamation but actually presented a bogus $3 million check to the president of the city's largest bank to get the project rolling.

Like many aspirants to greatness in the sometimes dreamlike atmosphere of San Francisco, Norton's surroundings often didn't match his vision. Far from being a castle, Norton's residence was a six-by-ten-foot room with a threadbare carpet and broken furniture at Eureka Lodging House, where the nightly rent of fifty cents was probably paid by the Masons, of which he was an ardent member of long standing. His room featured portraits of foreign rulers—though, in his lifetime, he met only one of his "peers," Emperor Don Pedro of Brazil—and his hat collection.

Most of Norton's genuine proclamations reflected his idealism and concerned serious matters, chiefly international relations and the Civil War. But humorists haunted Norton and distributed bogus proclamations in his name on matters of less moment. Some of their rude jokes involved the emperor's own marital status. Once a fake proclamation was issued in his name to the effect that while the emperor contemplated marriage, he wished to arouse no jealousy among the females of the realm, so he was leaving it to the women themselves to decide which of them was to become empress. Another, apparently successful, hoax played in the last days of his reign was an attempt to induce Norton to believe that by a match with Britain's Queen Victoria, he could bring the two nations closer together. Among his final effects were found congratulatory telegrams purportedly signed by Czar Alexander of Russia, President Ulysses Grant, Lord Beaconsfield of Britain, and others, expressing their happiness over the proposed marriage.

One of Norton's least favorite people was anti-Chinese labor leader Denis Kearny. Kearny articulated both racist prejudice and resentment by white workers of the effects of Chinese immigration in cutting wage levels and increasing unemployment. Norton once ordered that Kearny be decapitated. When the emperor died, a telegram was found in his pocket, purportedly sent by the emperor of China, suggesting Kearny be exiled to that country.

Another of Norton's causes in later years was his 1876 agitation against President Ulysses Grant's efforts to be re-elected to a third term, including an unsuccessful order to the state senate that it officially protest Grant's efforts.

One of the few indications of Norton's Jewish origins was that while he frequently mentioned God in his proclamations, he never referred to Jesus Christ.

Norton suffered a stroke on January 8, 1880, at the age of 60, while standing on the corner of California and Grant streets in San Francisco's Chinatown, and died within minutes. An enormous crowd, variously estimated from ten to thirty thousand, came to his funeral. Norton left an estate of one two-dollar gold piece, three dollars in silver, and an 1823 franc. The established Jewish community considered Norton something of an embarrassment, and he was buried in a Masonic cemetery.

"Poor, sometimes soiled and shabby, pathetic and philosophic, but always with a noble mind," says historian Cowan, "he bore himself with dignity amid squalid surroundings . . . with one fixed purpose, the welfare of his people."

The Stingiest Man in San Francisco

Michael Reese was another legendary Jewish San Franciscan character of the mid-and-late nineteenth century. Unlike Emperor Norton, Reese was one of the richest men in San Francisco and, it was said, the stingiest. He once told Methodist minister and writer (later bishop) O. P. Fitzgerald: "My love of money is a disease. My saving and hoarding as I do is irrational, and I know it. It pains me to pay five cents for a streetcar ride, or a quarter of a dollar for dinner."

A man whose wealth was estimated at up to $20 million, Reese was known for stepping into a German bakery at the corner of Montgomery and Sacramento Streets in San Francisco's financial district, going to the table where waiters cut the bread, gathering up a plateful of discarded pieces and eating them with a cup of coffee.

Reese was born in Bavaria in 1817, arrived in the United States in 1837 and came to San Francisco in 1850. He arrived in California with a reported capital of $120,000, derived from importing and other businesses, and multiplied this sum many times over. He was renowned for his refusal to give to charity and was reported to have assaulted a tailor who charged him ten cents for repairing the seat of a pair of pants.

Rev. O. P. Fitzgerald recalls calling on Reese for a charitable contribution:

Seeing that he was intently engaged, I paused and looked at him. A man of huge frame, with enormous hands and feet, massive head, receding forehead, and heavy cerebral development, full sensual lips, large nose, and peculiar eyes that seemed at the same time to look though you and to shrink from your gaze—he was a man at whom a stranger would stop in the street to get a second gaze. There he sat at his desk, much too absorbed to notice my entrance. Before him lay a large pile of one-thousand-dollar United States Government bonds, and he was clipping off coupons. That face! It was a study as he sat using the big pair of scissors. A hungry boy in the act of taking into his mouth a ripe cherry, a mother gazing down in the pretty face of her sleeping child, a lover looking into the eyes of his charmer, are but faint figures by which to express the intense pleasure he felt in his work. But there was also a feline element in his joy—his handling of those bonds was something like a cat toying with his prey. When at length he raised his head, there was a fierce gleam in his eyes and a flush in his face. I had come upon a devotee engaged in worship. This was Mike Reese, the miser and millionaire. Placing a huge hand on the pile of bonds, he gruffly returned my salutation.

"Good morning." He turned as he spoke and cast a look of scrutiny into my face which said plain enough that he wanted me to make known my business with him at once.

I told him what I wanted. At the request of the official board of the Minna Street Church I had come to ask him to make a contribution toward the payment of its debt.

"O yes; I was expecting you. They all come to me. Father Gallagher, of the Catholic Church, Dr. Wyatt, of the Episcopal Church, and all the others, have been here too. I feel friendly to the churches, and I treat all alike—it won't be fair for me to be partial—*I don't give to any!*"

That last clause was an anticlimax, dashing my hopes rudely; but I saw he meant it, and left. I never heard of his departing from the rule of strict impartiality he had laid down for himself.

Reese died in 1878 while visiting Bavaria. A newspaper account reported he died climbing a cemetery fence to avoid a toll gate, although it is not certain whether this was true in a literal or merely a literary sense.

According to the story recounted in Jackson Graves' *My Seventy Years in California*, Reese walked eight miles to the cemetery where his parents were buried. To save the pfennig (a small coin) the cemetery gatekeeper would have charged for entry, Reese, then over sixty years old, walked a couple of hundred yards from the gate and tried to climb over the cemetery wall, but fell off and broke his neck.

He did make one notable contribution while alive, that of $2,000 to the University of California for the acquisition of a scholar's personal library.

In his will, though, he actually left some $400,000 to charities, but this was considered extremely disappointing as a share of his huge estimated personal wealth. His estate provided $80,000 for the rebuilding of Chicago's Jewish hospital after its destruction in the 1871 Chicago fire, on the condition that the new hospital bear his name. Ironically, this began a myth of Reese as a great philanthropist, especially in Chicago, where much of his family lived. This new "counter-legend" grew to the point that the same newspaper that reported the cemetery fence story called for the building of a statue of Reese "the philanthropist."

Holy Moses

The King of Hawaii was intrigued with a traveling self-styled "rabbi" in 1887 and made him his soothsayer and astrologer. Soon the Jew, Elias Rosenberg, had such power over the king that the local press angrily called him "Holy Moses."

Blessed with some Hebrew knowledge and lots of *chutzpah*, Rosenberg got himself quarters in the royal palace. He impressed the king, David Kalahaua, with his chanting and "occult" powers and taught the monarch Hebrew. He spent much of his time practicing magic, reading the stars and chanting Bible stories. He persuaded the king to appoint him appraiser of customs.

But within a few months, a revolution limited the king's power and forced Rosenberg to return to San Francisco. In gratitude for his service, the king gave Rosenberg an inscribed silver cup, a gold medal, and $260.

For some reason, Rosenberg left with the king a Torah scroll he had brought to Hawaii. It was passed down through the royal family and lent to Honolulu Jews for services for many years.

Divine Sarah

Legends wrapped themselves about French-Jewish actress Sarah Bernhardt. Folklore had it she napped in a rosewood coffin lined with quilted satin, and that she'd domesticated a lion cub that, along with monkeys and other normally wild animals, lived in the garden of her mansion.

Throughout her American tour, the clergy trailed her with invective. A New York preacher called her "the European courtesan who has come to ruin the morals of the American people." But the criticism didn't keep people away. The passionate sermons preached against her by the bishop of Chicago proved such valuable advertising her manager sent the cleric $200 "for your poor."

The actress went on to sweep audiences throughout the country off their feet. At the end of one performance, an ecstatic audience gave her twenty-seven curtain calls. Critics praised the music of her golden voice, the expressiveness of her face with its beautiful crown of red-golden hair, the eloquence of her gestures, her feline tread. American women demanded clothes that would give them the tragedienne's "spiral silhouette."

In Boston, two wealthy art collectors decorated Miss Bernhardt's hotel suite with their most valuable paintings. In St. Louis, her manager insisted that her jewels be displayed in the window of a leading jeweler, who added costly items from his own stock and pretended that they were her property. On the night she left St. Louis, it was discovered that a gang of outlaws planned to uncouple her car from the train and relieve her of her jewels. Detectives shot it out with the bandits, foiling the plot.

Local folklore of Rochester, Iowa, claims "the divine Sarah" was born there. According to this story, she was Sarah King, who ran away from Rochester, joined a traveling troupe of actors, later entered a French convent in St. Paul, and eventually went to Paris to make theatrical history.

Bathing in Milk— Naughty Anna Held

Anna Held was a petite French-Jewish actress with enormous dark eyes. Determined to make her a queen of musical comedy, her husband Florenz Ziegfeld decided to wrap her in legend.

The American public was soon startled by the news that, for the sake of her beauty, Miss Held took a daily bath in milk. Gallons of milk were ordered delivered to her hotel daily. Ziegfeld actually escorted a group of skeptical reporters to her suite to view her immersed. Soon wealthy women everywhere were sitting, up to their necks, in tubs full of milk.

Before this sensation died down, there was another. A man at a party bet he could kiss Miss Held 200 times with what he called "undiminished ardor." Miss Held declared him the loser after 162. The furor growing out of this story added to a reputation for seductiveness not easily matched. Ziegfeld's plans were realized, and the appearance in a musical comedy of the five-foot-tall actress with the famed eighteen-inch waist became a magnet that attracted capacity crowds.

The couple wouldn't let well enough alone in building Miss Held's reputation as a symbol of glamour, chic and French "naughtiness." Ziegfeld let it be known he had paid $20,000 for one of her gowns. Miss Held challenged any American woman to race her by auto from New York to Philadelphia; the challenger had to drive an American car, she would drive a French one.

Miss Held gave Ziegfeld, her second husband, the idea for his famous "Follies," and starred in its first performance in 1907. Her two most popular songs were "Won't You Come and Play Wiz Me?" and "I Just Can't Make My Eyes Behave."

He Made the Stars

David Belasco was an actor, director, and playwright—but above all, he was a starmaker, and one of the most colorful figures of the turn-of-the-century American theater. A school of drama was given the name "Belascoism," emphasizing spectacular sets that meticulously represented reality. Belasco affected a theatrical personal appearance, wearing a clerical suit and collar, his heavy-lidded dark eyes smoldering under thick black brows. He spread the false rumor he'd been educated in a Canadian monastery. He generally acted the role of David Belasco, amazing personality.

The public bought the legend of starmaker Belasco too, which, as he put it, made him a "ferocious monster who would stop at no limit of physical violence to compel my actresses to do my bidding." This side of the Belasco image grew out of a highly publicized lawsuit in which he'd described in court the training he'd given his first big star, Leslie Carter.

He told of rehearsing Mrs. Carter in the scene of the play *Oliver Twist* in which Bill Sykes murders Nancy, dragging her about by the hair and beating her head against the wall. His vivid account of the scene led the press to report, as Belasco put it, that in order "to stimulate her emotional fervor," he had mauled the actress with "fiendishly calculated brutality."

Another young actress whom Belasco made a star was propitiously named Frances Starr. A frail-looking, high-strung girl, she greatly admired the French-Jewish actress Sarah Bernhardt. He gave Miss Starr the lead in his play *The Rose of the Rancho,* and her performance convinced him she could excel in roles requiring "intense emotionalism," if only, as Belasco put it, "I could contrive somehow to stir her imagination to even higher pitch."

When he got the script for *The Easiest Way,* a play about a "kept woman," Belasco gave the starring role of Laura Murdock to Miss Starr. In the climactic scene, Laura, trapped by her own false words and abandoned by the man who tried to redeem her, grabs a gun with the thought of killing herself. She lacks the courage to do it, and with a shriek of terror, throws the weapon down.

Belasco felt this scene had to be worked up to the highest possible emotional intensity. He wanted a scream that would describe a "soul in torment." He rehearsed the scene scores of times, but Miss Starr could not satisfy him. To get what he wanted, he humiliated her, driving her to greater and greater upset; he rehearsed her over and over and over for hours, while the rest of the cast looked on in silent anger, and Miss Starr became more and more desperate. Still she did not satisfy him. Finally, he remembered what she had often told him of her worship of Sarah Bernhardt.

"And *you* want to be as great as *Sarah Bernhardt,*" he said, the most contemptuous sarcasm in his voice, "*it makes me laugh!*"

At that, Miss Starr screamed hysterically and passed out on the stage. When she came to, he told her, "That's what I want! That's exactly what I've been working for these last three hours."

Levy's Gold

Dave Levy was a pioneer tavern-keeper in Boise, Idaho. One day, he asked workmen laying a new sidewalk around his house to lift part of the walk. When they did, he pulled out a pot of gold.

It created a sensation. Levy made frequent trips to Rocky Canyon north of Boise; this, on top of the "pot of gold" incident, led to the belief that Levy had a buried fortune.

Dave Levy was murdered in 1902. After his heirs failed to find the gold he was supposed to have hidden, it was thought that his hoard was stored somewhere in the canyon. For many years, a favorite pastime around Boise was to spend a day in the canyon searching for Dave Levy's gold.

5

DWELLING IN DARKNESS: THE EARLY AMERICAN-JEWISH COMMUNITY

Blows passed in a certain synagogue in New York on Kol Nidre evening, because one party insisted that, at the close of the service, the Adon Olam be sung first, and then the Yigdal, while the other insisted on the opposite.

—New York newspaper, 1846

*   *   *

I dwell in complete darkness, without a teacher or companion. . . . The religious life in this land is on the lowest level.

—Rabbi Abraham Rice, 1849

*   *   *

Here a man qualifies himself, ordains himself; he is his own college, his own professor, his own diploma. He is what he claims to be.

—Rabbi M. Jastrow, 1885

Mordecai Moses Mordecai: The Tide of Intermarriage

A well-repeated story that ties the American Revolution into the conflicts that beset early Jewish colonial communities concerns a Philadelphia Jew (and former rabbinical student) named Mordecai Moses Mordecai.

Mordecai came with his wife to attend a ball being given in Easton, Pennsylvania, then a frontier settlement by the forks of the Delaware River, on July 26, 1782, to honor General George Washington, commander of the Continental forces. Among the distinguished townspeople attending were Myer Hart, Mordecai's brother-in-law and reputedly the wealthiest Jew in Northampton County, Pennsylvania. Myer and his wife Rachel brought along their twenty-year-old daughter, Judith, and all were introduced to Washington's party.

During the course of the party, a romance developed between Judith and James Pettigrew, "a dashing officer" and a Christian, who had worked on Washington's staff. Within a few months, it was clear Judith was pregnant. Her father was hysterical. The rumor spread that the two had actually been married during the party by a Protestant Continental Army chaplain.

Rachel begged Uncle Mordecai to make another trip to Easton to "restore peace in the family." Mordecai, described by contemporary sources as "irrepressible," did so, promptly arranging an agreement between the couple and the enraged father providing that the two young people would raise any daughters as Jews and any sons as Christians.

While this agreement calmed the family, word soon got out that during his visit, Mordecai had also taken it on himself to perform the then unheard-of act of marrying Judith and James in the traditional Jewish ceremony. Officials of Philadelphia's Congregation Mikveh Israel were outraged that a congregant would presume to perform a Jewish wedding with a Christian, nonconverting partner. The congregation's president called Mordecai before a *Bet Din*s (religious court) and convicted him of the illegal act. Mordecai, known as a pious and orthodox Jew who had sat on earlier Mikveh Israel *Bet Din*s himself, refused to accept the court's judgment, denounced everyone involved and likened the proceedings to the Spanish Inquisition. In the absence of any rabbinic authorities in the colonies, something of an impasse developed. Three years later, this incident would be recalled when Mordecai again led a revolt against traditional procedures.

When Benjamin Clava, a Jew who had been married to a Christian woman, died in 1785, another Mikveh Israel *Bet Din* agreed with congregational officials that it was time to take a stand against the rising tide of intermarriage, ruling that although Clava could be buried in the Jewish cemetery, he would not be accorded the traditional burial rites. He would be buried instead in the section of the cemetery reserved for suicides, prayers would not be recited at the burial, and his body would not be ritually washed and dressed.

Mordecai Moses Mordecai apparently disagreed with this decision and, at the prompting of Clava's widow, led a group of community rebels into the room where the deceased's body lay and ritually washed and clothed the body. Again, the officials of Mikveh Israel were enraged, but again, in the absence of local rabbinic authority, they were at pains to decisively quash Mordecai and his rebel faction.

At length, they sent anguished reports on both cases against Mordecai to the Chief Rabbi of Amsterdam. His response, if any, and any subsequent action taken against Mordecai, have not come down to us.

Jewish in New Orleans

Early American-Jewish religious life was often disorganized and even chaotic. Jewish communities outside the Eastern Seaboard were generally small and relatively isolated. Not only were settlers separated from the milieu that had supported traditional practices but, until 1840, there was not a single ordained rabbi in the United States. In smaller communities, especially in the West and South, where Jews were few and tended to be less traditional, the synagogue might typically not have a building and the "rabbi" might be part-time or unpaid. But New Orleans was still special.

That city, exotic, cosmopolitan and decadent, occupies a special niche in early American-Jewish folklore, with its small, worldly and highly assimilated community of Jews that yet continued to maintain a distinct kind of Jewish identity. Perhaps New Orleans had a special place in folklore because it captured the dilemma of the American Jew writ large, the traditional person separated from his roots and dropped into an alien golden world full of money, temptation and often-friendly Gentiles of all colors.

The New Orleans synagogue Shaaray Chesed (Gates of Mercy), founded in 1828 by a merger of Sephardic and Ashkenazic congregations, had neither Torah nor shofar until 1833. The Torah scrolls it acquired that year was described by an observer as "so shot through with holes . . . no one would have ventured to read it." Manis Jacobs, a layman considered a relative scholar because he could read Hebrew, was "rabbi." (Rabbi Jacobs was to die in 1839, folklore tells, six days after feasting on a hearty Yom Kippur midday dinner, and be succeeded by the legendary Albert "Roley" Marks.)

The special climatic and topographic conditions of New Orleans also lent themselves to a unique folklore. In New Orleans, for example, burials actually took place in water. It was generally impossible to dig more than several inches into the swampy earth before hitting water. New Orleans' unique topography, the laxity of Jewish observance, and the continuing link many of its Jews yet kept with that identity led to one of the stranger burial stories on record, in which a deceased woman was buried in the presence of her husband's new second wife. "Rabbi" Jacobs officiated.

A Jewish couple lived outside the city. When the wife, Leah, became very ill, she made her husband promise to bury her at the Jewish cemetery in town. After her death, the level of the waterway connecting their area with the city was too low for a boat to pass, and it was considered too dangerous to travel the route by land, through wet marsh filled with crocodiles. Her body was preserved in a barrel filled with alcohol while the family waited for the rains to come and the waterway to rise. The dry spell continued, and soon *Shloshim*, the traditional thirty-day mourning period, passed, and still Leah lay in her alcohol barrel. Some rain finally came, but only lifted the rivers enough for one man in a canoe to safely navigate. The bereaved husband had to make a business trip to the city. During this trip, he met a woman and became engaged. By the time he got home, the riverway was high enough for safe transport and the burial was scheduled.

At the burial the husband, dressed in a black suit, came with his new wife, dressed in white. Holes were bored in the side and bottom of the wooden coffin, as usual, so that the water would enter and the casket stay submerged. The coffin was lowered beneath the damp earth until it floated, perhaps a foot below the surface, on a pool of water. Two black gravediggers than jumped on either end of the coffin, which quickly filled with water and sank, and they scrambled hurriedly back to land. After the prayers were completed, the tomb was covered with a mud mound.

Holy Roley

When Manis Jacobs died in 1839, the congregation hired a comic actor, part-time fireman and part-time customs inspector named Albert "Roley" Marks, who had also been functioning as its part-time secretary, to be its part-time rabbi.

Roley was barely over four feet tall, a pudgy, round-faced, good-natured British Jew. His true work was the theater; he was known as a character actor who played old men in humorous parts. But since he wasn't able to make enough to support his family from New Orleans theater alone, he'd accumulated a number of part-time jobs. There was some dispute over whether Roley first got his nickname from his physical appearance or his performance as the character Rowley in the play *School for Scandal*.

His stage laughter was renowned. A contemporary theater critic wrote: "It would do your heart good to see one of his laughs—I say *see*, for nothing is *heard* when he laughs; a turning up of his eyes, a filling up of his cheeks with wind, and suddenly letting it burst forth, at the same time giving himself a half-turn, winking at the audience, swinging his cane about—and it is done."

Rabbi wasn't a natural role for Roley. He was married to a Catholic, had had none of his sons circumcised, kept neither the Sabbath nor *kashrut*, and ate bread openly on Passover. Given the state of religious observance in Jewish New Orleans, this was not in itself unusual; a contemporary survey found only two New Orleans Jewish families observed the Sabbath, four kept kosher, and less than a third of even congregational members had their sons circumcised.

One Purim evening, Roley wasn't even in *shul* to read the Megillah; he was out fighting a fire, becoming something of a local joke and raising congregational discontent. Gentiles were laughingly calling Roley "chief rabbi" of New Orleans. Meanwhile, an orthodox faction in the congregation was pushing to bar the intermarried majority from even synagogue membership.

The following Rosh Hashanah, as Roley assumed his position to lead services, an angry congregant named Gershom Kursheedt, a German-Spanish Jew who'd become a leader of the orthodox anti-Roley faction, demanded he step down from the pulpit. Roley asked why. Kursheedt said he had no right to lead the services, charging him with a long list of religious breaches. Roley pounded the pulpit angrily and shouted: "By Jesus Christ, I have a right to *daven* and no one will dare stop me!" Roley Marks's reign as New Orleans' "chief" and only "rabbi" ended shortly thereafter.

Rebecca Gratz's Sunday School

In 1838, Rebecca Gratz founded the first Jewish Sunday school in the New World, in Philadelphia, modeled after the Christian Sunday schools of that city. Miss Gratz began the class with a prayer starting, "Come ye children, hearken unto me, and I will teach you the fear of the Lord." At first, the school used Pyke's Catechism, with "Who formed you, child, and made you live?" and the response, "God did my life and spirit give." Scriptural lessons were taught from a small illustrated work published by the Christian Sunday School Union. Rosa Mordecai, Gratz's grandniece, spent many long summer days pasting strips of paper over answers unsuitable for Jewish children.

Rabbi Isaac Leeser of nearby Mikveh Israel, a constant visitor to the school, soon replaced the catechism with his own material and the King James Version of the Bible with his translation of the Holy Scriptures.

Rosa Mordecai recalled the school in her memoirs: Rabbi Leeser's "pockmarked face, gold spectacles and inexhaustible fund of ever-ready information," Rabbi Sabato Morais, "always ready to lead Hebrew hymns or take the class of an absent teacher," and the distribution of prizes, books chosen by Gratz and handed to each child, along with an orange and a pretzel.

Folklore has it that Gratz was the model for the character Rebecca in Sir Walter Scott's novel *Ivanhoe*. She was a close friend of American writer Washington Irving, who apparently praised her effusively and described her in detail to Scott during a European visit. Rebecca and her two sisters were called the three "graces," a pun on "Gratzes," by Philadelphia humorists of their day.

Finally, a Real Rabbi

In 1840, Abraham Rice, the first ordained rabbi in the United States, arrived in New York from Bavaria (from which a majority of America's Jews of that time had come). After unsuccessfully trying to re-establish a synagogue in Newport, Rhode Island, he ran into a *landsman* from Germany, Aaron Weglein, then president of the Baltimore Hebrew Congregation. Weglein brought Rice back to Baltimore, where he preached on Rosh Hashanah 1840. Rice would stay at the congregation for nine years.

Although the congregation was, like the rabbi, predominantly Bavarian and theoretically Orthodox, the membership and rabbi soon ran into problems much like those that would plague other congregations throughout American-Jewish history.

Most congregants believed in the Sabbath, for example, but often felt they personally couldn't afford to observe it. Rice first insisted that those who worked or kept their businesses open on the Sabbath be denied *aliyot* (the honor of being called to chant the blessings over the Torah). He hadn't accounted for how large a proportion of the congregation this would put him in conflict with, nor how much the donations that accompanied *aliyot* meant in financial support for the synagogue.

So the rabbi fell back to another position—although Sabbath-breakers would be permitted to say the blessings over the Torah, the congregation would not respond with the customary *amen*s. A later edict excluded persons keeping their businesses open "in the city" (tacitly excluding traveling peddlers) from holding congregational office, but this too proved unenforceable. The problem of Sabbath violation was continually on the congregational agenda, as even the synagogue's president, vice-president and treasurer were charged with doing business on the Sabbath. Congregational minutes report the decision was made "to postpone discussion on these charges indefinitely."

In 1842, another revolt broke out against Rice when he tried, at a congregant's funeral, to stop lodge brothers of the deceased from performing Masonic and Odd Fellows rites at the graveside. A segment of the congregation seceded after this incident to form Har Sinai, which would become the first permanent Reform congregation in the United States.

"The heavens may vanish and the Earth wear out with age," said Rabbi Rice, in a faithful Orthodox view, "but still not an iota will vanish from our religion." In frustration, he resigned his post in 1849 and wrote to his old teacher, Wolf Hamburger, a Talmud scholar at the Wurzburg *yeshiva* where he had studied:

> I dwell in complete darkness, without a teacher or companion. . . . The religious life in this land is on the lowest level, most people eat foul food and desecrate the Sabbath in public. . . . Thousands marry non-Jewish women. Under these circumstances my mind is perplexed and I wonder whether it is even permissible for a Jew to live in this land. I am tired of my life. . . . I often think of leaving and going to Paris and put my trust in the good Lord.

In 1853, the rule prohibiting Sabbath violators from being called to the Torah was formally taken off the books of the Baltimore Hebrew Congregation.

To make a living after his resignation, Rice started a grocery and dry goods store.

As rabbi, Rice had agitated vigorously against the activities of the American Society for Meliorating the Conditions of the Jews, a missionary organization. The congregation had voted indigent Jewish families a $3-a-month stipend to help them resist the blandishments of such Christian societies. After his resignation, a delegation from the Society, adding insult to injury, visited Rice at his home, apparently imagining it might possibly convert the biggest catch in town; it was not well received.

In 1851 Rice organized his own small synagogue, which he served as rabbi but from which he received no income.

He wrote to Isaac Leeser:

I have made it a practice not to make religion a means of livelihood. I do not want to have anything to do with Jews. . . . In Baltimore, all is lost for it is "a people that has broken loose."

Ironically, in 1862, the last year of his life, the Baltimore Hebrew Congregation invited him back and he agreed to serve, but he died after the High Holidays that year. In line with his instructions, no eulogies were said at his funeral.

An Anti-Semitic Incident

The independent pioneer spirit and the ideals of the new land grew within the immigrants so they might react with the most extreme indignation to infringements that would have seemed trivial in Europe. A San Diego Jew, Lewis Franklin, wrote about what he called an "anti-Semitic" incident that occurred in his community on Rosh Hashanah 1858, which Franklin said "disgraced civilization."

He went on in this vein in a letter to the editor:

Were I to say that unmitigated disgust fills my bones I would scarcely express myself, as a wrong I shall here relate to you, knows no parallel in the annals of the civilized world—and I, in common with all my co-religionists, call upon you to give publicity in the matter, so that the perpetrators may be marked with the rebuke of scorn by a free and independent press.

The incident in question, which may have more reflected ignorance and carelessness than anti-Semitism per se, involved a Jewish grape grower, Moses Menasse, who traveled fifty miles from his homestead to attend Rosh Hashanah services in San Diego. A deputy sheriff appeared at the synagogue and asked Menasse to appear before a grand jury sitting that day. Menasse replied he could not, that he was worshipping. Later, the deputy returned with a subpoena requiring Menasse to testify. The congregation insisted en masse that Menasse was needed for the *minyan* and that the deputy had no right to serve a subpoena during services.

The third time, the deputy reappeared with a posse that took Menasse to the grand jury by force. Brought before the jury, the Jew refused to testify. The sheriff then released Menasse to return to services; he came back to the jury after sundown and answered the routine questions put to him.

Other incidents of this kind were reported in California during this period, and the militant tone of the Jewish response says something about the degree to which, by the 1850s, even the tiny minority of Jews in the West had come to expect full religious freedom as a matter of right in the New World.

Pistol-Packing Rabbi

Conflicts between rabbis and congregations are nothing new in America. In Europe, a rabbinic post was often a lifelong sinecure, frequently even guaranteed by the state. The rabbi was traditionally a man renowned for learning, piety and wisdom. But in America, arrangements were far less stable. Highly qualified rabbis were few. The rabbi became more of an employee to be hired and fired at will by a congregational board of directors. The situation was worse in earlier times when many Jewish communities, typically with only one real synagogue, were indecisive about which way to go in the struggle between Orthodoxy and Reform.

Common as conflict was, a nadir may have been reached in 1880 by Rabbi Moses May and Portland, Oregon's Congregation Beth Israel.

Although not formally ordained as a rabbi, May was hired by the congregation over twenty-one other applicants in 1872. He introduced the Reform prayer book to the nominally Orthodox but transitional congregation. May was not known for his tact or patience, and by 1876, Beth Israel was already advertising for a new preacher.

But May and his faction fought back hard. Charges and counter-charges multiplied but May held on. In 1878 the congregation resumed advertising for what it called a "moderate Reform" rabbi. In January 1879, a "public hearing" was set up to air all the charges made against May so they could be openly investigated. Among the formal charges were: that May had acted "as a libertine and a rake" during a recent visit to San Francisco; that he had "blackmailed" several members of the congregation; that he had slandered the married women of the congregation generally, referring to them as "ladies of easy virtue"; that he had called officers and members of the congregation "outlandish names," opened mail addressed to others in order to prepare slanders against the letters' authors, and threatened to join the Unitarian Church if the congregational president were re-elected.

After a year of investigation, the board of directors decided to absolve May of all charges against him and to cover over the pages in its minute book charging him with various offenses.

But on October 1, 1880, tempers flared again. The rabbi and a prominent congregant named Waldman confronted each other on a Portland street corner—directly under the window of a hotel where President Rutherford Hayes was then staying. May was angry with Waldman for having allegedly misquoted him. When Waldman appeared to gain the advantage at fisticuffs, May pulled out a pistol and fired two shots at the congregant. He missed; passers-by separated, and police subsequently arrested the two.

May, who became known to folklore as "the pistol-packing rabbi," left town shortly. The board of directors voted to reverse themselves and reopen the minutes detailing the earlier charges against him. And, once again, Beth Israel advertised for a new spiritual leader.

Isaac Mayer Wise: Albany and Beyond

When Isaac Mayer Wise, the young German missionary of Reform Judaism, tried to "reform" his first congregation, Beth El in Albany, New York, in the late 1840s, he faced considerable opposition. While not concealing his ideas from those hiring him, he introduced reforms that still shocked a large portion of the congregation. Wise, who would become the leader of American Reform and a guiding force in the founding of Hebrew Union College and the Union of American Hebrew Congregations, replaced Hebrew prayers with English and German hymns sung by choirs, abolished the women's gallery, and even refused to "sit *shiva*" (seven days of mourning) when his daughter died. Opposition to the changes built and eventually led to a congregational split.

On the Sabbath after Shavous, 1850, Wise found his rabbinic regalia had disappeared. Wise preached that day in his suit. Friends had a new gown made for him.

Wise went to see a temple board member who had opened his store on the Sabbath. He begged the member not to set a bad example and reminded him of the temple rule that board members must observe the Sabbath. The member refused to either close his store or quit the board. Some of the congregation feared Wise would raise the issue from the pulpit.

Congregational president Louis Spanier had been pro-Reform and a friend of Wise, but he'd begun to turn against both Wise and his Reform ideas. During Sabbath services the sexton handed Wise a note from Spanier: "The *parnass* (president) serves notice to you not to preach today." Wise went to the pulpit at the regular time. Spanier rose in front of Wise and said threateningly, "I tell you, you shall not preach today." Wise ignored Spanier, and began his sermon, speaking in a loud voice and drowning out the president.

Next the congregation refused to pay Wise's salary. Parents of children in the temple's religious school who opposed Wise stopped paying tuition, although the children kept attending school. Formal charges were offered against Wise: that he had written on Rosh Hashanah, that he had ridiculed the *mikveh* (traditional ritual bath for women), that he had been seen "swinging on a swing" on the Sabbath, and that he preached "a God of Reason" quite different from the traditional Hebrew God the congregation worshipped.

The congregation was bitterly divided. An eight-hour congregational meeting on what to do about Wise gave neither side a decisive advantage. At eleven o'clock the night of that meeting, president Spanier would still not entertain a motion for adjournment. At some point, the congregational vice-president made a motion to adjourn, a vote was somehow taken, and the vice-president declared the meeting adjourned, leaving with his supporters. After they'd left, Spanier declared the meeting still on, and the remaining rump session voted to oust Wise and not pay him back salary apparently due him.

Now the congregation was split into warring factions. On Rosh Hashanah 1850, Wise went to the synagogue, put on his rabbinic gown, and came to the *bimah* to find one of Spanier's supporters in his chair. He took another seat. The choir sang the Ain Komocho prayer, announcing the start of the Torah service. Wise relates in his memoirs what happened next:

At the conclusion of the song, I step before the Ark in order to take out the Scrolls of the Law as usual, and to offer prayer. Spanier was in my way, and, without saying a word, smites me with his fist so that my cap falls from my head.

This was the terrible signal for an uproar, the like of which I have never experienced. The people acted like furies. It was as though the synagogue had suddenly burst forth into a flaming conflagration. The Poles and Hungarians, who thought only of me, struck out like wild men. The young people jumped down from the choir gallery to protect me and had to fight their way through the surging crowd. Within two minutes the whole assembly was a struggling mass. The sheriff and his posse, who were summoned, were forced out until finally the whole assembly surged out of the house into Herkimer Street.

"Louis Spanier," I said to him, "there is the law to which I can appeal." He answered: "I have $100,000 more than you. I do not fear the law. I will ruin you."

I finally reached home, bowed with pain and inexpressible grief. The constable came and arrested me as the ringleader of a rebellious mob at a public service. He seized me by my coat and thus led me to the police station through the streets of Albany. The whole rabble was present in order to feast their eyes on the sight of their rabbi appearing before court on New Year's Day, but their hopes were disappointed, for the police judge went into an adjoining room and received me there. My friends had informed him of what had taken place, and he dismissed me on my word of honor. Three months later the constable died of a stroke of paralysis, one day after his discharge.

Who can describe that terrible day? Not I. It was agonizing, hellish torture.

Fortunately for Wise, Albany was not the peak of his rabbinic career.

In 1854, Wise went West, settling in Cincinnati, Ohio, the "Queen City of the West," a part of the country he felt would be more amenable to an "American Judaism." He started an English-language Jewish newspaper, *The Israelite*, and the German-language *Die Deborah*, reaching those who read English and German, the vast majority of American Jews of that time.

Wise was the first real organizer of American Jewry. In 1873, twenty-five years after he had first proclaimed his hopes for a union of American Jews, Wise finally succeeded in creating the Reform Union of American Hebrew Congregations. Two years later the Hebrew Union College, which he founded and which is now the oldest surviving Jewish theological school in the Western Hemisphere, opened its doors to students. By 1889, he had rallied the Reform-minded rabbis of the country into the Central Conference of American Rabbis.

In later years, when the Great Migration of Jews from Eastern Europe began, Wise remained a leader of the Americanized, German, Reform segment of American Jewry and was considered by many Russian immigrants a spokesman for "uptown" wealth, arrogance and even apostasy.

His enthusiasm for the Russians' style was limited too. When Wise was reported to have made comments like "We are Israelites, they are Jews," many downtowners retorted, "We are Jews, they are *goyim*." Wise had a style that particularly suited the "downtown" Russian image of "uptown" Germans, for example in his anti-Zionist comment: "We want no Jewish princes or government; we prefer President Hayes to a Jewish prince." In another frequently quoted remark he called Zionism simply "a momentary inebriation of morbid minds and a prostitution of Israel's holy cause to a madman's dance of unsound politicians."

The First Woman Rabbi?

Though never ordained, Rachel (Ray) Frank Litman preached widely in synagogues throughout the West in the 1890s and was actually offered her own pulpit in Chicago and elsewhere. She emphasized a message of reconciliation in the Jewish community between rich and poor, Orthodox and Reform, Jews of German descent and culture and the poorer and more numerous Russian-Polish immigrants.

A descendant of the Vilna *Gaon*, Rachel Frank was born in San Francisco in 1865 to Orthodox, Eastern European parents. She taught children in a mining camp in Nevada, settled in Oakland in the 1880s, where she taught Bible classes and, in 1891, became superintendent of Oakland's First Hebrew Congregation's Sabbath School. She was a gifted speaker and was soon lecturing the congregation. At the same time, she worked as a freelance journalist.

Her "rabbinic" career started on Erev Rosh Hashanah, 1890, when she arrived in Spokane Falls (now Spokane), Washington, and asked directions to the synagogue of a prominent Jew who had heard of her reputation as a speaker in Oakland. She was informed the town didn't currently have a synagogue but that, if she would give a sermon, a service would be arranged anyway. The local opera house was filled to hear her plead for construction of a new synagogue and religious school. After this sermon, Spokane Jews persuaded her to remain throughout the High Holidays.

From then on, she was in demand as a speaker to Jewish audiences throughout the West. She was famed for her abilities to articulate the identity American Jewish audiences felt with victims of persecution abroad as well as their desire to overcome internal dissension here. Dubbed "the latter-day Deborah," she studied for several months in 1893 at Hebrew Union College and became known as "the first woman rabbi." She was offered rabbinic posts but turned them down. Despite her trail-blazing role as a public speaker, she was quite conservative. She opposed the women suffragists of the 1890s, saying women were not yet "in the proper frame of mental development to go into politics." Although childless herself, she called motherhood "the culmination of womanhood" and warned that "every innovation, every change, is not progress."

On an 1899 European trip, she met Simon Litman, a Russian Jew whom she subsequently married. In 1908 she left Oakland to accompany her husband to Urbana, Illinois, where he'd taken a position as an economics professor. "Ray" Frank Litman receded from the public eye after the 1890s and never achieved the stature her youthful promise as an orator or writer appeared to foretell. She did serve as a healing voice during that period and a role model for a more active public place for women in the American-Jewish community.

6

THE JOYS OF PEDDLING

The Pack

"The pack," generations of immigrants were told, "will give you food to eat, teach you to talk, help you learn the country, emerge from your greenness." For new Jewish immigrants with no capital or experience of agriculture, and often some knowledge of business, peddling was often the path of least resistance to getting started in the new land, particularly before the era of mass-production industry.

While peddling, a man would fitfully learn English, meet people and see the country, getting a sense of its very different tone and pace. And he would hopefully save money toward the day he could open his own store.

The peddler garnered unfamiliar names. The Cherokee Indians called him *Jew-wedge-du-gish*, or "egg eater," for the eggs that often filled his pockets as he tried, at least at first, to adhere strictly to the traditional *kashrut* dietary laws in the new land. Philadelphia Jewish leader Isaac Leeser dubbed him "Son of the Weary Foot." The general public noted his guttural accent that called to mind the Dutch (or German "Deutsch") and often called him "Dutch" or "Dutch Peddler."

*   *   *

. . . None of us is able to observe the smallest commandment. Thousands of peddlers wander about America: young, strong men, they waste their strength by carrying heavy loads in the summer's heat: they lose their health in the icy cold of winter. And thus they forget completely their Creator. They no longer put on the phylacteries; they pray neither on working days nor on the Sabbath. In truth, they have given up their religion for the pack which is on their backs.

—Diary of Abraham Kohn, peddler, Upper Ohio Valley 1842–43

Pretty Sally Solomons

The isolated peddler in the American West usually had no one to pray with and, even more seriously, no one to marry. A popular ditty of the early nineteenth century sang of a peddler who has found his "Pretty Sally Solomons."

Though every place I rove,
A peddler by my trade
And soon I fell in love,
With a very pretty maid . . .

. . . one day, instead of calling my shoestrings I cried "Sally Solomons, all a penny a pair"; so de people laughed, and I looked like a fool—

And 'twas all for Sally Solomons,
Pretty Sally Solomons,

Oh, listen love, to me;
Would you be Mistress Ab'rams,
How happy should I be . . .

No girl in Duke's Place should compare
Bid her to buy and sell:
She made such bargains you would stare,
And so in love I fell.

Hyman Lazarus and the Steamboat

Most peddlers who worked on the Ohio River and its tributaries were happy with the advent of the steamboat; they stood to benefit handsomely from the speedier travel and the greater number of passengers traveling the rivers. One peddler, though, didn't follow the trend; he was immigrant Jew Hyman Lazarus, whose base was the town of Malta, Ohio, where Isaac Baker had built the state's first mill. The mill's base rested on two flatboats. Lazarus was said to be watching a vision on the horizon one day—one of the river's first steamboats—as it churned up the Muskingum River heading for the riverbank. Hysterical with alarm, Lazarus reportedly ran through town screaming: "Mr. Baker! Mr. Baker! Your mill haf got loose, und he is coming oop the river a-grinding like the Devil!"

Lost Language

A *hazzan* (cantor) reported in the 1850s that he had been traveling on a boat and had seen a peddler, a recent arrival from Germany, pacing the deck, evidently in great distress. Asked if he had a problem, the immigrant replied, in German, "I have lost everything! I have lost my English language." The man didn't understand.

"You don't understand? I arrived in New York, and after I paid off what I owe, I had twenty-five dollars left. So they said 'Pfeiffer, you buy a basket for six shillings, and twenty-four dollars worth of *kuddel muddel* (notions), and then you go out peddling in the country.' But I said, 'The country speaks English, and I do not. How can I get along?' They told me, 'That makes no difference. We'll write it all down for you.' They gave me the basket filled with *kuddel muddel* and wrote down the English language for me on a piece of paper and they sent me on my way. Now I've lost my English language and am completely helpless."

The American Jew comforted the anguished peddler, asked him to write down in German the sentences he thought he'd need, and in turn wrote down their English translations. This pleased the immigrant greatly, although it didn't completely solve his problems. He learned these sentences quite well, but in no particular order, and continued to approach customers and say things like: "You fant to puy sumdink? Can I shtay mit you all nacht?"

Sorry

Whereas in the old country, entrenched antipathy to Jews was common among the peasantry, in America the wandering peddler often encountered instead a naive and relatively benign ignorance. This was illustrated in a brief tale from Tennessee folklore:

A Jewish peddler was heading, exhausted, down a trail and encountered a hillbilly who had just "got religion" at a camp meeting. "Ain't you a Jew?" the mountaineer inquired. "I never seen a Jew," he allowed, "but I calculate you is one." The peddler cautiously responded that he was.

"Put your pack down," said the native, and proceeded to hit the surprised peddler. "What did you do that for?" he protested.

"What for?" repeated the hillbilly, "You crucified our Lord, that's what you done!"

The Jew told his attacker this had happened more than 1,800 years before and that, at least, he personally had had nothing to do with it. The man became suddenly apologetic.

"I'm sorry," he said in a tone of genuine remorse. "I was told at the camp meeting that the Jews crucified our Lord, and I figured you was one of the men that did it." He shrugged and added, "I never heard about it before today!"

Peddling in California

The practice of peddling was even harder in far western California, with its huge distances and difficult terrain; California peddlers often carried astounding loads. Folklore had it that the brawniest gold prospector could not lift even one of the two packs customarily carried by Russian-born peddler Abraham Rackovsky. When going on a steep climb uphill, Rackovsky would drag each pack to the top one at a time, then roll each down.

Slave to Servant

As a spokesman for American Jews of his time, Rabbi Isaac Mayer Wise learned of and in turn articulated the frustrations of the weary and often isolated Jewish immigrant peddlers, struggling to make their way in the New World.

Rabbi Wise passed on the folklore that the American Jews of those days could be divided into the following classes: (1) The basket peddler, altogether dumb and homeless; (2) the trunk carrier, who stammers some little English and hopes for better times; (3) the pack carrier, who carries from 100 to 150 pounds upon his back and indulges the thought that he will become a businessman some day.

Then there was the aristocracy, which could be divided into three classes: (1) The wagon baron, who peddles though the country with a one-or two-horse team; (2) the jewelry count, who carries a stock of watches and jewelry in a small trunk and is considered a rich man even now; (3) the store prince, who has a shop and sells goods in it. At first one was the slave of the basket or the pack; then, the lackey of the horse, in order to become, finally, the servant of the shop.

That's Business

Even in more recent times and more urban environments, peddling continued to provide both opportunities and terrors for the new immigrants, as noted in these reminiscences by Joseph Morgenstern of Cleveland (ca. 1907) about his uncle's horse and wagon peddling.

> Instead of heading toward the isolated farms away from the city, where the farmers were eager to receive peddlers amicably, my uncle, who was the manager of our business, rode out only a mile or so from our house. He began to "huckster" at the top of his voice: "Paper! Rags! Paper! Rags!" But the only immediate response to this announcement was the jeering cries of

the street-urchins: "God-damn-Jew-Sheeny!" These insults cut me to the heart and their bitter taste was more than I could bear.

When the uncle grabbed junk out of private backyards, the boy objected, but his uncle was unmoved: "That's the business! That's the business of peddling! Everything goes into the wagon. If you're too finicky you'll never make a living."

7

LEARNING THE ROPES: GREENHORNS AND THEIR ADVISERS

Hope must be beyond us. . . . If I had known . . . nothing could have induced me to go.

—Emigrant traveling in steerage from Hamburg at age twenty, writing in the ship's diary, 1848.

When I left for America, I was told the streets were paved with gold. When I got there, I found that not only were they not paved with gold, they weren't paved at all. And not only weren't they paved, but I was expected to pave them.

America

If one has no means of livelihood, he is free to die of hunger.
If one is unemployed, he is free to knock his head against the wall.
If one breaks a leg, he is free to walk on crutches.
If one gets married and hasn't enough to support his wife, he is free to go begging alms with her from house to house.
If one dies, he is free to get buried.

—Sholom Aleichem

The Presser

The Presser said:

Be submissive to thy boss, for he is thy God.
The machine is thy Law, and the table at which
thou workest is the altar upon which thou sacrificest
thy blood and sweat to the money God.

This is the way to live in America.
Bread and salt shall be thy food,
Water from the hydrant thy drink,
the floor in the shop thy bed,
and 18 hours a day shalt thou work.

Abadiah ben Charlie

Abadiah the son of Charlie said: Consider three things and you will be
able to exist in America: Forget who you are, wear a mask before those
who know you, and do anything you can.

—Parodist, ca. 1890.

Hold fast, this is most necessary in America. Forget your past, your
customs, and your ideals. Select a goal and pursue it with all your might.
No matter what happens to you, hold on. You will experience a bad time
but sooner or later you will achieve your goal. If you are neglectful,
beware for the wheel of fortune turns quickly. You will lose your grip
and be lost. A bit of advice for you: Do not take a moment's rest. Run,
do, work and keep your own good in mind. . . . A final virtue is needed
in America—called cheek. . . . Do not say, "I cannot; I do not know."

—Immigrant Guidebook, ca. 1890.

(Translation reprinted by permission of Moses Rischin.)

No Sin

A recent Russian-Jewish immigrant, worried in the early 1880s about
having to work on the Sabbath, was advised by an American cousin that
there was a twenty-four-hour difference in time between America and
Russia, so that when it is Saturday in America it is Friday in Russia and
when it is Sunday in America it is Saturday in Russia; therefore, one who

works on Saturday in the New World committed no sin as long as he rests from work on Sunday.

Counting Streetcars

In those days, a Jew who had been in America for a while would notice an obviously "green" newcomer standing on a corner laboriously counting the streetcars. The "veteran" approached the greenhorn and asked gently in Yiddish what he was doing. The new arrival would patiently explain that he'd been told to take streetcar number 67. Thus far, only 22 streetcars had passed the stop. So, he said, he would continue counting until before long, the sixty-seventh would arrive.

Modern Wonders

Many were the shocks new immigrants faced before learning the facts of life of the 'modern' world. Practical jokers among their own people didn't smooth the process, and their depredations began before the prospective greenhorn had even descended to steerage. One told a trusting young Jew, for example, that he could avoid the plague of seasickness by buying a fifth of whisky and drinking it all straight down as soon as he got aboard his ship.

There are seemingly infinite stories about greenhorns confronting the wonders of modern life in America. One greenhorn, for example, had never seen an ice cream cone before, and didn't know what to do when a generous American friend bought him one, so he stuffed it in his pocket.

Another true story tells of the greenhorn who happened upon an outhouse (outdoor bathroom) with two toilet bowls. He had no idea how to use them. Under the pressures of Nature and confusion, he put one foot in one bowl, the other foot in the second bowl, and defecated between them.

* * *

Many immigrants had never seen glass display windows before. One girl marveled at the clothes and toys piled high in the clean transparent store windows, not realizing that glass separated them from her. "How wonderful," she said to her friend, "in America, anyone can take whatever they want."

Escalators

Perhaps the classic greenhorn marvel was escalators. *"America goniff, me steht und me geht,"* was the famous reaction, which means roughly, "So clever, America, people stand still and yet they move!"

A Golden Land

Sometimes the immigrant generation were only too impressed with a modern land and technology that they would never really understand. This led them at times to make errors, as in the case of the elderly woman on a trip from New York to Baltimore. After a stop at Philadelphia, she got back on the wrong train, headed in the opposite direction. Before the conductor could come by to discover her mistake, she struck up a conversation with another Yiddish-speaking woman across the aisle.

"Where are you going?" she asked her.

"Boston."

"Isn't America marvelous?" beamed the first, filled with genuine wonderment. "I sit on this side of the car and go to Baltimore and you sit on the other side, and go to Boston! It's truly a *golden medina* (golden land)!"

A Wonderful Place

An immigrant Jew, fresh off the boat from Europe, sees a clean-shaven man, dressed in American-style clothes, smoking a cigar on the Sabbath, sitting on a park bench reading a Yiddish paper. "America is a wonderful place!" he exultantly tells his friends later. "Here even the *goyim* read Yiddish!"

Coney Island

A new immigrant, intrigued by stories of Coney Island, got up the courage to ask a woman friend to go there with him. The next day he met a friend.

"So, how was it?"

"A disappointment, really," said the greenhorn. "The Tunnel of Love was so wet we both caught cold."

"Your boat leaked so much?"

The newcomer looked aghast. "There's a *boat*?"

Even Keel

Meyer, a Jew from Russia, decided to emigrate to America. On the fifth day at sea a terrible storm broke out. The captain shouted disembodied orders through a megaphone, women screamed, children cried, sailors lowered lifeboats, and everyone else milled around the deck in confusion. Everyone else except Meyer; he alone maintained a tranquil mood, watching the hysteria with detached amusement.

"How can you be so calm when the ship's sinking!" demanded a fellow passenger. "Are you crazy?"

"What are you so excited about, uncle?" retorted Meyer. "What, does the boat belong to you?"

Don't Fix the Country

The story has come down of the Russian Jew who has just met his younger brother, a radical intellectual, at Ellis Island. The younger man has just landed after his two-week sea journey from Europe and, within minutes, the new arrival is setting forth his ideas for making the United States a better place.

"You want to do your big brother a favor," the elder, a world-weary sort, would say, *"Fix mir nicht dos land."* (Don't fix up this country for me.)

Fifth Avenue

Kirstein got his first steady job, as a bus driver. The first day his box held $60, the second $70. On the third day it held over $500.

"What happened?" asked his supervisor.

"To tell you the truth," said Kirstein, "after a couple of days on your route, I figure it's a dog. So I say, 'enough already!' I went over to Fifth Avenue; uncle, *that* route is a gold mine!"

Learning English

Marcus Ravage, a Rumanian-Jewish immigrant, later a noted writer and journalist, worked as a bartender as a teenager recently arrived from Europe, employed by a generous couple named Weiss. Mr. Weiss, he related, paid for his haircuts and offered to teach him English. "Of this I did not avail myself," Ravage wrote later, "because I noticed he always referred to Mrs. Weiss as 'he'."

No Headway

The principal visited a New York night school English class for Yiddish speakers. "Good evening," he said cheerfully, and the entire class stood and replied, in student fashion, "Good evening, Mister Principal."

"Are you making any headway?" he inquired of the class.

Everyone shook his head and said, in unison, "No, sir!"

The principal gave the teacher a confused look. Then he wrote his question on the blackboard. "Now," he said, pointing to it, "translate that word *headway*."

"*Kopf-weh* (headache)," they replied.

The principal smiled. "Now I understand," he said, "why you're making no headway."

Give Me Your Tired

Not like the brazen giant of
    Greek fame,
With conquering limbs astride
    from land to land;
Here at our sea-washed sunset
    gates shall stand
A mighty woman with a torch,
    whose flame
Is the imprisoned lightning
    and her name
Mother of Exiles. From her
    beacon-hand
Glows world-wide welcome; her
    mild eyes command

The air-bridged harbour that
    twin cities frame.
"Keep, ancient lands, your
    storied pomp!" cries she
With silent lips. "Give me your
    tired, your poor,
Your huddled masses yearning to
    breathe free,
The wretched refuse of your
    teeming shore.
Send these, the homeless, tempest-tossed
    to me,
I lift my lamp beside the golden door!"

So beckons the Statue of Liberty in New York harbor. This paean to America as haven of the oppressed, Emma Lazarus's "The New Colossus," almost went unwritten, and once written was almost forgotten.

Walt Whitman, Mark Twain and Bret Harte, among others, responded with alacrity in 1883 to a call to donate works to be auctioned off in the drive to raise $300,000 to build the statue's pedestal, but Emma Lazarus refused. She said she "could not possibly write verses to order."

"Think of the goddess of liberty standing on her pedestal yonder in the bay and holding the torch out to those refugees you are so fond of visiting at Ward's Island," Constance Cary Harrison patiently wrote back to Emma. Two days later, Mrs. Harrison received the manuscript of "The New Colossus." It was auctioned off for $1,500, published in Mrs. Harrison's souvenir portfolio, and forgotten.

President Grover Cleveland dedicated the Statue of Liberty on October 28, 1886. Emma Lazarus, ill with cancer, not even invited. She died the next year at the age of thirty-eight. In 1903, sixteen years after her death, New York artist came across a copy of the portfolio in a bookstore. Moved by the sonnet, the artist, Georgiana Schuyler, had it engraved on a bronze plaque and obtained permission to have it affixed to the base of the statue.

Emma Lazarus was born in 1849, the daughter of a wealthy Sephardic sugar refiner. She achieved some recognition as a poet and translator. Among her early translations were renditions from the German of some of the Hebrew poems of Solomon ibn Gabirol and Judah Halevi. But it was after the summer of 1881, when she saw Jewish refugees huddled at Ward's Island in the East River, that her work about her people saw new life.

In May 1882, *Century Magazine* carried her answer to an article by expatriate Russian noblewoman Madame Ragozin, who sought to whitewash the recent Russian pogroms. Emma's reply was a passionate protest against persecution of all kinds. Invited to write a poem for the closing exercises of New York's Temple Emanu-El's religious school, she composed *The Banner of the Jew*, a flaming call for a new prophet Ezra to lead his people. In *The Dance of Death*, a poetic drama based on an incident in the persecution of Jews in Germany in the Middle Ages, she wrote: "I have no thought, no passion, no desire, save for my people."

She began to study Hebrew and later translated several works of great Hebrew poets into English. In a series of sixteen articles called "Epistles to the Hebrews," she made ringing appeals for united Jewish action on behalf of the persecuted Jews of Europe, for reforms in Jewish education, and for the restoration of Palestine as the Jewish homeland.

Emma Lazarus will best be remembered, of course, for those reluctant verses she wrote in a day, "to order," past which millions of American immigrants have since sailed, verses she died thinking were forgotten.

Boobelah

An immigrant Jewish mother always called her son "Boobelah." Before she sent him off for his first day at school, she admonished him, "Be a good boy in school, boobelah. Pay attention to everything the teacher says, boobelah. Boobelah, darling, there's nothing to be afraid of. The teacher will love you, boobelah."

When he came home late that afternoon, his mother was beaming. "Well, boobelah, so what did you learn your first day in school?"

"I learned," the boy said quietly, "that my name is Irving."

8

EAST SIDE STORIES: LIFE IN THE NEW GHETTO

Furnishings

Do as I have done. Put the spring over four empty herring barrels and you'll have a bed fit for the President. Now put a board over the potato barrel and a clean newspaper over that and you'll have a table. All you need yet is a soapbox for a chair and you'll have a furnished room complete.

—Anzia Yezierska, *Bread Givers*

Hooking a Boarder

It ain't so dark. It's only a little shady. Let me turn up the gas for you—you'll quick see everything like sunshine. . . . You can't have Rockefeller's palace for three dollars a month. . . . If the bed ain't so steady, so you got good neighbors. . . . I'll treat you like a mother! You'll have it good by me like in your own home.

—Anzia Yezierska, *My Own People*

Fear

An old man, recalling his boyhood on the East Side, told of his chronic fear on returning home from school each day that his cot in the dining room would be taken over again by a new family member just arrived from Europe and taken in by his parents.

Advice from Your Banker

"Sometimes," a Yiddish journalist recalled, "they would try to prevent their customers from withdrawing money. . . . A shopgirl would want to take out a hundred dollars to get married, and the banker would say, 'What's the hurry? You're still young, you can wait a few years.'"

*   *   *

STRICTLY KOSHER!
THE SHOCHET KILLS HIMSELF
EVERY MORNING!
—Sign from a Maxwell Street,
Chicago, butcher

*   *   *

When an East Side *landsman* society refused, in 1896, to pay the wife of a deceased member a death benefit because of a rule that anyone whose husband died living above Houston Street was ineligible for the benefit, the *New York Times* headline read: "DIED TOO FAR UPTOWN."

The same society, the *Times* noted, was also being sued by a Mrs. Nathan Greenstein for not paying her a death benefit. There was disagreement as to whether assessments had been properly kept up, and the *Times* headline read:

"WHEN HE FAILS TO PAY AN ASSESSMENT,
BECAUSE HE IS DEAD IS NO EXCUSE"

*   *   *

The prominent financier Otto Kahn was riding through the Lower East Side one day when he saw a huge sign in a store window reading: "Samuel Kahn, cousin of Otto Kahn." When he got to his office, Kahn immediately phoned his lawyer, ordering him to get the sign changed at once. The next week, Kahn drove down the same street. The sign had been changed; it now read: "Samuel Kahn, formerly cousin of Otto Kahn."

Lincoln, Bakunin, and de Hirsch

When, in 1891, the Baron Maurice de Hirsch established a fund of more than $2.4 million to help Eastern European Jews resettle in the United States, his picture went up in many immigrant homes beside their honored portraits of Washington, Lincoln and Russian anarchist Mikhail Bakunin.

Rumors swept the East Side that the baron would give each Jew a large amount of money, set him up in business, and send his children to college.

One of the many real contributions of the de Hirsch Fund was a free public bath built in 1893 at Henry and Market Streets, introducing one of the first German rainbaths, or, as we know them today, showers, in the New World.

Jewish Asthma

In the early years, tuberculosis ran rampant among the immigrants, becoming so endemic it acquired the folk name "Jewish asthma." Some people got around New York regulations barring consumptives from factories by having themselves certified by doctors as having "Jewish asthma." Samuel Ornitz, in his novel *Bride of the Sabbath*, depicts how a consumptive mother, in order to prevent spreading the dread disease to her children, stops eating with them, kissing them, and even picking up her baby. Only years later can the children understand that their mother's sudden coldness was out of love for them.

Yom Kippur Balls

Grand Yom Zom Kippur Ball with theatre. Arranged with the consent of all new rabbis of liberty. Kol Nidre Night and Day in the year 5651 after the invention of the Jewish idols, and 1890, after the birth of the false Messiah . . . The Kol Nidre will be offered by John Most. Music, dancing, buffet, Marseillaise and other hymns against Satan.

—Ticket to Yom Kippur ball

*   *   *

On Yom Kippur 1889, the anarchist group Pioneers of Freedom sponsored the first of what would become an annual event on the East Side: the Yom Kippur Ball. At these now-legendary sacrilegious celebrations, on the holiest day of the traditional Jewish year, when all Jews are commanded to fast and afflict their souls, tea with milk would be served with ham sandwiches that, some observers claimed, were heavily spread with mustard to kill their taste. Some of the young people actually lingered in front of synagogues where most Jews spent their Day of Atonement fasting and praying and *noshed* their ham sandwiches. The first year's ball was marred by an Orthodox protest and resulting fights. Over the years, the event became better organized, at one point charging 15 cents for general admission and 30 cents for the press. A *New York Times* reporter came up with the extra change and then complained "the proceedings really were tame."

The Anarchists, in their efforts to loosen the bond of religion and radicalize Jewish workers, ran up against the contradiction that many of their apparent supporters continued also to be relatively observant Jews. This paradox was not absent even in their own ranks. The story has come down about the young man at a radical meeting, held in defiance of the Sabbath, who lit a cigarette and was pounced on for this indiscretion. In frustration, he said, "What would you say if I told you I didn't believe in God altogether?"

Blind Justice

To be tarred with a red brush by the surrounding society required only association, not agreement, with Jewish radicals. Once a group of militant conservatives tried to break up a Socialist meeting on the Lower East Side; one of the group called the police to report the Socialists had started rioting. When the police arrived, they charged in, recklessly battering radical and conservative alike with their clubs. "But, Lieutenant," shouted a rightist, "I'm an anti-Socialist!"

"I don't give a damn what kind of Socialist you are," the cop shouted back, "you break it up!"

❈

The intellectual, passionate Jewish socialists introduced to New York a political style with which the local Democratic Party was totally unfamiliar. "We got our bookworms, too," one Tammany man advised a Socialist, "but we don't make 'em district leaders: We keep 'em for ornaments on parade days!"

❈

We not only wanted labor laws and bread, we wanted roses too.
—Rose Schneiderman

*   *   *

New York labor leader Rose Schneiderman once visited a shop owner about whom female employees complained that he habitually pinched them as they passed. Accompanied by a woman who worked in the shop, Schneiderman told the owner the women resented this treatment.

"Why, Miss Schneiderman," the man replied, "these girls are like my children."

The woman from the shop shot back, "We'd rather be orphans."

Romance at the Settlement

Not so long ago, American Jews were seen less as the source of idealistic young people going out into the world to help the poor and downtrodden than as the downtrodden themselves.

A century ago, young white Anglo-Saxon Protestant social workers would visit Jewish neighborhoods to stare the hard life in the face and try to improve the lives of the destitute. The University Settlement House on the Lower East Side was the scene of much of this activity, and the backdrop for one of the most famous and legendary romances of the immigrant period, between J. Graham Phelps Stokes and Rose Pastor.

Stokes was the stuff of legend before he met Rose Pastor. Thirty-one years old, tall, handsome and idealistic, the scion of a wealthy and aristocratic family, Stokes worked as a settlement house worker. Putting aside the one key objection, that he was not Jewish, he may have seemed from the typical Lower East Side girl's romantic eye to be perfect: he was a millionaire (bank and railroad president) but at the same time, an idealist and a socialist. And, though he never practiced, he was even a doctor (M.D., Columbia).

Rose Pastor's family had left Poland when she was two and she spent her childhood in London. She worked from age twelve through twenty-three as a cigar maker in a Cleveland factory. Though she had no formal education in the United States, she was a voracious reader and began publishing poems in New York's Yiddish newspaper *Tageblatt.* She came to New York and was hired by the paper to report and write an advice column for the English page. One day in late 1903, a few months after she wrote an advice column to a young woman struggling with the issue of intermarriage (warning her in the strongest terms against it), she was assigned to interview Stokes, the aristocrat turned settlement worker. The rest, as they say, is history. This is an excerpt from the 'interview':

> Mr. Stokes is a deep thinker . . . his youthful face takes by virtue of its fresh earnest and kind expression. One glance at his face and you feel that

he has sown his black young curls with the bleaching cares of half a
million men. . . . Mr. Stokes is very tall and I believe, six feet of thorough
democracy. A thorough-bred gentleman, a scholar and a son of a millionaire, he is a man of the common people, even as Lincoln was. . . .

"If I thought as much of Mr. Stokes as you seem to," her editor is said
to have told her, "I would take care not to let anybody know it."

When Stokes read the article, he invited Miss Pastor to dinner. Soon
she began working with him at the Settlement House. In April 1905, this
was a front page headline in the *New York Times*:

> J. G. PHELPS STOKES
> TO WED YOUNG JEWESS
> Flattering Article by Miss Pastor
> As Reporter May Have Brought
> About The Engagement

The ceremony was performed by Stokes' brother, an Episcopal
minister. The couple honeymooned in Europe and visited the *shtetl*
where Rose was born. On their return, the Stokeses continued working
together to improve the lives of East Side tenement dwellers. In the fall
of 1906, *Harper's Bazar* carried an article, "Mrs. J. Phelps Stokes at
Home," showing how the ever-active Rose practiced shortcut house-
keeping—for example, using disposable Japanese napkins instead of
table linen. Popular writer Anzia Yezierska wrote a novel, *Salome of the
Tenements*, that seemed to have been modeled on the Stokes-Pastor
marriage, in which the Pastor-figure finally leaves the Stokes-figure,
denouncing him as an "all-right-nik!"

Two years after Yezierska's novel appeared and twenty years after
they married, in 1925, the two did divorce. By then, Rose was a noted
writer, Communist and birth control activist, while Stokes had grown
more conservative. In any case, the two created a romantic legend in
their own time and managed to lend, as *Poor Cousins* author Ande
Manners put it, "an aura of fabulous romance" to the University
Settlement House. "The legend of a poor Jewish girl from the East Side
who had 'caught' a handsome socialite millionaire socialist—who was
also a doctor—" Manners wrote, "proved that at such institutions
anything was possible."

Upstairs

A pious old rabbi lived over a store on the East Side. On the grocery's door was a sign: RABBI RABINOWITZ IS UPSTAIRS. When the rabbi died around 1912, he left no money to pay for his funeral nor relations who could. His congregation, such as it was, at great effort raised the funds for a funeral and a plot in a Jewish cemetery. But when the next year passed and it was time to put a stone on his grave, the poor congregation couldn't afford the extra expense. One of his flock decided they would take the old sign from the store and put it above the tomb. So those passing the rabbi's grave see the simple epitaph: RABBI RABINOWITZ IS UPSTAIRS.

Advertising

A man on the Lower East Side finds that the gold watch, given him by his grandfather for his bar mitzvah many years ago in Europe, is broken. He goes out on the street and finds a little shop with a giant clock in the window. He goes inside but no one seems to be there. He calls out, "Hello, hello!" After a minute a little old man comes out. "So, what can I do for you?" he says in a weary voice.

"I have this watch I want to get fixed."

"Watch? Watch? What do you come to me? I'm not a watchmaker, I'm a *mohel*."

"A *mohel*? I thought you were a watchmaker—why do you have that giant clock in the window?"

The old man looks at the younger, amazed. "What do you want I should have in my window?"

A young man walked briskly up the street to catch up with a friend. Finally he reached the other man and slapped him hard on the back, only to discover the object of his greeting was a total stranger.

"I'm so sorry," he said, "I thought you were my friend Goldberg."

"Even if I was Goldberg," demanded the stranger angrily, "what's the point of hitting me so hard?"

"Hey, listen," demanded the first, now annoyed himself, "what's it to you how I treat my friend Goldberg?"

🌼

The comedian Buddy Hackett used to quip: "When I was a kid, my mother used to say: 'Drink your milk till you see Standard Oil on the bottom of the glass!'"

Today this joke may need a little explanation. In the early years of the century, Standard Oil of New York made *yahrzeit* candles—memorial candles for the dead—from paraffin wax, a petroleum by-product. Once the *yahrzeit* candle had been burnt out, thrifty Jews would save the empty glass. The glasses, being heat-resistant, were considered a special find, since in addition to serving standard glass functions (such as cold milk), they could also be used for hot tea.

A Good Question

The story is told about Benny Leonard, lightweight boxing champion of the world (1917–1925), who was riding on a Pullman train on his way to a bout in Chicago. It was almost sunset when the door to his car was yanked open and a huge, muscular, aggressive-looking fellow stepped in. The man looked belligerently to the right and then the left and barked loudly, "Is there a Jew in this car?"

Leonard nearly jumped from his seat, red in the face with anger. Billy Gibson, his manager, pulled him back. "Take it easy, Benny," he said, "the guy's a drunk!" Leonard sank back in his seat, cooled himself down, and the man left the car.

But a few minutes later the same tough-looking fellow returned. Again, turning to the right and to the left, he demanded gruffly, "Is there a Jew in this car?" This time the now-livid champ wouldn't restrain himself. As Gibson struggled to hold him down, Leonard broke away, leapt up, and assumed a defiant stance facing the big guy, saying, "Yeah! I'm a Jew! What do you want to make of it?"

The man's expression turned slowly from a scowl into a grin. "Thank God," said the giant, "now we have the tenth for a *minyan* so we can say *mincha* in the empty car up ahead!"

Born Benjamin Leinert, Benny became Leonard after an announcer mangled his last name and the nervous new fighter didn't bother to correct him. He kept the name in a short-lived attempt to keep his new career from his parents. Benny learned to fight in Lower East Side gang wars. His home was near the local public baths; "You had to fight or stay in the house," he recalled later, "when the Italian and Irish kids came through on their way to the baths." He was good at it and became the "champion of Eighth Street"; he was credited with routing a gang that attacked an old Jewish woman and taking on hoods who tried to deface a synagogue. He fought his first match with gloves at age eleven and his first paid bout at fifteen; he lost it and got paid $4, one dollar of which went to his "manager" and another that was split between his two seconds.

Another story has it that Leonard's first pro bout took place after he fell from a skylight he was perched on at a neighborhood club because he couldn't afford a price of a ticket. To pay for the broken glass, he offered to replace a fighter who failed to show up; this fight, he won.

When his parents thought he was out looking for a job, Benny would be working out at New York's Tompkins Square Park. When his mother found out what he was really doing, she begged a relative to give the boy a job in his printing plant. Leonard showed up for work one morning with a black eye; he was told he'd have to quit fighting or quit the job. He quit the job.

Leonard became lightweight champion of the world in May 1917, knocking out then champion Freddie Welsch. Immigrant Jews and their children found in Leonard their first major American Jewish sports star and took enormous pride in the young boxer. During Leonard's eight-year reign as champion, some synagogues actually offered a *gomel benshen*—prayer of thanksgiving—on the Sabbath following each of his successful bouts. He was probably the best-known Jew in the United States during his tenure as champion. Leonard's success excited particular attention given the generally non-violent and non-athletic way of life of the immigrant generation. Editor Arthur Brisbane said Leonard did "more to conquer anti-Semitism than a thousand textbooks." Sports historians have rated Leonard one of the greatest lightweights of all time and the best Jewish boxer in history.

Leonard was known to plaster his hair down before a fight and challenge his opponent to muss it; folklore has it that in all of Leonard's more than 200 fights, no one ever did.

Dan Parker, a veteran sportswriter, once wrote: "Leonard moved with the grace of a ballet dancer and wore an air of arrogance that belonged to royalty. His profile might have been chiseled by a master sculptor. . . ."

What none of his challengers could do a sick Jewish mother did. Leonard retained the championship undefeated for eight years while, all the while, his mother urged him to quit the ring. In 1925, when she was ill, he voluntarily gave up the crown—the first lightweight champ in history to retire undefeated. He was not yet thirty. A 1932 comeback attempt was unsuccessful. He died while refereeing a bout in New York in 1947.

Unto You, Peace

Mrs. Aaron Jacob Mankiewitz was so impressed with the Yiddish writer Sholom Aleichem, whom she'd met on a transatlantic voyage, that she planned a big testimonial in his honor in her city, St. Louis.

Sholom Aleichem ("peace be unto you") was the pen name of Sholom Rabinowitz, known for his humorous tales of poverty-stricken Russian Jewry of the late nineteenth and early twentieth centuries. In Jewish Eastern Europe, of course, the phrase "sholom aleichem" was part of the core of everyday life for centuries as a greeting, song and blessing; in America, it was less familiar. When the St. Louis affair finally took place, Mrs. Mankiewitz presided and introduced the guest of honor: "Ladies and gentlemen, my task at this moment is a simple one, since you all know who our famous guest is. Without wasting any more of your time, I will call on the world-famous writer, *Alav Ha-shalom*! ("May he rest in peace.")"

Once in 1906 Sholom Aleichem and Mark Twain appeared together at the Educational Alliance in New York in 1906. Sholom Aleichem was introduced as the "Jewish Mark Twain." Mark Twain responded, "I am the American Sholom Aleichem."

Sholom Aleichem's stories *Tevye's Daughters*, depicting family and community life in the loving, enclosing and despairing world of the

Jewish *shtetl* of Easter Europe, achieved the greatest fame among his works through their adaptation into the acclaimed musical and movie *Fiddler on the Roof.*

When Sholom Aleichem died in 1916, he was buried at Cypress Hills Cemetery in Brooklyn, known as a pantheon for Yiddish literary figures. Before his death, he asked that these verses be inscribed on his tombstone beneath his name:

Here lies a simple-hearted Jew
Whose Yiddish womenfolk delighted;
All the common people, too
Enjoyed the stories he recited.
Life to him was but a jest,
He poked fun at all that mattered;
When other men were happiest,
His heart alone was bruised and shattered.

On his *yahrzeit* (anniversary of death), in accordance with his will, family, friends and Sholom Aleichem buffs gather to read from his works.

The judge in the New York courtroom was getting progressively more irritated with the distinctive attitude of the little old Jew who seemed to be the only person who could explain the circumstances of a crime. After hours of wandering, inconclusive testimony, he finally lost his patience. "Witness!" he demanded angrily, "Why must you always answer a question with another question?"

The Jew, taken aback, turned and faced the judge; "Vy not?" he said.

The *Schnorrer*

The tradition of the *schnorrer*, the *shtetl* beggar who, as legend had it, more demands than begs for his rightful portion, made the transition to the Lower East Side and for many years was a familiar figure there and in similar predominantly Jewish neighborhoods around the country. His survival depended on the Jewish tradition that it was each person's responsibility to give *tzedakah*—charity—to those in more dire need than himself. *Schnorrers* would frequent Jewish cemeteries and the sites of Jewish weddings, and would often be found at the synagogue door. Many East Side shopkeepers left outside their door a *pushke*, or small container, which held a handful of pennies from which each *schnorrer* would take his one-cent ration. The Yiddish word *Schnorrer* is believed to derive from the sound of musical instruments commonly carried by *shtetl* beggars.

A Grand Street bank at one time had a special counter for *schnorrers* where they could roll up their pennies, nickels, and dimes for deposit without slowing lines at the other windows. In the early days when there were many newly-arrived immigrants, there were numerous women *schnorrers* as well as men, some of whom would hire a neighbor's child for twenty-five cents a day to increase their appeal as an object of *tzedakah*. Another standard trick was the faked dispossession notice.

A chronicler of the *schnorrer* in New York was *Times* reporter and author Meyer Berger, who wrote about the innovative female *schnorrer* he called Beckie who faked illnesses in order to get free bed and board at hospitals. She apparently had medical knowledge, as she was able to consistently fake symptoms in such patterns as to be allowed to stay. Beckie had "eyes which under duress of suffering could be so eloquent as to tear your heart-strings" and seemed to know when a new doctor would be riding the ambulance, so she'd be more likely to get into the hospital unrecognized. Depending on how long she needed bed and board, she would feign varying illnesses. "If a long period of time were needed to study obscure symptoms and differential diagnosis," Berger wrote, "this meant, of course, bed, security and food."

The traditional Jewish view allowed the *schnorrer*, while driven to an undesirable economic position, to still retain his or her dignity. The *schnorrer* was seen as fulfilling an important social function by giving others a chance to perform good deeds, a view that helped less successful Jews survive and maintain their sanity in a larger world that gave them no quarter, in which long periods of unemployment, low wages, child labor, and a virtually complete absence of any form of public assistance were the order of the day.

A typical story from the folklore is of a certain *schnorrer* who stood in front of a Wall Street building with a box of pencils. One broker, every day of his working life, dropped a dime in the beggar's box without ever taking a pencil. Then one day, after the broker had dropped in his usual dime and was heading for his office, he felt a tap on the shoulder. It was the *schnorrer*.

"I'm sorry, mister, but I've had to raise my prices," he said. "A pencil now goes for a quarter."

※

The *schnorrer* presented his case, and the rich man was moved.

"I really would like to give you something," he said, "but I don't have my wallet with me. Could you ask me again tomorrow?"

"Mister," shot back the *schnorrer*, aggravated almost beyond endurance, "you have no idea what I lose each year by extending credit!"

※

The traditional *schnorrer* was always supposed to have a quick response ready.

"You have two good arms," one man asked. "Why do you *schnorr*?"

"What!" responded the *schnorrer*. "For your measly nickel, I should cut off an arm?"

※

A *schnorrer* got this from a woman:

"Aren't you ashamed to be *schnorring* here on the street?"

"What do you want, lady—I should open an office?"

※

A *schnorrer* approached a rich man for a donation as he climbed the steps to his brownstone, but the man said he had no money. "Will you be good enough to let me have something to eat?" asked the *schnorrer*.

"Sorry. We have nothing in the house."

"So, why sit around?" demanded the *schnorrer*. "Hurry up and get your bag, and we'll go *schnorring* together!"

※

A *schnorrer* enters a rich man's house without wiping his shoes, and smoking an evil-smelling pipe.

The rich man is indignant. "If you *have* to come *schnorring*, you should at least wipe your shoes and remove your pipe," he remarks.

"*Reb yid*," says the *schnorrer*. "Are *you* going to teach *me* how to schnorr?!"

✳

A well-to-do Jew was surprised by a pathetic-looking beggar one morning and so affected by his desperate appearance that, out of character, he impulsively gave the man two quarters. A half hour later, the rich man passed his favorite dairy restaurant and, right in the window on the street, saw the mendicant gorging himself shamelessly on bagel and lox. "You've got a nerve," shouted the enraged donor, storming into the restaurant and heading for the beggar's table, "did I give you a half dollar so you could treat yourself to bagel and lox?"

The poor man, unflustered, stood his ground. "What a ridiculous man!" he responded. "Before, I didn't have fifty cents, so I couldn't afford bagel and lox. Now, with God's help, you gave me the fifty cents—and then you say I can't eat bagel and lox." The beggar stood up, stared the rich man in the eye and demanded so all could hear, "So, tell me, wise guy, when do I get to eat bagel and lox?"

Rabbi Harvey Franklin recalled from his tenure in Long Beach, California, that hobos debarking from boats in nearby harbors would habitually stop at the synagogue for handouts. He used to wonder whether they were really all Jewish, as they claimed, or merely cashing in on traditional Jewish openhandedness to the *schnorrer*. One day, he recalled, he asked a tramp if he knew what Pesach (Passover) was. "Sure," the man replied, "that's a Mexican dollar."

Dr. Levine, the big specialist, examined Blum the *schnorrer*.
"What's the cost?" asked Blum afterwards.
"Fifty dollars."
"Fifty dollars! Where am I going to get fifty dollars?"
"Too much? That's my normal charge. So, if you don't have it, make it twenty-five!"
"Twenty-five dollars! That's totally out of the question!"
"All right," said the frustrated Levine, "so—make it ten dollars!"
"Ten dollars! Who has ten dollars? I'm a poor man!"
"So if ten dollars is too much, what do you have?"
"I have nothing!"
The doctor was annoyed. "You have nothing? So why do you come to a high-priced specialist like me?"

"When it comes to my health," shouted Blum, "*nothing* is too expensive!"

❊

A wealthy Jew was struck one morning by the peaceful, contented appearance of an older Jew who stood on a street corner, begging for alms. The beggar was friendly to all and appeared to be quite enjoying himself. Numerous passers-by freely gave him change. When a crowd had passed, the rich man strolled over to the poor man and addressed him confidentially.

"My friend, you have family?"

"Oh, yes, six fine children—three boys, three girls."

"You're all on good terms?"

"Oh, yes—they're over almost every Shabbas!"

"How are they doing?"

"Oh, quite well! Really well!"

"They could support you?"

"Sure—if I'd let them!"

"Well, why not?"

"*What!*" said the poor man, enraged. "And lose my *independence?*"

9

GREETING THE MISHPACHA: UPTOWN VERSUS DOWNTOWN, REFORM VERSUS ORTHODOX

America is not a poorhouse, an asylum for the paupers of Europe.
> —Moritz Ellinger, Hebrew Emigrant Aid
> Society (HEAS) (1882)

Father, What Is an Israelite?
"My son, an Israelite is a rich Jew."
"And what is a Jew, my father?"
"A poor Israelite."

> —*Puck* (1879)

The reputation that every Jew has is no higher than that of the lowest who professes his religion. We cannot therefore afford to permit this influx of poor deluded and oppressed Russians to become the standard upon which we shall be judged in the future.
> —*The American Israelite*, Cincinnati (1882)

One easy way of determining if an agency were established by Americanized (primarily German) Jews, or Russian Jews, in the 1880s when the rush of immigration began, was that the German agencies used the word *emigrant*, as if the persons being referred to were outside the country and only prospective Americans, whereas the Russian Jews used the word *immigrant*, emphasizing that they were already quite here.

Bridging the Gap

Efforts to narrow the gap between Russian and "American" German Jews with attempts at friendliness and humor were often not successful, with the downtowners often ending up somehow insulted. At one annual ball of the Russian-American Hebrew Association, a German-

Jewish lawyer named Greenbaum apparently tried to cross the abyss with little success. A Yiddish newspaper reported:

> Greenbaum, the German Jew who is active in many charities, honored the ball with his presence and, naturally, with his speech. At the beginning he said: "Who would have believed that this is a gathering of Russian Jews? Why, everybody here looks human!"

At another Russian-Jewish gathering, a similarly well-meaning Russian Gentile declaimed, with similar aplomb:

> And these are our Russian Jews? It is wonderful! What have become of their bent backs, of the fearful look in their faces! See how they walk in an upright manner!

The Harmonie Club, considered the most elite German-Jewish men's club in the country in the 1890s, adopted this position: "More polish and less Polish."

Bad Dreams

Sometimes the Russians had their revenge, sometimes without even knowing it. The classic nightmare of the successful Americanized Jew was to have his medieval Russian "poor cousin" dropping in and humiliating him in front of the "real" Americans who were only, at last, coming to accept him. One version of this nightmare was lived out by Mark Gerstle of San Francisco, in the days when Russian migration was still a relative trickle.

Gerstle, scion of a prominent, wealthy and assimilated German-Jewish family, belonged to the prestigious law firm of Olney, Chickering and Thomas. In his third year with the sedate old WASPish firm, Mark's wife had a son. Louis Greene, a cousin of Mark's and an incurable practical joker, called every *mohel* (ritual circumciser) in San Francisco's City Directory and made appointments for each to visit Olney, Chickering and Thomas at half-hour intervals to solicit Mark's business.

Dressed uniformly in traditional black, wearing high hats, long beards and ritual curls, the men arrived at the firm, dutifully requesting an audience with Mark every half-hour for three straight days. Mark had no idea who had sent them and no way to stop their seemingly endless flow.

The *Tzimmes* Revolt

The first place where tension between uptown and immigrant Jews broke into open warfare may have been the legendary *Tzimmes* Revolt at the Ward's Island Shelter (sometimes called the Schiff Refuge) run by HEAS (Hebrew Emigrant Aid Society), where Jewish Ellis Island new-comers were frequently referred in the early 1880s.

Immigrant complaints about the refuge were legion: the food was said to be filthy and worm-ridden, there was not enough soap and water for the newcomers to keep clean, there was no work, education, or diversion of any kind available, and the staff was reputed to be brutal and authoritarian. Immigrants were expected to obey arbitrary orders without complaint.

Tension was at a particularly high level one October day, after persistent complaints had been ignored. An immigrant delegation had once again approached the shelter's superintendent that day with complaints about his assistant, Zadok, and got no response, the story goes, but insults. At dinner that night, *tzimmes*, a traditional Eastern European dish of carrot and potato pudding, served in the shelter on special occasions, was offered. (*Tzimmes* was also a Yiddish expression for a "big deal," something blown out of proportion.)

A waiter deliberately failed to ladle out *tzimmes* to one immigrant, Jacob Rabota, with whom he'd previously had words. When the newcomer protested, Zadok was summoned and threatened Rabota, who angrily grabbed a bowl of the *tzimmes* and threw it in the official's face. A melee broke out with Rabota and the other immigrants against Zadok and his kitchen staff. Within a half hour, club-swinging police arrived from the Harlem precinct house and began arresting immigrants, many of whom fought back, the men with sticks, the women and children with bites. Mobs of immigrants stoned staff residences and a gang of enraged women searched for Superintendent Blank—who had, unknown to them, fled through a window, jumped into the East River and swum to shore, where he'd been rescued by police. By the time a larger contingent of police arrived to restore order to the island, the immigrants had already elected a provisional government of ten notables.

The next day, the HEAS committee that ran the refuge came out to the island to investigate, heard immigrant complaints, fired Blank and Zadok, and tried to institute reforms. The refuge closed in 1883 and HEAS itself ceased functioning the following year.

❀

The larger community, including its large anti-Semitic elements, were not oblivious to the conflict, as these parodies from a popular magazine show:

Two Ends of the Line

I don't recognize him, my frent,
I ain't dot kindt of Shoo;
I own a shtore, un'bay my rent,
Und make it bay me, too.
De besht of goots are on the shelef,
Bei Moses Cohen un'Co.—
Oh, I begun like him, myself—
Bot dot vas long ako.
I vear dot lovely di'mond pin;
My son dot Sixty-Nint' is in—
Dey call him Sheeny Ike.
You bet zwei tollar un'a helef,
I'am Moses Cohen un'Co.
Vell, I vas vonce like dot myself
But dot vas long ako.

—*Puck*, 1882

Immigration

. . . Ike Diamondstein the Jew exclaims:
Ah, Izzy, ain't dat grandt!
Ve yangees haf such nople aims
und vill together standt,
Ve've got der goods, ve're nach ralized
"Americavich is civlzized
So keep dose aliens outen!"

No, Thanks

Splits between German and Russian Jews, analogous to the tensions dividing New York's uptown and downtown Jews, were felt in other cities as well. In Atlanta in 1896, the established Hebrew Ladies Benevolent Society and the local Council of Jewish Women (the national organization that would eventually come to be known in some Russian-Jewish circles as the "Council of Jewish Vermin") had opened, respectively, a low-cost bathhouse and a Sabbath school— the latter organized more on the model of the American Sunday school than the traditional Eastern European *cheder*— for the benefit of the new Russian and Polish arrivals.

The tensions between Germans and Russians exploded after the local *Jewish Tribune* commented that these measures had been initiated in response to public school teachers' complaints about the immigrant children's appearance and from a growing feeling they didn't understand "true Judaism." The school was then described thus:

> A strenuous effort to instill patriotism into these young minds is made and "America" is most heartily sung by all. Generally speaking, the ignorance of these people is sadly striking. They know nothing at all of the Ten Commandments and the fall of Adam and Eve is a news story to them.

The Russians were outraged and forced closure of the Sabbath school. Two leaders of the Russian-Jewish community responded to the editorial:

> We do not need forced baths, nor do we need a guardianship as to our lavatory exercises. . . . Charity is a great virtue but the charity which seeks notoriety in newspapers ceases to be a virtue and becomes a simple advertising medium. . . .

Marshall Law

The prominent German-Jewish attorney Louis Marshall became a major spokesman for the Jewish community and a symbol of uptown power. His father had come to America in 1849 with his name spelled Marschall but, Louis claimed, had been seasick for the full fifty days of his ocean journey to America and, on arriving, promptly dropped the *c* from his name.

Once, when arguing a case before the United States Supreme Court, Marshall went over the time allotted him and Chief Justice Edward White reportedly leaned forward and said, somewhat apologetically: "Mr. Marshall, one of the most unpleasant duties presented to the head of this Court is that he sometimes is obliged to shut off the light."

Marshall was known for a pomposity downtowners regarded as characteristically uptown and German. Marshall was also known more favorably to downtowners for championing an uncharacteristic firmness against anti-Semitism. Once New York's prominent Union League Club, which refused to admit Jews, asked him to lend the club some paintings from his private art collection for an exhibition. Marshall replied:

> I can scarcely reconcile myself to the incongruity of finding my property welcome where I would be excluded. Your invitation, while a great tribute to the universality of Art, does not, however, modify the regret with which I regard the manifestation of the narrowness and intolerance of man, as disclosed by the records of your organization.

Due to his influence, some claimed the American Jewish community was "under Marshall law." Others called him "Louis XIX."

"As Rich as Jacob Schiff"

Marshall's partner as spokesman for the uptown community was financier and philanthropist Jacob Schiff, whose wealth and philanthropy both became so legendary it sometimes seemed he was the person to go to for money, whatever the cause.

An immigrant woman once saw Schiff when he visited the Henry Street Settlement House, which he had helped establish. The woman asked to see Schiff; she wanted him, she said, to buy her daughter a piano. Schiff's assistant asked the woman if the girl were talented.

"How would I know?" she shot back disdainfully. "She hasn't got a piano!"

Richman and the Pushcart Peddlers

Julia Richman, the Lower East Side's German-Jewish school district supervisor, became a downtown public enemy in 1908 when she urged that unlicensed pushcart peddlers be "sent back to the country from which they came."

Richman, a pioneer in progressive education after whom a downtown Manhattan high school has been named, was the first woman to become a Manhattan district supervisor, and was credited with introducing special education for the retarded, parent-teacher associations and the dispensation of eyeglasses in the New York schools. She had also served notably in the Jewish community as, among other things, the first president of the YWHA and a founder and director of the Educational Alliance.

In those days, New York City issued a maximum of 4,000 licenses for pushcart peddlers. Each peddler was legally required to have a license, which cost $15 when they were available. More than 10,000 such operators also worked illegally, and could usually avoid penalty if they paid a bribe—which ran only about $5—to the police.

Although from the uptown standpoint, pushcarts were mainly a source of crowding, noise, ugliness and fire hazards, for downtown they were vital both as sources of income for their operators and of cheap food and clothing for everyone else.

Richman, who was known, according to a contemporary observer, for her vigilance against "evils or irregularities," demanded the law be enforced.

In a celebrated exchange, New York Police Commissioner Theodore Bingham was said to have told Richman: "You don't want to be too hard on the poor devils; they have to make a living." To which she replied: "I say, if the poor devils cannot make a living without violating our laws, the immigration department should send them back to the country from which they came."

While Richman kept insisting on deportation of pushcart ordinance violators, the East Side organized a petition drive to force out "this self-constituted censor of our morality and . . . patron saint of the slum" to another school district. When Louis Marshall was asked to sign the petition, he responded:

> Is a lifetime spent in good works to go for naught because of an occasional over-emphasis of expression? . . . Her methods may not have been the best, her words, on occasion, have been unwise, her discretion may sometimes have lapsed, but her motives have been unimpeachable.

Richman survived as district supervisor until her death in 1912, and the pushcart peddlers survived, too. Downtown kept its objections to Richman alive, the *Forward* remarking in 1911: "When she visits a school, it's like *Yom Kippur*."

The peddlers' legal status remained ambiguous until the 1930s, when the administration of Mayor Fiorello LaGuardia established a centralized market for them. He told the peddlers, who all wore white coats for the historic dedication ceremony: "Now, you're merchants."

*   *   *

In the 1930s, the roles were reversed as Russian Jews acted as host and benefactors to desperate German Jews escaping Nazism. The tension remained, still with the Germans looking down at the Russians. A joke of that time went: A haughty German dachshund snubs a friendly terrier, saying: "Don't think I was always just a dachshund; back home in Germany I was a Saint Bernard!"

*   *   *

When, in the 1930s, a Russian Jew broke through and won admission to Philadelphia's exclusive German-Jewish Philmont Country Club, members reportedly circulated the remark, "This year we got the Russian Jews—next year we get the Japanese beetles."

How Many Synagogues

A Jewish adventurer is shipwrecked on a previously uninhabited island for five years. When finally discovered, he proudly shows his rescuers around the island, pointing out his large house, the orchards and pastures, the irrigation system he's built, everything done completely by himself. "And those," he says, pointing in the direction of two structures on the far corner of the island, "are the synagogues."

"*Two* of them!" his guests laugh. "But you're all alone by yourself here!"

"Well," explains the modern-day Crusoe, "*this* one," pointing to the closer, "is the one I pray in. And the *other* one," he says, with a look of profound disgust coming to his face, "I wouldn't go in if you *paid* me!"

The *Treifa* Jollification

Few incidents captured the rift between Reform and traditional Judaism in nineteenth-century America like the July 11, 1883, banquet in Cincinnati honoring the first four rabbis ordained by the Reform movement's Hebrew Union College. There is disagreement about what actually happened, and versions of the incident passed into the realm of folklore.

From what can be gathered, something like this did occur: HUC, founded a few years before, planned a huge banquet for the happy occasion. Only four of the class' original fifteen members had made it to graduation: the majority, Reform leader Isaac Mayer Wise saying, having attended "only to kill time and at the command of their parents." The graduation was held concurrently with the tenth annual meeting of the Union of American Hebrew Congregations, the national association of Reform temples. (Reform was by then a unified movement with its own widely-recognized and functioning institutions.)

A broad range of local and national Jewish and Christian figures attended, including representatives of more than 100 congregations from across the country. The banquet was to be perfect—it was held atop beautiful Mount Adams outside the city. The Reformers billed it the "largest body of representative Israelites from all parts of the country ever assembled on the Western continent." Considering the ambition of the event, the *Cincinnati Enquirer* puckishly called it a "Jewish Jollification."

The banquet committee, made up of wealthy Cincinnati German Jews, used the same caterer who served the city's Jewish social club. Committee members would insist for decades afterwards that the caterer had been strictly warned to observe *kashrut*—the traditional Jewish dietary code—out of respect for those guests Wise disparaged as "kitchen Jews."

The first course served was littleneck clams. Two outraged rabbis rushed from the room in a huff. Others soon followed. The courses continued—one, if it were possible, more *treif* (nonkosher) than the next. Shrimp salad, soft-shell crabs, creamed frogs' legs—fancy French dishes the uninitiated couldn't tell how kosher or *treif* they might be.

The *treifa* banquet was roundly denounced as far away as St. Petersburg, Russia. Congregations across the East pulled out of the UAHC. Wise fought back. "Be no fanatic," he argued in his characteristic tone. "Be intelligent and allow your reason to govern your passions, propensities and superstitions!" But the damage had been done; animosity between Reform and Orthodoxy grew stronger than ever, and Jewish spokesmen rushed to position themselves vis-à-vis the profound, though possibly unintentional, statement the banquet appeared to represent.

Chief Rabbis

The acrimonious and unsuccessful struggle by the New York Orthodox community to pick a "Chief Rabbi of America" in the late 1880s and early 1890s was not without humor either. In 1893, Rabbi Chaim Vidrowitz, recently of Moscow, gathered several small New York *hasidic shuls* to his side and hung out a sign on his door, "Chief Rabbi of America." Vidrowitz became the third claimant to the position at the time, and, when challenged as to who gave him the title, he replied with candor: "The sign painter."

Emil Hirsch: Closed on *Shabbes*

Rabbi Emil Hirsch was known as a radical Reformer and something of a rugged individualist. After serving in pulpits in Baltimore and Louisville, he came to Chicago in 1880 and became the most prominent Reform rabbi in the largest Jewish community outside the East Coast. Hirsch pioneered a number of ritual changes, one of which was the holding of Sabbath services on Sunday.

A California rabbi who was a student of Hirsch's told the story of his grandfather, Louis Mayer, a Chicago peddler, who used to ask his friends who they thought was the most pious rabbi in Chicago. The friends, who typically answered a question with another question, would bounce the issue back to him and he answered, "Rabbi Emil Hirsch."

His friends, Orthodox traditionalists, scoffed, denouncing Hirsch as no better than a *goy*.

"Oh, no," Grandpa Mayer would say, "he's the only rabbi in Chicago who's closed on *Shabbes*."

Hirsch was known for his blunt, critical approach. Once he conducted a wedding in three minutes flat, much to the surprise of all concerned. Asked why, he replied, "They wanted it short, so I made it short."

In one of his most widely-repeated cracks, the antitraditional Hirsch nonetheless chided Jewish girls for having their noses bobbed, remarking, "You might change your noses but you can never change your Moses."

Solomon Schechter, a leader in the emerging Conservative movement, was known neither for diplomacy nor affection for Reform. When a Reform rabbi once turned down his offer of a cigar, saying he didn't smoke, Schechter riposted, "so what do you do on the Sabbath?"

An Orthodox Joke

Three Reform rabbis were arguing over which had the most modern, progressive temple. "In our temple," bragged the first, "we have ashtrays in the pews so congregants can smoke during the Torah reading."

"That's nothing," snorted the second. "In our temple, we serve a big Yom Kippur morning meal—ham sandwiches with milk!"

"Not bad," said the third rabbi, "but in our temple, when Rosh Hashanah and Yom Kippur come around, we just put out a big sign: 'Closed for the Holidays.'"

Forced to Close

The Temple, in Atlanta, became known as one of the most extreme of Reform congregations. "We stand today for the ideals of Israel spiritually interpreted, a minority of a minority people," Rabbi David Marx said in 1909. "Our services are cast on a high plane of sanity, which, while recognizing the importance of sentiment, does not degenerate into hysteria so prejudicial to the intellectual side of Man's religious nature."

When Rabbi Marx started Sunday morning worship services in 1904, these attracted more attendance than the usual Friday night and Saturday morning services combined. But the congregation's Gentile choir, whose members wanted to attend their own churches on Sundays, eventually forced the Temple to convert its Sunday service into a mere lecture series.

One woman dropped out of The Temple, reporting that when her son brought Chanukah candles home, he didn't know what to do with them. "I heard him in his room," she said. "He lit them and sang Christmas carols."

S. S. Wise—Truth Bravely Uttered

"It's a sin to carry money on *Shabbes*," Rabbi Stephen S. Wise used to joke as the collection basket passed around Carnegie Hall, where his Reform Free Synagogue met. "Empty your pockets here!"

Few Jews in the twentieth century articulated the prophetic tradition as forcefully and effectively as Wise. He managed to bridge the gaps between religion and politics as well as between uptown and downtown Jews. The Republican New York *World* called him the "professional denouncer of the times." And Wise observed: "In a world of shame, the truth bravely uttered is bound to sound sensational."

One of America's most prominent rabbis and social activists, Wise led repeated fights to purge corruption from New York politics. After he urged then-governor Franklin Roosevelt to remove Mayor Jimmy Walker from office, the mayor suddenly left for England. Another Tammany mayor Wise had no love for was "Red Mike" Hylan. When the two were introduced during Hylan's second term, the mayor allowed, "I ought to know Rabbi Wise; he's attacked me often enough."

"Mr. Mayor," Wise replied enthusiastically, "I may have attacked you often—but *not* often enough!"

Wise became an outspoken public figure championing the rights of—in addition to Jews—workers, blacks and women; he was a major spokesman for Zionism and against Nazism. He became a familiar New York figure to Jew and Christian alike. Once Rabbi Jonah Wise, son of American Reform movement founder Isaac Mayer Wise, was stopped by a New York cop and identified himself as Rabbi Wise. "If you're Rabbi Wise," the burly policeman said knowingly, "I'm Lily Pons!"

As a Reformer, Wise got mixed reviews from New York's Orthodox rabbinate, which in 1925 actually excommunicated him as a heretic after a sermon entitled "Jesus the Jew." Wise, however, was not a "classical" radical Reformer and had his own problems with Jews lacking knowledge of the tradition. He often recalled the time he asked a groom if he were *frum* (religious) and the young man replied, "Yes, I'm from Brooklyn."

Wise came from a long line of rabbis. His grandfather, Joseph Weiss, was Hungary's chief rabbi and renowned for gifts of prophesy. In fact, after Wise gave a trial sermon for his first pulpit at the Madison Avenue Synagogue, one of the trustees later told the congregation's president, "That sermon must have been written by this young man's father (Rabbi Aaron Weiss, formerly of Budapest)." The president retorted: "Well, if this young rabbi has sense enough to preach one of his father's good sermons instead of his own bad one, that only goes to prove how fit he is for the position we're offering him."

Within the Jewish community, Wise's most famed controversy was with the trustees of New York's wealthy "Establishment" Reform Temple Emanu-El, which led to Wise's own founding of the Free Synagogue.

When, in 1905, that richest pulpit in the country was vacant, Wise became a candidate to fill it. Emanu-El was ready to hire Wise. The young rabbi, demanding an "absolutely independent pulpit," noted that he had led a political reform movement in Oregon and must have the freedom to do the same in New York, "no matter who it affected."

Louis Marshall, speaking for the temple's lay leadership, frankly told Wise this was impossible. "The pulpit of Emanu-El," he said, "has always been and is subject to and under the control of the Board of Trustees." Jacob Schiff, on the other hand, told Wise privately to take it.

But Wise wouldn't accept under these circumstances. He followed up with an "Open Letter" to Emanu-El's trustees:

> A pulpit that is not free can never powerfully plead for truth and righteousness. . . . The chief office of a minister . . . is not to represent the views of the congregation but to proclaim the truth as he sees it.

In 1909, he founded the Free Synagogue—which not only gave him, as rabbi, the freedom to preach as he saw fit, but was to be "free from the evils of the pew system, dues or involuntary giving" and, while Reform, "vitally, intensely, unequivocally Jewish." The Free Synagogue, among other things, aimed to eliminate distinctions of wealth in membership privileges. In fact, largely due to liberal positions Wise kept taking that upset wealthy members, construction of the Free Synagogue's own building kept getting put off.

Years later, Wise invited Louis Marshall to speak from the pulpit of the Free Synagogue and introduced him as "the inspirer of the founder of the Free Synagogue" without, reportedly, either man cracking a smile.

Wise became used to rubbing elbows with presidents. Once, when Woodrow Wilson expressed distrust of Britain, Wise was surprised, saying, "You have not a drop of non-British blood in your veins, but you do not seem to trust England. I, on the other hand, have only Jewish blood in my veins and not a drop of British blood, but I trust and revere England."

Wilson remained unimpressed. "I know my family better than you," he replied.

Wise was generally popular for his sarcastic retorts to both open and subtle anti-Semitism. After a Daughter of the American Revolution had emphasized at a public meeting how her ancestors had taken part in signing the Declaration of Independence, Wise got up and noted: "My ancestors were present when Moses promulgated the Ten Commandments at Mount Sinai."

When a Russian peasant pilgrim told him to get his "Jewish hands" out of "her" Jordan River, Wise told her through an interpreter: "My fathers bathed in this river long before yours had ever taken a bath!"

Some people thought Wise thought too much of himself. He garnered numerous nicknames from "God's Angry Man" to "The Pied Piper," from "High Priest Caliphas" to "Doctor Angelicus." The story was told of Wise being admitted to Paradise, where it's decided to offer him the vice-presidency. Wise, however, is offended; he wants nothing less than the Number One spot, which he prepares to contest with God.

Along these lines, Wise used to tell about the "free analysis" he got from Sigmund Freud. The father of psychoanalysis reportedly asked Wise who he considered the four greatest living Jews.

"Well," said Wise, "I would name you and Einstein—and then, Weizmann—and finally, I think, Brandeis."

"But what about yourself?" Freud asked.

"Oh, no, no, no, no!" Wise exclaimed, gesticulating vigorously.

"It seems to me you protest too much," Freud observed.

"You see?" Wise would say, recalling the encounter. "I got a free analysis."

Wise once wrote his wife-to-be, advising her of what he called his

One miserable, unpardonable, besetting weakness, an unrighteous ambition which deadens the best within men in public life—love of fame, applause, popularity.

Although Wise was often in the newspapers, once when he was to address an international Jewish conference in Zurich, *New York Times* readers searched in vain to read what the rabbi had said—until they got to the shipping page. The makeup editor put it there after seeing, in the headline, "S. S. Wise."

10

MILK AND MONEY: GETTING BY IN BUSINESS

To begin with, the country itself, a land flowing with milk and honey. People make plenty of money; you dig into money with both hands, you pick up gold by the shovelful! And as for "business," as they call it in America, there is so much of it that it just makes your head spin. You want a factory—so you have a factory; you want to, you push a pushcart; and if you don't, you peddle or go to work in a shop—it's a free country! You may starve or drop dead of hunger right in the street—there's nothing to prevent you, nobody will object.
—Shalom Aleichem character Berl-Isaac describing
America to his fellow villagers in Kisrilevka

Promise You'll Be Rich

"Ach, Gott, what a rich country America is! What an easy place to make one's fortune! Look at all the rich Jews! Why has it been so easy for them, so hard for me? I am just a poor little Jew without money."

"Poppa, lots of Jews have no money," I said to comfort him.

"I know it, my son," he said, "but don't be one of them. It is better to be dead in this country than not to have money. Promise me you'll be rich when you grow up, Mickey."

"Yes, poppa."

—*Jews without Money*, Michael Gold, 1930

Lately

A man goes to his best friend and says, "Joe, would you lend me two hundred dollars or they'll take our home away, and we'll be kicked out on the street!"

"No," says Joe.

"What do you mean, no?" the first man replies, astounded. "Don't you remember, back in 1923, when you wanted to start in business, you came to me, asked me for five thousand dollars, I gave you ten thousand. Then, your boy was born, I gave you another ten thousand. In 1933, with the Depression, you're wiped out, another twenty thousand I gave you, set yourself up again. Then when your daughter's engaged, in 1939, I gave you another five thousand, she should have a nice wedding."

"That's all true, I admit it," said Joe, nodding thoughtfully. "But what," he asked, "have you done for me lately?"

Imagine

A poor Jew from Riga came to New York, hearing the old story that the streets were paved with gold. Finding they weren't and having no trade, he became, like so many others, a peddler of pins and needles. It was a hard life and he was always looking for something better. When he heard a synagogue on Attorney Street needed a *shammes* (sexton), he was first to apply. "Can you read and write English?" the president of the congregation asked.

"No," he admitted.

"I'm sorry," the president told him. "In America a *shammes* has to be able to read and write."

The poor peddler went sadly home that day. But in time, he found other paths to success. He went into real estate and over the years became a successful businessman, eventually close to a millionaire. One day, he went to his banker to arrange a loan. Naturally, he got it without question. "Write your own check," said the bank president, handing him his own personal pen.

The realtor blushed. "I—I can't," stammered the embarrassed tycoon, "I can't write at all. I can't even read English. I haven't yet learned to sign my own name."

"How wonderful!" remarked the amazed banker. "If you've done so much without knowing how to read or write, imagine where you'd be today if you only did know how!"

The realtor's expression became pensive, then sad, and then even sullen, "*Sure*," he muttered, as if to himself, *sure*, then I'd be the *shammes* of the Attorney Street Synagogue!"

Salt

A man walks into a grocery store. An entire aisle is stacked exclusively with salt, all kinds, hundreds of different kinds of salt. The grocer is unloading a few cartons nearby. The man says to him, "You must really sell a lot of salt."

"Salt—me?" the grocer laughs. "Nah, if I sell one or two containers of salt a month, it's big business. I don't sell much salt. But," and the grocer's eyes brightened, "you oughta see the fellow who sells *me* salt—now, *he* sells a lot of salt! Boy, is he *good*!"

Odds

An Orthodox Jew buys a monkey as a pet. The animal learns to imitate his master's religious practices so well that his owner finally takes him to the synagogue and offers to bet anyone the monkey could lead the Sabbath service. Just when he's gotten the twenty-five or so regulars to bet with him and he brings the monkey to the *bimah* (pulpit), the pet fails to perform. He jumps and chatters, and bounds off the platform like a simple animal.

On the way home, the Jew shouts at the monkey for failing him for several blocks, while the animal keeps silent. Finally, the pet can no longer contain himself.

"Fool!" counters the simian, "just you wait till Yom Kippur, and see the odds we'll get!"

Joseph Jacobs

Joseph Jacobs, a native of Georgia, moved to Atlanta in 1884 and founded Jacobs' Pharmacy. Before 1885, the nickel was the smallest coin in general circulation in Atlanta; transactions were generally rounded off to the nearest nickel. Soon after opening, Jacobs ordered $1,000 in new pennies and started giving exact change, enabling him to reduce prices and underbid competitors, who in turn pressured wholesalers and manufacturers not to supply him. Jacobs retaliated with a number of successful antitrust suits, and by 1910 his drugstore had ten branches.

Despite this seemingly keen business judgment, Jacobs is also remembered for having exchanged his one-third interest in the new syrup preparation that would become Coca-Cola for some glass factory stock and a few bedpans, syringes and pill boxes.

It's a Living

Folklore has it that around the turn of the century, a middle-aged Jew disembarked at Ellis Island. Not obviously different from hundreds of thousands of men who arrived at New York before and since, he quickly faced the difficult task of making a living in an entirely new civilization.

Without trade, family or special skills, he became a New York version of the traditional *shtetl luftmensch,* a man who seems to live from "the air," always trying to wrest a little something out of what seems like nothing.

One of the few things there was no shortage of on the old East Side was the sick, and the man began visiting them. It was, of course, a *mitzvah* to visit the sick. Still without means of support, he hit on a scheme. Before ringing the doorbell, he would nimbly take apart the *mezuzah* (the case attached to the door jamb in traditional Jewish homes, containing verses for the Torah). He repeatedly pierced the parchment with a nail or pin and then reassembled and reattached it. He got so he could do this very quickly. He would then call on the household, sharing sadness and bringing encouragement. By the way, he would eventually ask whether anyone had recently checked their *mezuzah*, implying, in line with traditional superstition, that a damaged scroll might be the cause of an illness. Who would have checked it? When the damage was discovered, he would mention that among his associations was a religious organization that happened to offer a selection of *mezuzot*. Soon a sale was made and the man was off to another household stricken by illness. Presumably, though, people talked to each other, and before long the *luftmensch* would have to find another scam, city or job.

A Good Question

Two men meet on the sidewalk.

"Nu, how's business on Canal Street?"

"Can the clothing business ever be good again? Everybody goes uptown. Besides, the weather."

"What do you mean, the weather?"

"In summer, people go to a store that's air-conditioned. We stay, but we lose money. In winter, who wants to leave their warm homes to come downtown? So we lose more money."

"So why do you keep open altogether?"

"If I close shop, how will I make a living?"

Moshe the tailor came to New York from a little Russian town. He could not read or write, but he opened a clothing shop on the East Side. At one point, he went to the bank to open a checking account for his business. In place of his name, he signed two crosses on the bank documents.

With time, he prospered. He sold his original cloak-and-suit business and became a textile manufacturer. A few years later, he went to the bank again to open a new account. This time he signed the bank documents with three crosses. "How come three crosses?" the bank president asked, "you've always signed with two." Moshe blushed.

"Oh, you know how the women are, fancy-shmantzy," he muttered, shaking his head in embarrassment. "Now my wife, she wants me to take a middle name."

A Penny Fan

Mrs. Bernstein stood for more than an hour next to the pushcart, handling every fan the peddler had, smelling, feeling, weighing, trying to decide which to buy. Finally, she settled on one. "I'll take this penny fan," she said, giving the disgusted man her coin and heading home with her prize.

The next morning, first thing, the peddler turned around to see Mrs. Bernstein standing again at his pushcart. "What is it now, Mrs. Bernstein?" he said tiredly.

"I want my money back!" she demanded.

"What? How much did you pay?"

"A penny."

"And how did you use it?"

"What do you think—it's a fan—I waved it from side to side in front of my face."

"So, *that's* how you use a penny fan, Mrs. Bernstein!" shouted the enraged peddler, gesticulating vigorously. "No! No! That's what you do with a nickel fan! With a penny fan, you hold the fan still and you wave your head!"

"How much is this fan?" asks old Mrs. Shapiro.

"A cent," says the peddler.

"Too much," says Mrs. Shapiro.

"So make me an offer!" says the peddler.

Visit to Bloomingdale's

There's the story of the older Jewish couple who came over from Europe, ran a grocery, and, for forty years, lived in a little room in the back of the store. They never even ventured out of their East Side neighborhood.

One day the man goes to Bloomingdale's. He looks around a bit, is quite impressed, and walks up to one of the floorwalkers and asks if he could see Mr. Bloomingdale. Although surprised, he agrees to show the old man to Bloomingdale's office. They go up to the office and Bloomingdale happens to be free and receives him graciously. "What can I do for you?" asks Bloomingdale curiously.

"Vell, Mr. Bloomingdale," says the old man, quite pleased with himself, "I would like to buy your store."

Shocked, then amused, Bloomingdale decides to play along and says, "I wasn't really planning to sell, but—who knows—I might."

"How much you vant for it?"

"Oh, maybe—about fifty million dollars."

"Could I use your telephone?"

"Sure." The old man goes to the phone and calls his wife. "Hello, Ida. Now, listen, Ida, you listen careful, you go to the back of the kitchen to the closet, up on the third shelf on the right-hand side you find a shoe box. In the shoe box you find a paper bag. You'll bring me the box right away to Bloomingdale's store."

In ten minutes, their son arrives at Bloomingdale's office with the paper bag. The old man opens it and starts taking out wads of bills, all denominations. He starts counting. A hundred, a thousand, ten thousand. This goes on for hours, with Bloomingdale goggle-eyed. He's up to thirty-five million, then halfway between forty-one and forty-two million, and there's nothing left. He's quite irritated, clicking his tongue, shaking his head. And he says,

"Mr. Bloomingdale, could I use your phone again?"

"Sure!"

"Ida, vere'd you get that box?"

"On the fourth shelf."

"No, no, I told you the third shelf shoe box, not the fourth!"

In an alternative ending, after he gives Bloomingdale the money, Ida bursts in:

"Don't buy the store, Sam, don't buy it!"

"Whatsa matter Ida, it's a beautiful store."

"Nah, but Sam I looked, it hasn't got a room in the back!"

Why did God invent *goyim*?
Somebody had to buy retail.

Bernard Baruch

Bernard Baruch once made almost a million by observing Yom Kippur.

In September 1901, the legendary financier was selling Amalgamated Copper stock short. That meant he was betting the stock would go down by selling shares at their current price, but not having to deliver them until some contractual future date, when he hoped to get them for a lower price, thus making a profit.

The company's board met on Friday the 20th and cut its dividend from $8 a share to $6. The stock fell from 107 to 100. Baruch knew the next Monday would be the crucial day. He planned to keep selling short until the price hit 97. Then he got a phone call from his mother.

"Son, you know Monday will be Yom Kippur?"

Baruch had grown lax in religious observance but decided he must keep this holiest of holidays. He told his broker to keep selling copper stock short but not to bother him Monday.

That Monday, the stock fell past 94. When he found this out after sundown Monday, Baruch was shocked; he knew he'd have stopped selling at 97. But with this much momentum, he felt the stock was bound to plunge further. He keep selling short; by December, the stock hit 60 and Baruch had made about $700,000—his biggest stock market success to that point.

Baruch's was a legendary story of Wall Street success. After graduating from New York's City College, he worked as a $3-a-week glassware wholesalers' apprentice, then a Wall Street clerk, and then as a gold miner in Colorado. In five years, he was worth $3.5 million through stock market speculation. Renowned for his business judgment, Baruch kept his fortune by getting out of the stock market in 1928, a year before the cataclysmic 1929 crash. He noted: "I liked hard cash around, especially in times of trouble."

Born in South Carolina, Baruch was the son of a former Confederate surgeon. His family claimed descent from Baruch the Scribe, known for compiling the biblical Book of Jeremiah.

When Baruch was twenty-two, he quit his Wall Street job and headed West, where he became a pick-and-shovel miner near Cripple Creek,

Colorado. Harassed by the camp bully, he proved he was no Eastern weakling and beat the guy up. Then he "broke the bank" at the Branch Saloon by hitting the right combination on the roulette wheel twelve times in a row.

The first stock he ever bought was in the "San Francisco Mine." After buying the stock, he went to work in a shaft next to that of his mine and realized the stock would never pay like the fast talker who'd sold it to him had said. This was Baruch's first big lesson in money making. He went back east to Wall Street, sadder but apparently much wiser.

His Wall Street fame established, Baruch became an adviser to presidents starting with Woodrow Wilson, who appointed him chairman of the War Industries Board. Wilson called Baruch "Doctor Facts" because of the relentless way he sought out all the facts in his various governmental assignments. Baruch worked for a succession of presidents in a variety of high-level posts and was considered something of an expert on presidential personalities. He was known as an admirer of Roosevelt, Hoover, and Eisenhower. Of Harding, though, he noted that while the office of the presidency usually makes the man, Harding was the exception that proves the rule.

Baruch's suggestions for stock market investing:

1. Don't speculate unless you can make it a full-time job.
2. Beware of barbers, waiters, beauticians—and anyone else— with "tips" or "inside" information.
3. Don't try to buy at the bottom and sell at the top; "This can't be done—except by liars."

The "elder statesman" par excellence, Baruch defined the term thus: "An elder statesman is somebody old enough to know his own mind and keep quiet about it."

Last Wills

Sam knew his days were numbered and called his wife and children to his bedside.

"Hana, my wife, are you there?"

"Yes, Sam."

"And Rivke, my daughter, my first born?"

"Yes, Dad."

"And Davey, my boy?"

"Yes, Dad."

"And Bracha?"

"Yes, Dad."

"And Sarah, my baby?"

"Yes, Dad."

The sick man marshaled his limited strength and sat up suddenly. "If you're all here," he said, "who's watching the store?"

Nathanson, the big millinery supply wholesaler, was dying. He asked his wife to come to his bedside.

"Leah," he said, "I put off, I never drew up a will. Now listen," he continued in a weak voice, "listen to what I tell you. First of all, I'm leaving the business to Irving."

"Oh, no!" his wife protested. "Irving has only one thing on his mind—horses. He'll destroy the business! Listen—you'd do better to leave the business to Max. He's smart, serious, and he's a *mensch.*"

"Okay," sighed Nathanson, weakly shrugging his shoulders, not having the strength remaining to fight, "let it be Max. The summerhouse in the Catskills, I leave to Rachel," he went on.

"Rachel! Are you serious?" exclaimed his wife. "What does Rachel need the house in the Catskills for? Her husband's got plenty of money. Why don't you leave it to Julia, who's so poor?"

"Good, fine," said the dying man resignedly, "give it to Julia. As far as the car," he resumed, "I leave it to Benny."

"Benny? Benny?" asked the surprised Leah. "What does Benny need the car for? He's got one already! Louis could make so much better use of it."

The sick man was silent but an exasperated expression grew on his face. Gathering his remaining power he pleaded, "Leah! Who's dying around here—*you* or *me?*"

Let Them Work for It

Henry Zweig was using his last bit of strength to dictate his will. "To my son David, I leave $100,000. To my daughter Ellen, also $100,000; to my niece Sylvia, $50,000. . . . "

"Wait a minute," said his lawyer. "Your whole estate doesn't come to $10,000. What are you trying to do—how can you expect your kids to get $100,000 or even $50,000?"

"Get it?" Zweig croaked. "So? Better they should work their heads off for it, like I did!"

Slonim the banker is drowning off Coney Island. "Help!" he screams. The lifeguard comes and drags him toward shallow water.

"Now," he asks, "can you float alone?"

"What?" gasps Slonim. "Is this a time to talk business?"

11

JEWS OF THE UNDERWORLD

Sam "Killer" Kaplan, a hit man for the notorious gang Murder Incorporated, which operated as the Syndicate's dreaded enforcement arm during the 1930s, was badly wounded in gang war crossfire in Brooklyn's Brownsville section. He barely managed to escape the scene, the story goes, crawling on hands and feet the three blocks to his mother's apartment. Bleeding profusely and barely able to make his way up the stairs to the second floor, he summoned all his remaining strength to bang desperately on the door. "Mama, it's me, Sammy," he cried out. "I'm hurt, Mama, I'm hurt bad!"

"Sit down and eat," his mother is said to have replied as she slowly pulled the door open. "Later, we'll talk."

The Early Days

Among pre–World War I Jewish criminals, a pimp was known as a *simcha,* a detective a *shammas,* and a ne'er-do-well a *trombenik.* Members of the New York Jewish underworld called the *chutzpadik* owner of a sleazy bar *Kishkes,* a gang boss "Rabbi," and a proverbially kind-hearted prostitute "Chanele."

Criminal activities certainly didn't mean the miscreant no longer considered himself a Jew. "Stiff Rivka," in fact, specialized in *shul.* "She knows Bible, *davens* splendidly, and is as well-versed in Judaism as a woman can be," reported a journalist. Rivka became notorious, in fact, for her High Holiday habits. She would pick out a front-row seat in the synagogue from which she had a clear view of the congregation and pick out a woman "well bedecked." On her way out of the synagogue, she would jostle the woman and steal her brooch.

Hudis and Leah were known for stealing chickens from New York's wholesale kosher poultry markets and then, on Friday afternoons when demand was brisk, selling the pilfered pullets at bargain prices. The

Schorr brothers—Ikie, Sam, and Max—religiously frequented weddings and funerals, where they brushed up against guests and relieved them of jewelry and cash.

Doing What Comes Naturally

Pickpocketing was a skill East Side Jews were charged with "taking to naturally." East Side pickpocket bosses ran training schools they called *cheders*. A *melamed* (teacher) like Dopey Benny Fein would help his poor young *talmidim* (students) out with money or a room.

Young pickpockets would typically create a disturbance on the street, perhaps a fight between themselves. When a crowd gathered to watch, the smallest member rifled spectators' pockets. Or one of a gang might pretend to be learning to ride a bike and wobble his two-wheeler through a congested street. He would fall into a crowd of women shoppers; while the fledgling cyclist struggled to right his vehicle, his cohorts busily snatched purses and picked pockets.

Besides marketplaces and parks, streetcars were among pickpockets' favorite venues. Surface transit was preferred to the subway due to the greater ease of escape it provided. While passengers were distracted by one commotion or another, a youth could "lift" a purse or watch and jump off the streetcar before his theft was noticed.

"Big" Jake and "Dopey" Benny

Former pickpockets went into bigger things, sometimes legitimate and sometimes not. Big Jake Zelig started picking pockets and worked his way down to murder-for-hire. He is best remembered for his public relations maneuvers. He was known for an incredible ability to turn on his tears to bring judges and even victims into his corner.

Once Zelig stole a man's wallet and diamond ring. Zelig's tears so overcame the man with remorse for accusing him that, the story goes, the victim bought the baby-faced thief a new suit of clothes by way of apology. Another classic Zelig ploy was hiring a frail consumptive girl to beg the judge at each arraignment not to send the father of her baby to jail. It often worked.

Dopey Benny Fein went from running a school for pickpockets into more thoroughgoing gangsterism. He specialized in labor racketeering—but only for the labor side. "My heart lay with the workers," he declared, explaining his long standing refusal of lucrative offers from management. In 1912, for example, a "white goods" manufacturer set fifteen thousand-dollar bills in front of Benny. This was a lot of money for a guy whose gang charged only $500 for a murder.

"No, sir," Benny told the businessman, "I won't take it. I won't double-cross my friends." Manhattan's assistant district attorney said of Dopey Benny:

> He had standards of a sort. . . . The man really had a conviction that he was helping along in his own way a cause in which he believed. He would talk with glowing eyes of the way he turned down offers to guard the shops of employers.

Horses and Hoods

Horse poisoning was another common and feared criminal activity in the early East Side community. "Yoski Nigger," born Joseph Toblinsky, was called "King of the Horse Poisoners." His Yiddish Black Hand Association ran a protective racket that poisoned to death hundreds of horses whose owners wouldn't pay up.

But horses were not always simply victims, as is seen in the story of Chicago's Sam "Nails" Morton. Morton was widely credited with protecting Chicago's Jews from Italian hoods, and some five thousand Jews attended his funeral in 1924. Morton died by violence, which wasn't in itself unusual in the underworld. But rather than at the hand of man Morton died at the foot of a horse. Morton loved to ride horseback in Chicago's fashionable Lincoln Park, where the society people also rode. One day in the park, a horse threw Morton and stomped him to death. Morton's O'Banion gang, in time-honored fashion, headed down to the riding stable and, with guns drawn, seized the animal. They coolly led him to the exact spot where Morton had been killed. Then, in traditional style, they executed the horse with four slugs to the head.

❋

Protection rackets came in many shapes and sizes, run by characters colorful or just vicious. Max Hochstim's "association" held an annual outing for which tickets cost five dollars. A ticket read, somewhat ominously:

> The Association will assemble at Headquarters, Number 47 Delancey Street at eight o'clock A.M., sharp, and march in a body to the boat.

"Your Honor," Hochstim, an attorney, once flattered a New York judge in court, "you sure look swell in your judicial vermin."

One of Max's clients was Charles "King" Solomon, also known as "Silver Dollar Smith" for his Silver Dollar Saloon on Essex Street. The entire floor of the tavern, true to its name, had silver dollars cemented into it.

Only in America

Prostitution, like pickpocketing, became a common feature of East Side life, shocking the sensibilities of most immigrants from the *shtetl*, where such things were unheard-of among Jews. Some women searched the streets of the East Side for customers. Jennie Silver was known for always carrying a milk can with her as insurance against arrest. If asked by police to explain herself, she would predictably respond that she had been looking "high and low" for a quart of milk but that all the stores seemed to be closed.

"Mother" Rosie Hertz, the East Side's most prominent madam, was considered something of an American success story. She began working in 1882 as a "migratory" prostitute, going from one coal cellar or working basement to another. Soon she opened her own brothel and by 1909 was one of New York's most successful madams. She gathered her "girls" from a daily "accounting" and often followed this with an intendedly inspirational lecture on how to succeed in business and through what "trials of strength and endurance" she had built her empire. A judge called her "as much a fixture of the Lower East Side as the Brooklyn Bridge." She contributed to both major political parties and was not generally bothered by the police. She gave local children pennies and was known for speaking of and to God much of the time. A contemporary observer said of her: "She wears a wig as a pious Jewess would, and a large white apron. And when she smiles . . . she pinches your cheek in a motherly fashion." But, others charged, she had been the mentor of more prostitutes than any other woman in the world.

Out in the West, where they were less common, Jewish prostitutes had special status. A Jewish prostitute was considered exotic and usually commanded higher prices, especially if she had red hair. The reputation grew of the "Jew girl" as a "turned-on tart." Nell Kimbrell, in the book *Her Life as an American Madam*, said that in San Francisco, "a redheaded Jew girl was supposed to be just pure fire and smoke." Idoform Kate was known as the big Jewish madam of San Francisco. The operator of some twenty brothels, she stocked each with a "genuine" Jewish redhead, swore her hair was natural, and claimed each was in fact "a pious Jewess" struggling to save enough to bring her family over to America.

Ma Crime

The most prominent member of the nineteenth-century Jewish underworld and, many have said, the leading criminal in all late nineteenth-century America, was "Mother" ("Marm") Fredericka Mandelbaum, also known as "Ma Crime," "Queen of the Fences" and "Felonious Fredericka." Mandelbaum weighed a relatively dainty 150 pounds in 1849, when she arrived in New York from Prussia, but this nearly doubled by the time the gang she ran was committing 80 percent of America's bank robberies.

A widow with four children, at the height of her power Mandelbaum commanded an army of burglars and pickpockets and ran a school for training children in the criminal arts as well as what she called a "little notions business" in her small dry goods store on the corner of Clinton and Rivington streets. She lived in two floors above this store, her "eclectic but handsome furnishings," as author Ande Manners put it, "harvested from some of the most opulent homes in New York." She reportedly received a large share of booty harvested by looters during New York's Civil War draft riots, as well as the later and more distant Chicago Fire. Those in her orbit qualified for legal services from a questionable but pricey firm she retained for $5,000 a year. While known as a tight-fisted businesswoman who would rarely pay a thief more than 10 percent of the value of a stolen item, she was generous with expense money and open-handed in donating for her minions' health care and retirement.

"She was scheming and dishonest as the day was long," recalled one devotee nostalgically, "but she could be like an angel to the worst devil as long as he played square with her."

During more than thirty years of illegal activity in New York, "Marm" was known for wearing a tiny feathered black bonnet over a mass of tightly rolled hair. Vile language was unacceptable to her; she commanded respect from the crudest ruffians. Her dinner parties, where she brought her thieves together with representatives of straight society, were considered the high point of underworld social life.

"Marm" Mandelbaum had imitators but no successors. "Black Lena" Kleinschmidt set herself up as "Queen of Hackensack (New Jersey)" and tried to rival Marm's "family" and social circle. But, among other things, she lacked Marm's discretion. One of her dinner parties headed straight downhill when a guest recognized Lena's emerald ring as the same one recently lifted from a friend's handbag.

For most of her career, Marm enjoyed cordial relations with New York's police. But in 1884, in her sixties, she was finally nabbed at the behest of an uncharacteristically incorruptible Manhattan district attorney and charged with grand larceny and receiving stolen goods. She spent only one night in jail before skipping bail and fleeing with her son Julius to Canada, where she lived the rest of her life.

Gyp "The Blood" Horowitz

Perhaps it is possible, through the distance of generations or even centuries, to smile at some of the antics of the early Jewish criminals in

America. This gets much harder with those of more recent vintage, some of whom were simply brutal killers. This is not to say that all of the old school of gangsters were charming, but some had charming stories. Sort of.

Gyp "The Blood," whose real name was Harry Horowitz, was an example without such mitigating charm. He once won a $2 bet by grabbing a stranger and cracking his spine in three places. He claimed he could break any man's back by bending him across his knee, and gave proof of this several times. Once asked why he was so eager for bombing assignments, Gyp explained: "I likes to hear de noise." This friend of all mankind was electrocuted by the State of New York at the age of twenty-five.

"Lepke" Buchalter

There is even less light or amusing to say about Louis Buchalter, dubbed "Lepkele" by his mother and "the most dangerous criminal in the United States" by FBI director J. Edgar Hoover. Mobster Lucky Luciano even disdained the morals of this labor racketeer who specialized in breaking labor.

"With the rest of us," recalled Luciano, "it was booze, gambling, whores, like that. But Lepke took the bread out of the workers' mouths." By 1932, when he dominated a variety of superficially legitimate businesses and was on his way as the "feudal lord" of the New York underworld, he was known as "Judge Louie" or simply "The Judge." An associate, Sholem Bernstein, put it this way: "I don't ask questions. I just obey. It would be more healthier." It was said of him: "Lep loves to hurt people." Buchalter was the only one of eleven brothers and sisters to turn to crime; among his other siblings were a rabbi, a dentist and a pharmacist.

Lepke's modus operandi was extorting "protection" money and hiring his gangs out to manufacturers to forcibly prevent unionization of their shops. Rival Buchalter unions would sometimes be installed to "represent" workers. By the 1930s, Buchalter was said to dominate New York's bakery and pastry drivers, milliners, kosher poultry market, taxicab business, fur truckers and shoe trade.

Buchalter became the first top underworld figure of his generation to be executed by the state rather than the mob, for the murder of a Jewish garment industry trucker he'd run out of business and who'd threatened to tell his story to the district attorney. Buchalter was tricked into surrendering on a Manhattan street to FBI boss Hoover and columnist Walter Winchell, thinking a deal had been worked out that would reduce the penalties he'd face on a variety of counts. While in custody, he was implicated on murder charges.

"Kid Twist" Reles

"Kid Twist" Reles, once one of Murder Incorporated's top gunmen, was the fellow who implicated Buchalter. Long before Joe Valachi, he pulled what in 1940 was called the biggest "canary act" in underworld history, helping to solve forty-nine murders in Brooklyn alone (including several the law was unaware had happened) and to execute several major gangsters. Reles was credited with giving the authorities their first real inside look at the underworld. In 1941, under guard by six New York policemen and reportedly never left alone, he "fell or was pushed" from a Coney Island hotel window.

A. R.

Arnold "The Brain" Rothstein, also known as A. R., was a prototype of the smooth, well-dressed, nonviolent gangster who moved gracefully through all levels of society and never spent a day in jail. He was widely considered the model for gangster Meyer Wolfsheim in F. Scott Fitzgerald's *The Great Gatsby* and was dubbed "The Brain" by writer Damon Runyon. Rothstein was probably best-known for arranging the "Black Sox" fix of the 1919 World Series that sullied the reputation of major league baseball. Inside the underworld, he was known largely for bringing order and businesslike rationalization of the extreme and destructive competition until then prevailing between rival gangs. An 'equal opportunity' gangster, he was a prominent believer in underworld alliances independent of ethnic considerations.

Rothstein's taste in clothes was legendary. Once he suggested Lucky Luciano moderate his loud dress, characteristic of the Chicago Capone mob, as part of an effort to be less visible.

"I want you to wear something conservative and elegant," Rothstein advised Lucky, "made by a genteel tailor."

"What the hell are you talking about?" responded Luciano. "My tailor's a Catholic!"

Despite the aura he projected, Rothstein was not immune to the risks of the circles in which he moved. He once lost $320,000 in a single two-day poker game with two California gamblers. Word got out that Rothstein said the game was fixed and wouldn't pay up. A short time later, he was shot to death at his New York hotel. True to the underworld "code of honor," he wouldn't finger his assailant. Rothstein, whose father had been board chairman of New York's Beth Israel Hospital, was given an Orthodox funeral.

"Greasy Thumb" Guzik

Jake "Greasy Thumb" Guzik was treasurer of Al Capone's Chicago mob and got his nickname from the green stains he chronically had on his hands, from counting the mob's money. Guzik sued newspapers that called him a gangster. "I'm paying these judges," he argued. "Why shouldn't I use 'em?" Guzik, known as the Syndicate's financial wizard, was also known for never carrying a gun or venturing out of the house with less than $10,000 in cash, which bought off kidnappers three times. He was said to be the only man for whom Al Capone ever killed out of friendship. At the Senate's Kefauver hearings on organized crime in the 1950s, Guzik refused to answer questions, saying they "might tend to discriminate against me." At Orthodox funeral services for Guzik in 1956, it was said that more Italians attended his synagogue than ever before in its history. In an oft-quoted eulogy, the rabbi said Guzik "never lost faith in his God. Hundreds benefitted by his kindness and generosity. His charities were performed quietly."

"Dutch Schultz" Flegenheimer

Conscious of his image and cautious with his change, Arthur Flegenheimer reportedly took the name "Dutch Schultz" because it was short enough to fit into a newspaper headline. "If I'd kept the name Flegenheimer," he remarked, "nobody would have heard of me." He was known for never spending more than two dollars for a shirt or thirty-five dollars for a suit. "Dutch was the cheapest guy I knew," Lucky Luciano said of him. "The guy had a couple of million bucks and he dressed like a pig and worried about spending two cents for a newspaper."

With the help of math whiz Otto "Abbadabba" Berman, Flegenheimer figured out how to fix the Harlem numbers racket to make the smallest possible payout. A stickler for loyalty, he reportedly had an assistant who betrayed him "fitted" with a "cement overcoat" and dropped alive into the Hudson River. Flegenheimer was "executed" by two Murder Incorporated henchmen in a Newark restaurant men's room for defying Syndicate policy by threatening to kill New York prosecutor (later Governor and presidential candidate) Tom Dewey, then besieging the underworld with indictments. On his deathbed, Flegenheimer converted to Catholicism.

Meyer Lansky

Lansky's was one of the few Jewish names to be publicly associated with the underworld in more recent times. A character resembling him was featured in the "Godfather" movies. Long before John Lennon's controversial remark about the Beatles being "bigger than Jesus," Lansky was quoted as saying of the Syndicate: "We're bigger than U.S. Steel."

A studious young man who immigrated from Grodno, Poland, Lansky long stayed out of the underworld limelight. His luck was such it was said "the barrel of his gun was curved." Lansky built up a gambling empire that stretched from Las Vegas to prerevolutionary Havana. Lansky argued his acquaintanceships with underworld figures should not be held against him. "Who do you think comes to gambling casinos," he once parried a query about his associations, "*yeshiva* students and rabbis?" Lucky Luciano said: "I used to tell Lansky he may've had a Jewish mother, but someplace he must've been wet-nursed by a Sicilian."

Lansky was a long-time financial supporter of Jewish causes who reportedly helped Israel get arms during its 1948 War of Independence and was said to have killed an arms exporter who was supplying the Arabs. Facing prosecution on U.S. tax charges in 1970, Lansky fled to Israel but, following intense national debate and a protracted legal fight, Israel's Supreme Court found him ineligible for entrance, ruling he had "operated within the framework of organized crime" and agreeing he was "a person with a criminal past, likely to endanger the public welfare."

Jewish figures including Lansky, Rothstein and others were often credited with putting organized crime on a more rational and business-like basis that increased the take while reducing the violence to which the predominantly Italian underworld was prone. Some Italian gangsters had decidedly mixed feelings about the *Yiddishe* contribution to the underworld. Albert Anastasia, in conflict with Lansky over gambling in Havana, once lamented to a group of associates:

> You bastards have sold yourselves to the Jews. The traditions of the Honored Society have been forgotten. The old days were bad, maybe, but at least we could hold up our heads in pride. We had respect then; now we're a bunch of fucking businessmen.

12

STAGE, SCREEN, AND SONG: THE YIDDISH THEATER AND ITS CHILDREN

It Wouldn't Hurt

The following story is told of the death of the great Yiddish actor Yankel Leib. The theater manager is said to have come out at curtain time to solemnly tell the audience: "Ladies and gentlemen, I'm terribly sorry to have to announce that the great actor Yankel Leib has just now had a stroke in his dressing room and he has died, and we will not be able to have our performance tonight."

At this point, a woman in the balcony screamed hysterically: "Quick, give him an enema!"

"An enema?" said the manager. "Lady, the stroke was fatal!"

"*Give him an enema!*" she shouted again.

"But Yankel Leib is dead. He's left us. An enema can't possibly help."

And the voice resounded: "It wouldn't *hurt!*"

Sleep with a Baker

Boris Thomashevsky was at one time the best known and most financially successful actor on the Yiddish stage. A former cigar factory worker, he took his salary in gold, was first of the luminaries of the Yiddish stage to have a chauffeur-driven limousine, and employed a Japanese valet. He wore a cape and silk hat and sported a cane.

Thomashefsky had his apprenticeship as a boy playing female roles in amateur theatricals. Later he became a primary interpreter of plays that appealed to the broad Yiddish theater audience.

Thomashevsky was widely known for his romantic escapades, and as something of a sex symbol, although appearing corpulent and effeminate. He usually had an attractive woman waiting for him at the stage door. The story is passed down that, after spending the night with a young admirer, he gave her a pair of theater tickets.

"Oh, Mr. Thomashevsky," she cried, "I'm so poor! I don't need tickets—I need bread!" Summoning his dignity, the haughty actor is said to have replied: "Thomashevsky gives tickets—if it's bread you want, sleep with a baker!"

The Yiddish *King Lear*

Many of the devotees of New York's Yiddish theater were legendary for both their enthusiasm and eccentricity. There was one man who, it was said, would not miss a single performance by the renowned actor Jacob Adler in the title role of the Yiddish *King Lear*. When the actor delivered the famed line: "Will no one here give me even a piece of bread?" the man, with amazing predictability, ran into the aisle actually offering the actor bread and shouting, "Mr. Adler, come with me! Children are no good!"

An Actor's Theater

In the early days of the Yiddish theater, actors dominated to the extent that they were actually known for hazing playwrights, a situation described by Hutchins Hapgood in his 1902 book *Spirit of the Ghetto*. At that time, only the popular playwright Joseph Latteiner and M. Horowitz were regarded by the somewhat haughty actors as legitimate "ghetto" playwrights. Any other writers might face a variety of pranks. The actors might get the new playwright to try on, one after another, every costume in the theater, purportedly to help him better conceptualize his characters. Another popular prank was to locate the erstwhile playwright in the middle of the stage and ask him to read his script through aloud to "see how it sounded." The actors would supposedly go to sit in the galleries and listen, but, during the early course of his reading, they would all gradually file out of the theater, until the playwright realized he was reading only for himself.

Another indignity inflicted on playwrights, reported by Hapgood, would occur when the actors were seeming to rehearse a script. One actor would suddenly scream out, "He is coming, the great Professor Horowitz, and he will eat you!" and responding to the cue they would all run frantically off the stage and out the door, with, Hapgood wrote, "the panic-stricken playwright following close at their heels."

Jacob Gordin

Jacob Gordin, the prime "realist" writer of the Yiddish theater, strove to introduce what he considered higher literary and dramatic standards than previously characterized the theater. When Gordin's work was relatively new on the East Side, he found himself in a virtual war with the Yiddish theater's generally dominant actors over the issue of ad-libbing changes in scripts. In no serious theater throughout the world, Gordin argued, could actors do what they wished with the writer's text. The Yiddish actors felt this demand impermissibly cramped their roles; they viewed the theater as more of a vehicle for their spontaneous expression before an audience.

On the opening night of Gordin's *The Pogrom*, in the first scene, Gordin himself played the part of a police inspector (this also because he would not compromise on an actor who couldn't speak good Russian—and what real Russian police inspector, Gordin argued, spoke Yiddish?) who is a surprise visitor at the home of a wealthy Jewish family.

The lady of the house, played by actress Bina Abramowitz, welcomes him and invites him to sit down and enjoy wine and fish, and wishes him a good appetite. At this point, Miss Abramowitz turned to the audience and said, in a loud aside: "He should choke on it!" Apparently forgetting where he was, Gordin slammed his fist down on the table. "Stop it!" he screamed, "That's not in the script!"

A Fighter's Theater

The Yiddish theater differed from the general American theater in far more than its language. It was a far less inhibited environment, in which, for example, realist writer Jacob Gordin used to regularly come out on stage between acts of his plays to denounce his critics.

Labor leader and journalist Abraham Cahan, who would later become the longtime editor of the *Forward*, was at an early point a champion of Gordin's realistic writings, but conflict broke out between the two, whose first outbreak some traced to the 1895 run of Gordin's *The Russian Jew in America*.

The play attempted to be a critique of American life, filled with characters portrayed as corrupt opportunist. One of these was a Jewish labor leader named Huzdak, who was depicted as all too willing to compromise his principles to win concrete gains for his union. All through the play, Huzdak repeats the line, "What do I need brains for when I've got a Constitution?"

One night Cahan attended a performance of this play. Apparently feeling Huzdak did not provide a fair insight into the attitudes of Jewish labor leaders (like himself), when Huzdak first said this line, Cahan leaped spontaneously from his seat and shouted out in Russian, "That's a lie!"

Later, after a 1902 performance of Gordin's *The Slaughter* by what now was his own company, Cahan mentioned to one of the actors backstage that he thought Gordin's dialogue for one of the characters, a *shtetl* girl, seemed improbably intellectual, and the character thus unrealistic. Gordin apparently heard about the comment, and a few nights later Cahan was shocked to hear Gordin had gone on stage between acts for another of his customary midplay diatribes against critics—this time taking off against Cahan's word-of-mouth criticism, which had not appeared in print anywhere. Cahan angrily told the actor to whom he had spoken to assure Gordin that he, Cahan, would no longer have any opinion whatsoever about forthcoming works of his, and vowed to never again see another Gordin play.

Another time, a few days after the Orthodox *Tageblatt* had sharply criticized a new Gordin play, *Orphan*, the *Tageblatt* critic attended Gordin's theater to see another play in repertory with the critic of another Orthodox paper called the *Morning Journal*. When Gordin stepped out on stage for his customary attack on his critics, he spotted the two and cried, "There they are," pointing angrily at them, "sitting there, the two scroungers—they haven't even paid for their tickets!"

With the entire audience watching, the two men rose without speaking and walked out. A few days later the *Tageblatt* began a massive counterattack, denouncing the irreverence of Gordin's play, his personality, ideas and socialism.

* * *

Meyer was a legendary hanger-on of Yiddish theatrical and literary circles. He was close to the greats and his opinion was sought after. The Yiddish theater was full of jealousies and petty disputes. It was once argued that Maurice Schwartz, director of the Yiddish Art Theater, took all the good parts for himself, preventing younger men in his company from getting anywhere.

"That's an unfounded piece of gossip," disputed Meyer vigorously. "On occasion, Mr. Schwartz has been very generous with the leading parts. Take, for example, his recent production of the *Brothers Ashkenazi*. Tell me, did he play both brothers?"

The Jewish Caruso

At the age of four, Yossele Rosenblatt already showed signs of musical talent. Before he had learned to read, he was able to repeat to perfection, in a clear bell-like alto voice, all the chants of the synagogue. He even added flourishes of his own. When he was ten, the would-be audience that sought admittance to the synagogue where he was to chant was so unwieldy police reserves were called to maintain order. The chief performer made several attempts to break through the mass, but in vain. He waited patiently, laughing to himself. A man, seeing the boy so amused, asked him, "Little boy, why are you laughing? What's so funny?"

"What am *I* laughing for? If it weren't for me, those fellows over there would be out of a job."

He was offered $1,000 a night to sing in the opera *La Juive*. He could have Jewish women as his singing partners, kosher food would be prepared for him wherever he went, and he would not have to appear on Saturdays or Jewish holidays. Yet he turned the offer down, causing excitement in both the Jewish and non-Jewish worlds. The humorous Yiddish weekly *Der Groisse Kundess* featured a cartoon of the famous cantor running away from a siren in a gossamer gown, representing grand opera. "Come, Yossele," she beckons, "a thousand dollars a night." But Yossele, with his prayerbook in hand, crying "Shema, Yisra-El!" heads straight toward the synagogue.

Enrico Caruso, upon hearing Yossele sing, was so moved that he went up on stage and kissed him.

One of the many names given to Rosenblatt was "The Man with the $500,000 Beard." There were other great cantors on the scene—Kwartin, Hershman, Roitman, Sirota, Liov, Minkowsky, and Rovner. But they did not worry Yossele. "I am not afraid of rivalry. It is only of God and the barber that I stand in awe. My beard, you know, is in constant danger of the haircutters."

One poet wrote about him:

> Cantors and singers we get without quota.
> We've already heard both Kwartin and Sirota.
> But this must admitted be ev'n by his *son'im* (enemies)
> That Yossele king is of all the *Chazonim*.

The very first music heard in any American movie was in Hebrew. Yossele Rosenblatt's voice was on the sound track in the original *Jazz Singer*, which starred Al Jolson. Yossele sang the Kol Nidre on the condition that he would not be listed in the credits and that another cantor would stand in for the filming. He did not want to be connected with a "commercial enterprise."

Yossele and the Metropolitan tenor John McCormack used to greet each other: "Hello, Jewish McCormack!" "Hello, Irish Rosenblatt!"

Moishe Oysher

Moishe Oysher was one of a number of cantors who succeeded in American show business. During his entire career he remained the *hazzan* of the First Rumanian American Congregation on Rivington Street. He once told *The New Yorker*: "I keep so busy from Friday to Sunday, by Monday, look—I'm on a stretcher! . . . I sing in the synagogue, I sing at weddings, I sing at funerals, I sing at club dinners, I sing at benefits. For the High Holidays alone, I earn a figure in five figures. Once, when I told my grandmother that, she shook her head and said 'Moishe, your grandfather sang for a sack of potatoes!' Maybe I'd do the same in Bessarabia."

A Jewish woman watched a play from a second balcony seat near the place from which spotlights were thrown on the stage. She sat in the row behind another Jewish woman she knew. Every so often the woman in front would say, "Hooh hah, hooh hah."

After the show, they ran into each other. The woman in the back row said, "You really seemed to be enjoying the show."

"No, not particularly. Actually, I didn't much care for it."

"Well, you know, every so often, you kept shouting, 'Hooh hah, hooh hah.'"

"Oh, no," laughed the other, "that wasn't the show. That was the spotlights. Ooh, that gave me such a good bake on my shoulders!"

In the days of the Yiddish theater, a man bought a ticket to see a play. Before the show had gone fifteen minutes, though, he hurried out and asked the woman in the box office for his money back.

"You don't like the show?" asked the ticket seller.

"No, I like it; it's a nice show."

"Well, what then, you didn't have a good seat?"

"No, it was a fine seat."

"Well, what's the problem?" demanded the ticket seller.

"Frankly" said the man, "I'm just scared to sit alone in the theater!"

The Great Houdini

His name meant magic. A poster with his photograph hailed "Europe's Eclipsing Sensation," "The World's Handcuff King and Prison Breaker," and proclaimed, "Nothing on Earth Can Hold Houdini a Prisoner."

Houdini was born Erich Weiss, the son of Rabbi Samuel Meyer Weiss, in 1874. He often assisted his father in his work and celebrated his bar mitzvah in New York. In later years, he would help organize the Rabbis' Sons Theatrical Benevolent Association (that also claimed as members Al Jolson and Irving Berlin), which held volunteer benefits for charitable and patriotic causes.

He began to practice magic at fourteen. In one of his first acts, he was tied up, placed in a tightly secured sack, and locked up in a large case bound with rope. The case was further placed inside a cabinet. In three seconds, Houdini had somehow exchanged places with his partner outside; she was now bound up in the sack and was wearing a coat she had borrowed from a member of the audience. Her hands were tied behind her back just as Houdini's had been.

Houdini and Handcuffs

Houdini used to start his act by inviting anyone in the audience who cared to, to handcuff him in regulation police cuffs. There was never any shortage of takers. After examining what he called the "prison jewelry," Houdini had himself manacled by several pairs around his wrists; his feet were also shackled and the cuffs joined to his leg irons. Then placed in a curtained enclosure in the middle of the stage, Houdini took four minutes to completely free himself.

Houdini was continually challenged. A Dorchester, Massachusetts, doctor brought an ancient pair of handcuffs to a Boston performance and insisted on putting them on Houdini with his hands behind his back. Admitting he couldn't then remove them in that position, Houdini had to dislocate both his shoulders to bring his hands in front of him.

In Cologne, Germany, the police chief called Houdini "an impostor" and asserted the magician didn't really escape from his shackles. Houdini took him to court and won. The local court ordered the police chief to apologize publicly to Houdini. Instead, the chief appealed to a higher court, where police officials produced a special new lock that, once locked, could never be reopened. Houdini unlocked it in five minutes and won his case.

"Emperor of Straitjackets"

Houdini kept up a continual patter while doing his tricks. At Keith's Theatre in Boston, he held up a straitjacket and observed that he had never known anyone to free himself from such a device. The straitjacket, with heavy leather straps, was firmly strapped on Houdini by three men. When he was buckled in, he could hardly move. His hands had been tied behind him and pushed up inside the sleeves.

A contemporary newspaper review of his act read:

> He wriggles and squirms, humps and writhes, slips his head under his arm, skates along on one shoulder, chews a buckle or two, and peels off his crazy house trappings as a boy does his bathing suit. Chains which cut into the flesh and are padlocked are a mere bagatelle. Houdini slips out of them without bothering with the lock. All these things are done in full view of the audience.

The "Prison Breaker"

Onstage was a wooden cell, raised above the floor and locked from outside, without any panels or visible means of access except one door. Houdini was placed in an iron-hooped barrel, the ends fastened with straps and padlocks. The barrel was placed inside the cell and the door locked. A canopy was drawn over the cell. Within five minutes, Houdini emerged, bowing and smiling.

Time after time, people thought at last they had nailed and jailed their "prisoner." Employees of a desk company equipped a six-foot rolltop desk with secret locks. Every known device for securing the desk cover was used. Houdini took longer than usual to get out of this "jail." He entered the desk at 10:08 P.M.; before 11, he was free.

On the Ground, in the Air . . .

As Houdini's acts grew more sophisticated, some people came to believe he had supernatural powers. The Chinese Water Torture Cell escape, one of his inventions, made him an international sensation.

In this trick, Houdini was placed upside down in a large steel box filled with water. His ankles were locked securely in the middle of the box's massive cover. He escaped in two minutes. A $1,000 award was offered to anyone who could find air in the "Chinese Water Torture Cell."

A large metal container, whose neck had barely enough space for a person to squeeze through, was brought onto Keith's stage in Boston. Stage-hands filled the container with water. Houdini, dressed in a bathing suit and handcuffed, climbed in. A metal cover was fastened securely over him with six padlocks.

A stagehand stood at the ready with a hatchet to smash the container open and revive Houdini if he didn't appear on time. But, at the end of two minutes, Houdini was out, drenched and breathless.

Some of Houdini's challenges were tougher than others. In one, handcuffed and shackled, he was locked into a steel boiler measuring six feet long and two feet wide. Six riveters sealed Houdini in as the audience watched. Houdini struggled for an hour to get out. Like many a man who has spent an hour inside a boiler, his clothes were covered with dust, his collar gone, his hair disheveled.

Five men spent fifteen minutes fastening Houdini to a long ladder. His feet were shackled to one end of the ladder with a padlock. A chain tied his neck to the other end. His hands were tied crosswise between the rungs of the ladder and behind his back. In seven minutes, Houdini signaled he was free.

In the "East Indian needle trick," Houdini swallowed two papers of needles and a ball of thread. He then drew the thread from his lips with the needles strung on it at regular intervals.

Houdini took up flying and was called the first "birdsman" to fly in Australia. In Chicago, at a benefit exhibition for a fellow magician's widow, Houdini was shackled hand and foot, and flown up in a plane over Lake Michigan. While the plane flew 50 feet above the water, Houdini leaped overboard, plunged into the water, somehow freed his hands and legs, and swam ashore.

Houdini's Brother

Another prominent magician, known as Hardeen, was Houdini's brother, born Theodore Weiss. Rabbi Weiss would have liked to have called his boys "My sons, the lawyers," the story goes; instead they turned out to be world-famous magicians and escape artists.

Hardeen was not as much of a showman as his more celebrated brother and didn't deliver the same entertaining stage patter. But some observers claimed that, as a sensational performer, Hardeen was actually superior to Houdini. Handcuffs were child's play to Hardeen—he released himself from half a dozen handcuffs and leg irons at once. In his tours of the world, he found his way out of Siberian prisons, Chinese dungeons, a German fortress, and the rock-hewn chambers of Gibraltar. Like his brother, he escaped straitjackets, water-filled iron boilers, packing cases, "crazy cribs," and beer kegs. An audience saw him "walk" through a brick wall.

Houdini willed his show to Hardeen on his death.

Houdini the Human

"It requires years to build a reputation, but only a single performance to break one," Houdini said. "Let an audience once discover that a performer has met his match, and no time will be lost in spreading the news from one end of the world to the other."

Houdini was not "Superman"; he was thoroughly human and always alert to the danger of being confronted with the impossible.

Houdini carried his own typewriter with him on tour and reportedly answered every letter that came to him. In his spare time, he invented a tri-colored typewriter ribbon arrangement, an envelope that could not be unsealed by steam without revealing the word *opened,* and a wash that removed printer's ink from paper.

He claimed his abilities were largely inherited. "While my father was a rabbi," he said, "there were locksmiths in our family, and I guess I got my lockpicking talents from them.

"What I do takes a lot of study, intuition, strength, physical endurance, and quick action, both of body and mind."

Houdini took a strong interest in the reputation of magic, calling it "the most sadly misrepresented of all professions." He wrote a book, *The Unmasking of Robert-Houdin*, in which he denounced the French magician from whom he'd borrowed his stage name as a "sorry impostor, a prince of pilferers," who "unscrupulously robbed dead-and-gone magicians of all credit for their inventions and accomplishments." He also commissioned the study, *Houdini's History of Magic in Boston*.

Houdini's Strange Death

Houdini was meeting in Montreal with a McGill student who'd written an article about him. The student brought two friends; one of them, believed to have been an amateur boxer, asked Houdini about his claim that he could withstand an all-out punch to the midriff. Houdini agreed that it was true. Apparently misunderstanding this casual remark, the student bent over and punched the reclining Houdini in the abdomen with all his might. The magician gasped, jumped up, and belatedly explained he hadn't been ready, that it was necessary first for him to brace his muscles. Houdini had recently also snapped an ankle, which may have made him more vulnerable to infection. Despite growing weakness and fever, Houdini kept up his schedule but, three days later, he collapsed during his act and was found to have a ruptured appendix and peritonitis—at that time, before sulfa drugs, a usually fatal illness. He died several days later, at fifty-two.

Include Me Out: The Legend of Sam Goldwyn

Sam Goldfisch was one of the world's top glove salesmen by the time he was eighteen, but his real fame would come as Samuel Goldwyn, a Hollywood baron who mixed up his own lines to the lasting amusement of the American public.

A Hollywood legend has it that when Goldwyn first became an independent producer he called in the head of his publicity department and said, "David Belasco became a famous producer by wearing his collar wrong side around. What can I do to make myself famous?" Shortly after, the "Goldwynism" was born.

A more popular theory is that "Goldwynisms" were merely typical examples of the thousands of humorous malapropisms and mixed metaphors by Eastern European Jewish immigrants as they learned English, and then by their descendants who, despite speaking English well, continued into today some of their forebears' speech patterns in changed forms. The fact that movie mogul Sam Goldwyn was supposed to have said them made them especially quotable. Goldwyn, in fact, claimed to never said half the "Goldwynisms" popularly attributed to him, blaming many on press agents and hangers-on from his studio. Some "Goldwynisms" follow:

"Anybody who sees a psychiatrist ought to have his head examined."

"Include me out!"

"This atom bomb is dynamite!"

"Every Tom, Dick and Harry is named Sam."

"The publicity for this picture is sweeping the country like wildflowers."

"A verbal contract isn't worth the paper it's written on."

"I had a monumental idea this morning, but I didn't like it."

"I want to make a picture about the Russian secret police—the G.O.P."

"Our comedies are not to be laughed at."

"They're always biting the hand that lays the golden egg."

"I'll write you a blanket check."

"I never put on a pair of shoes unless I've worn them for at least five years."

"The trouble with this business is the dearth of bad pictures."

"Excuse me, I'm going out for some tea and trumpets."

"You're always taking the bull between the teeth."

*   *   *

In 1916, after being squeezed out of a movie production company partnership with Cecil B. DeMille, Sam Goldfisch founded a new company with two Broadway producers, Edgar and Arch Selwyn; by combining their last names, they got the name Goldwyn Pictures. Apparently tired of "goldfish" jokes, Sam liked the new company's name so much he adopted it as his own. The company was making silent movies with big stars, but in 1919 it needed cash badly and sold $7 million in stock to the DuPont family; this led to Sam getting squeezed out of his own company. He himself was never part of the MGM whose *G* bore his name, and it was as an independent producer that he achieved his fame.

After leaving Goldwyn Pictures, the magnate formed Eminent Authors Pictures, Inc. He was forced to play up his writers since Goldwyn Pictures already had most of the big-name movie stars under contract. Ever ready to pioneer, Goldwyn first thought he could advertise the names of the writers in big lights and the names of the stars in small ones. He imported some of the best-known writers to Hollywood, including numerous prominent Europeans.

Goldwyn had trouble with Belgian playwright Maurice Maeterlinck, whose *Blue Bird* (from which came the expression "bluebird of happiness") was creating a sensation in European literary and theatrical worlds. Maeterlinck spoke no English and had never heard of Goldwyn or his Eminent Authors, but he had heard of American currency, especially when expressed in five figures.

The story has it that Maeterlinck's first Hollywood effort was a film adaptation of his play *Life of a Bee*, and that, on reading it, Goldwyn ran out of his office screaming, "*My God, the hero is a bee!*" None of Maeterlinck's writings ever made it to the screen. When the Belgian author left Hollywood, so the story goes, Goldwyn saw him to the railroad station, patted him on the shoulder, and consoled him: "Don't worry, Maurice, you'll make good yet."

Goldwyn was always ready to pay colossal sums for "big-name" writers. He tried desperately to snare George Bernard Shaw, but Shaw could not be had. Shaw said Goldwyn was too interested in art while he, Shaw, was only interested in money. Goldwyn's discoveries included Rudolph Valentino, Bebe Daniels, Pola Negri, Anna Sten, Will Rogers, Vilma Banky and Ronald Colman. Goldwyn is also credited with developing Eddie Cantor on the screen. Gary Cooper was on Goldwyn's payroll at $50 a week when he was discovered by another producer and signed up for $260 a week. Several years later Goldwyn got him back for $3,000 weekly. Goldwyn was so successful in securing a foreign market for his pictures that he was able to proclaim: "Gentlemen, I've invented a new slogan—Goldwyn pictures griddle the earth!"

Goldwyn was also known for having the worst temper in Hollywood. One associate said of him: "His voice breaks men down like a rubber hose. Sam argues a man into a coma or into a disorder resembling 'the bends.' His victims sign anything. . . ."

Goldwyn had a dispute with a rival studio over the services of screen writer William Anthony McGuire, who wrote *The Great Ziegfeld* (1936), and it seemed the only solution was to arbitrate. "All right," said Goldwyn, "I'm a fair man. I'll submit anything to arbitration. But remember, no matter what's decided, McGuire goes to work for *me!*"

Goldwyn was tall and broad shouldered and almost totally bald. One of the best-dressed men in Hollywood, he never carried any money, lest the lines of his suit be distorted. Although he had a regard for money, he threw it away like water to get the effect he wanted in a picture. When he didn't like his first version of *Nana* he scrapped it completely, throwing away the $411,000 he had spent on it.

"It's too caustic," a director once said when asked his opinion of a script.

"To hell with the cost!" snorted Goldwyn. "If it's a good picture, we'll make it."

The Dancing Cantor

"Do something about my grandson," the elderly woman told a social worker at the Educational Alliance. "The boy's mixed up with bad company. And another thing—*ehr vill eemer zingen und tantzen* (he always wants to sing and dance)."

The Alliance sent young Eddie Cantor to its Surprise Lake Camp at Cold Spring, New York. There he entertained fellow campers—one of whom was George Jessel—with an imitation of his grandmother's Polish servant girls' songs, dances, and impersonations. The camp director asked him to stay two more weeks. "That was the first time my act was held over," Cantor said later.

He was born Edward Israel Iskowitz on the Lower East Side, the son of a dreamy violinist. Eddie was orphaned at the age of two, and grandmother Esther started an employment agency, recruiting servant girls for families. She and Eddie lived in two rooms in a basement that also housed the girls before Esther found them jobs. "Overnight, I used to get as many as seven sisters and eight first cousins," Eddie recalled.

Eddie was headed for sure trouble and Grandma Esther had to keep him in tow. He stole fruit from vendors, robbed bicycle stores, ran away from home, and slept on roofs. His talents were used to hold the attention of street corner crowds while his buddies picked spectators' pockets. In desperation, Grandma Esther turned to the Educational Alliance.

Cantor's first stage appearance was made as an entrant in an amateur contest at the hard-boiled Miner's Bowery Theatre. When he was announced as "Mr. Edward Cantor, Impersonator," the toughs guffawed at the "Edward." During his routine, a heckler shouted, "Stick to it, kid. You're rotten!" Cantor stuck to it and won over his audience as well as the grand prize of five dollars.

Cantor did imitations and little sketches of his own in a downtown burlesque house with "The Indian Maidens." In a Yiddish Civil War sketch, a Chinese sentinel stood guard at a war conference between Lincoln and Grant. Lincoln kept whispering to Grant about the Chinese sentinel, *"Ich deink ehr eez a spion."* ("I think he is a spy.")

He became a singing waiter at Carey Walsh's saloon in Coney Island. His accompanist was the young Jimmy Durante. Eddie and Jimmy told customers the number wasn't written they couldn't sing and play. When somebody asked for a piece they never heard of, like "South Dakota Blues," Jimmy composed a melody on the spot and Eddie made up the lyrics.

When Eddie was fourteen, he met Ida Tobias, who became known to many as "the belle of Henry Street," and eight years later they were married. Ida's family felt Eddie would never amount to anything. During the run of the Midnight Frolic, however, Mr. Tobias introduced Eddie with "Meet-my-son-in-law-makes-four-hundred-dollars-a-week."

In 1927, Cantor developed pleurisy. The doctor gave him six months to live unless he quit work. He quit for a few months, but the stage drew him back. "I'd rather die working than be bored to death," he said.

On radio, Cantor introduced the use of the announcer as the comedian's "straight man." His trademarks were his bounce, the clapping of his hands, and his big round "banjo" eyes.

During the 1917 run of Ziegfeld Follies, Cantor passed the hat for charity. In 1936, he started the March of Dimes drive against polio, for which he was later cited by President Franklin Roosevelt.

"Jolie"

Al Jolson's favorite story was about the time he bought his father an overcoat for $200. He knew his dad wouldn't approve of such extravagance, so he had the salesman take out the price tag and put on one that read $20.

"Well, Pop," he said when he saw him later, "how did you like the coat?"

"Fine," his father answered. "You know what? I sold it to Uncle Moishe for $40. You didn't know your father was a businessman, did you?"

(Another version of this story is told about Earl Sher, a Hollywood actor born Isidor Sharnapolsky, who gets a telegram from New York a few days after sending his father a 'marked-down' $20 coat:

"Send six more overcoats at same price. Sold mine for $30.")

Born Asa Yoelson in Srednicke, Russia, he came to America with his family and settled in Washington, D.C. At fourteen, Al ran away from home and joined a circus as a singer in a side show. He made his stage debut as one of the mob of boys in Israel Zangwill's *Children of the Ghetto*. After a bit as a clown in a tent show, he moved on to the Dockstadter Minstrels and then to the Winter Garden in New York.

Jolie, as he came to be called, raised commonplace material to unimagined heights. In his mouth, a "Mammy" lost its maudlin sentimentality and acquired the quality of a folk ballad. After listening to Jolie performing what he said was his mother's favorite tune, *A Chasendel auf Shabbes* ("A Cantor of the Sabbath"), a writer wrote, "He laughed it, he wept it." Jolson used all the tricks he knew—the smashing abandon, the emotionalized talking off of the second verse of a song, the blackface appeal, and the big finish—to become one of the most individualistic and sensational performers ever.

Jolson was called "America's greatest minstrel singer." He didn't just sing his "Mammy" songs and his "Rockabyes"—he poured them out. It has been said that a Jolson show had the instant pull of a UJA drive in the midst of a Middle East war.

When he wowed his audience, Jolie would chuckle and shout, "You ain't heard nuthin' yet!"

In Washington, his father Cantor Yoelson served a congregation, and Jolie used to joke about entertaining the president at the White House in the morning and his father in the synagogue in the afternoon. The cantor was reluctant to go to the theater to see Al. When Jolie asked why he didn't come, the cantor answered, "A father doesn't call on a son."

Jolson and George Jessel engaged in one of Broadway's most famous feuds, which may have grown out of a dispute over a movie contract for *The Jazz Singer*, in which Jessel starred on the stage and Jolson in the movies.

Toastmaster General

"I've learned practically everything I know in the theater," George Jessel once said. "I can remember learning to read and write, but I still print." His grandfather was a tailor; while the older man's customers waited to have their pants pressed, he brought little George out to sing for them. Later, George entertained at Grandpa's lodge meetings.

George's mother, a ticket seller at a Harlem movie theater, arranged for her boss to hear George sing. It was the right move at the right time; the theater owner had just decided to try vaudeville, and Jack Weiner, Walter Winchell, and George became Leonard, Lawrence and McKinley, "The Imperial Trio." After the trio dissolved, George was kept on as a soloist. The theater marquee announced: "It's worth five cents alone to hear little Georgie Jessel sing."

Thirty years later Winchell wrote: "And it still goes."

1917 found Jessel without an act and too old for what he called "kid stuff." He tried to think what he could put across. Once, when some friends were visiting, he called his mother on the phone and started telling her funny stories. The friends found his side of the conversation hilarious and suggested he use a "Hello, Momma" routine as an act. It clicked and became one of his best standbys.

Jessel performed in vaudeville, theater and movies, wrote songs (one of them titled "Oh, How I Laugh When I Think How I Cried About You"), and produced a few shows.

He may have been best known, though, as "Toastmaster General of the United States." He presided at several hundred funerals and more than 300 banquets and raised more than $60 million on behalf of Israel Bonds alone. Fifteen years before his death, Jessel estimated he owned 600 thank-you plaques; 200 City of Hope torches and 188 honorary synagogue memberships. Will Rogers once said, "Every time Jessel sees half a grapefruit, he automatically rises and says, 'Ladies and gentlemen, we have here tonight . . .'"

Television was not among Jessel's many favorite media. Once an unauthorized announcement was made that he would go into TV; he bristled. "Someone quoted me as saying, 'I might be in television by May.' He misunderstood me," Jessel said. "What I did say was, 'I might be in Tel Aviv by May!'"

Forgot to Remember

Unable to sing or read music, Irving Berlin became one of the world's most prolific and popular composers. A native of a Siberian province, he wrote what has become a "second" national anthem of his adopted America. A Jew, he composed two of the most popular tunes associated with Christian holidays.

Where fact stops and legend begins is hard to say. Isidore Baline came to America with his family at the age of four. His father worked as a part-time cantor and certified meat in kosher butcher shops. When Isidore was eight, his father died; before his death, his father had already taught the boy the rudiments of music.

The youngster sold newspapers to help his mother make ends meet. One story has it that one May afternoon he was watching a merchant ship set sail for China. In his right fist the boy clutched his day's gross receipts of five pennies. Suddenly a crane, which had been loading coal nearby, caught him in its swing and knocked him into the East River. An Irish "wharf rat" kicked off his shoes and swam to the rescue. Although young Isidore was saved as he went down for the third time, his right fist still held all five pennies.

Berlin also worked as a "busker" or song plugger who, in the days before radio disc jockeys, used to play or sing songs to promote them. For a short time he plugged songs for Harry von Tilzer at Tony Pastor's Restaurant on New York's 14th Street. He led around Blind Sol, a Bowery character, and made occasional tips when he was allowed to sing.

In 1904 he got a job as a singing waiter at "Nigger Mike's" Pelham Cafe—a bar and restaurant owned by Mike Salter, a Russian Jew nicknamed so for his swarthy complexion. It was Herbert Bayard Swope, a reporter for the *New York World*, who, when the singing waiter refused to accept a tip tendered by Prince Louis of Battenberg, gave Berlin his first press notice. And it was at Nigger Mike's that the composer concocted a tinkly ballad that was later to sweep the nation—"Alexander's Rag-Time Band." Years later, a rumor spread that Berlin had paid an unknown black man ten dollars for the song and published it under his own name. When this sour note reached Berlin's ears, he bristled and barked, "And from whom did I buy my other successes?"

Folklore, not history, has it that Berlin, Walter Winchell, Eddie Cantor and Al Jolson all started as waiters at Nigger Mike's. In any case, Berlin didn't stay there long. In 1907, the story goes, he was fired when, left in charge of the cafe, he fell asleep.

His next stint was at Jimmy Kelly's on Union Square. It was here he wrote the words for "Marie from Sunny Italy." After that, he turned out more than 1,000 more songs. Yet he still had no formal musical education, was unable to read notes, and played in only one key—F sharp. His piano had a lever that shifted its works so melodies could be transposed from key to key.

In an interview, Berlin said, "I've got all the music textbooks home you're supposed to have, and the rhyming dictionary and the thesaurus, but I never open one of them. Rhymes just come to me or else they don't. And when they don't, it's just awful. I beat my brains out."

The classic example of words that didn't come is "Remember," one of Berlin's biggest hits. Berlin had the song all written except for the tag line. That he couldn't seem to get. He refused to release the song until he got an ending that satisfied him, and for two years it lay on a shelf. Then that line, the one that made the song, came to him. It was "You forgot to remember."

Berlin wrote "God Bless America" during World War I as the proposed finale of the musical *Yip, Yip, Yaphank*, but felt that the time was not ripe for it and so pulled it out. It was shelved for more than twenty years. In 1939, when asked to write a patriotic hymn, he recalled the old *Yaphank* finale, made a few changes, and decided it just fit popular sentiment at that time. Kate Smith introduced it and it became a smash hit overnight.

But the song caused an uproar. All kinds of people from isolationists to Communists saw hidden meanings in the song. It was attacked and defended in pulpits and editorial pages for months, and an especially bitter controversy arose as to whether it should supplant "The Star Spangled Banner" as the national anthem. With Pearl Harbor, the furor was forgotten. Berlin chose not to make any money from that song, turning over the royalties to a trust fund for the benefit of a number of youth organizations, primarily the Girl and Boy Scouts of America.

Two of his songs are focused on Christian holidays: "Easter Parade" and "White Christmas."

Berlin also wrote "Sadie Salome," about a Jewish girl who leaves her proverbial happy home to become a dancer. Her sweetheart begs her:

Don't do that dance, I tell you Sadie
That's not a bus'ness for a lady!
Most ev'ry body knows
That I'm your loving Mose
Oy, oy, oy, oy—
Where is your clothes?

Other ethnic specialties, sung by Eddie Cantor as part of his repertoire, included "Yiddishe Eyes," "Yiddle on Your Fiddle (Play Some Ragtime)," and "Good-Bye, Becky Cohen."

When, on January 4, 1926, Berlin wed Ellin Mackay, a Catholic member of the New York Social Register, the marriage caused a stir in New York society and was recorded in the "Dilatory Domiciles" section of the *Register*. The Berlins sailed on their honeymoon without the blessing of the bride's father.

Mrs. Berlin, however, always had their children celebrate the religious holidays of both faiths. One Yom Kippur she took them to Temple Emanu-El, where they heard a cantor chant. "Your grandfather was a cantor," Mrs. Berlin told the children, and daughter Mary Ellin responded, "Grandpa Mackay was a cantor?"

Berlin was an insomniac, and there is a wealth of insomnia stories about him. A typical one concerns one of his annual prewar trips to Europe. In the middle of the night a man fell overboard and there was a terrific hullabaloo. Lifeboats were lowered, whistles blew, officers shouted orders, women screamed, and everyone rushed on deck. But

Berlin was nowhere to be seen. The next morning he showed up rubbing his eyes. "You know," he moaned, "I couldn't sleep a wink last night. The quiet on these boats drives me crazy."

Victor Borge

Born Borge Rosenbaum in Copenhagen, he began to study violin but switched at age five to piano. He gave his first concért at eight. Victor Borge escaped to the United States, penniless and unable to speak English, in 1940; the chief target of the comedy-with-music for which he'd become famous in Europe had been Nazi leader Hitler.

Borge taught himself English by watching movies. His American career took off after he appeared on Bing Crosby's radio show.

Audiences came to see Borge, ready to giggle. One of his classic skits evolved from something he saw at a concert: a pianist playing Tchaikovsky fell off the bench. One incident at a Borge performance couldn't be repeated. A fly lit on his nose while he was playing. He twitched his nose, jerked his head, all the while continuing to play.

Borge once attended a concert in which the pianist played the opening chords of the Grieg A minor concerto, then slumped forward against the keyboard, dead. "If I did that, everybody would laugh," Borge said.

Borge was knighted by all four Scandinavian countries.

"Uncle Miltie"

Sandra was an ambitious Jewish mother. She entered her five-year-old son Milton in a Charlie Chaplin look-alike contest. He won and was on his way to a career that eventually made him, with the advent of TV, a folk hero. He reigned from 1948 to 1955 as "Mr. Tuesday Night."

Milton Berle's tremendous success—on Tuesday nights, many restaurants and nightclubs shut down—caused him to comment, "It took me thirty-five years in show business to become a star overnight."

He became known as a tyrant to those who worked with him in television and was called "King Lear." When a rival, inspirational show, *The Fulton Sheen Hour*, commanded higher ratings in the mid-1950s, Berle quipped, "Bishop Sheen has better writers than I have."

Oh, God!

After his Peewee Quartet won first prize in an amateur contest at a local Presbyterian church, George Burns was ready to convert. His mother asked, "Why don't you want to be Jewish anymore?"

"I've been a Jew for seven years and never got anything," he replied. "I was a Presbyterian for one day, and I got a watch."

When the watch broke, Burns became a Jew again.

Born Nathan Birnbaum on the Lower East Side, the ninth of twelve children, he claimed "We were so poor we couldn't afford parents." By the time he was in his midteens, he had begun performing in vaudeville as a trick skater and comedian.

Gracie Allen, an Irish teenager, joined his act in 1923, and they were married three years later. Before Gracie, George had always been the comic and his partner the straight man, but George and Gracie reversed this with far more successful results. Gracie took the role of a somewhat lame-brained but lovable wife to George's raspy-voiced straight man. Burns often said that whatever he had become he owed to Gracie.

At age eighty, Burns won his first Oscar for *The Sunshine Boys*. When he was eighty-four, he was offered the role of God in a new movie.

"Why would they pick me to play God?" he wondered. "I realized it made some sense. I was the closest one to his age. Since Moses wasn't around, I suppose I was next in line."

Burns was able to celebrate his hundredth birthday before his death in 1996.

13

NOTES FROM THE INTERIOR: THE CATSKILLS, GALVESTON, AND BEYOND

*   *   *

It was the promise of more space, with all that involved, that lured immigrants away from New York and toward the vast spaces of America's interior. A majority of Russian Jews did head first for New York and most of them stayed there; this was where there were family, *landsmen* and a familiar community. Many of them, of course, did settle in other cities—Chicago, Boston, Philadelphia—and some, adventurous or with family connections, headed further into the hinterland. Some, for health reasons or to escape the city's crowding, eventually tried to establish themselves in rural areas outside New York and other cities. German Jews, with their "Galveston Plan," tried without great success to encourage immigrants to settle in the middle of the country.

Of course, there was nothing unusual in Jews living outside New York. Earlier generations had long ago spread themselves across the entire continent and, in fact, had never been concentrated to the degree the new Russian immigrants were in the "Promised City." But, the earlier German and Sephardic immigrants were, if identifiable as Jews at all, still thoroughly integrated Americans, while the Eastern Europeans were a distinctive presence.

*   *   *

Many Jews who left New York for southern California couldn't say enough about their new "golden medina." One of them came back for a visit after a few years and spoke in Messianic terms about his adopted state. "It's God's country," he said, "the Paradise Moishe Rabbenu spoke of—a regular land of milk and honey!"

"I've been told," said one of his supportive listeners, "that in your city, you have sunshine 365 days a year; is that true?"

"Aah!" grunted the expatriate, "that's a conservative estimate!"

Southern Sabbath

Workers in the South in the early twentieth century generally got their wages on Saturdays, helping make it the busiest shopping day of the week. In addition, local ordinances prevented businesses from operating on Sundays, so the Jewish shopkeeper was forced to work Saturday or go out of business. The Yiddish poet I. J. Schwartz, who settled in the South in 1918, wrote:

> The joke was:
> That one worked on the Sabbath
> Even harder than on the weekday,
> Because on Saturday people got their wages;
> They fitted shoes and pants on Negroes,
> And talked their hearts out—
> But as soon as the stars appeared,
> The merchant immediately stopped his business,
> Withdrew quickly behind the partition
> And said the *Havdalah* out loud.

The Outcast of
the Grand Union Hotel

Judge Henry Hilton focused attention on anti-Semitism when he excluded prominent banker Joseph Seligman from his Grand Union Hotel in upstate New York. Hilton said that he admired "Hebrews" but disliked "Jews". The following ditty, taking off from this comment, is attributed to writer Bret Harte, who had one Jewish grandfather, Bernard Harte.

> You may give to John Morrissey supper and wine
> And Madame N. N. to your care I resign

You will see that those Jenkins from Missouri Flat
are properly cared for, but recollect that
Never a Jew
Who's not a 'ebrew
Shall take up his lodgings
Here at the Grand U.
You'll allow Miss McFlimsey her diamond to wear
You'll permit the Van Dams at the waiter to swear
You'll allow Miss Decollete to flirt on the stair,
But, as to an Israelite, pray have a care
For between me and you
Though the doctrine is new
There's a business distinction
Twixt 'Ebrew and Jew.

Milwaukee, you are a fine little town,
Your girls are so blond and your beer so brown,
There the Turners build a splendid house
And no Hilton throws a Seligman out.

—Doggerel circulating in Chicago, ca. 1878

Sol Levitan arrived in Baltimore from Lithuania in 1881, peddled his way through Pennsylvania and Ohio, and later settled in Wisconsin. He met with great success; by 1907, he'd founded the Commercial National Bank of Madison. At the same time, he'd become a close associate of Progressive Party leader Robert LaFollette. Levitan later became state treasurer of Wisconsin. He kept a homey sign on his office door in the capitol: "Uncle Sol, Your State Treasurer, Welcomes You." One day the building superintendent took down the sign, charging "it made the capitol look like a Jewish fire sale."

The Filth

Jews who bought property in farming areas, like upstate New York's Catskill Mountains, often found catering to boarders a more congenial and profitable activity than agriculture. Taking care of demanding Lower East Side boarders, however, was no bed of roses. Often separated by generations form the practice of agriculture, they frequently knew little of its reality. One older archetypal Hester Street resident was horrified when she learned manure was actually put into the ground right next to vegetables intended for eating. "Fe!" she shouted in disgust.

A True Story

A legendary Catskills farmer named Goldstein once bred a Guernsey cow with a Holstein bull and called the offspring a Goldstein. The calf, though, never went "moo-moo."
Instead, she went, "Nu?—Nu?"

The Borscht Belt

Most Jews who, for one reason or another, left the crowded, unhealthy city to try their hands at farming found agriculture too hard a row to hoe. Some had more success making a living renting out rooms to other Jews seeking to escape the city's summer heat, particularly in such areas as New York's Long Island and Catskill Mountains. In the latter region particularly, a number built hugely successful resorts, and the Catskills gained fame as the "Borscht Belt."

The most famed of the Jewish Catskill resorts was probably Grossinger's, in Sullivan County 100 miles northwest of New York City. When Selig Grossinger moved upstate after a nervous breakdown in the city and bought it in 1914, what would become one of the world's best-known resorts started with what the *New York Times* described as "a rundown seven-room house with an old barn and chicken coop on 100 acres of rock-strewn land that would intimidate any farmer."

After fifty-eight years of building under the guidance of Selig's daughter Jennie Grossinger (until her death in 1972), the 600-room resort entertained up to 150,000 guests a year and boasted its own landing strip, post office where mail was stamped "Grossinger's, N.Y.", and rooms with two adjoining bathrooms.

With a reputation as a luxury hotel, Grossinger's was known also for retaining elements of traditional Jewish quality and a personal family touch. The resort offered strictly kosher cuisine and prohibited smoking in public areas on the Sabbath. It offered free honeymoons for couples who'd met there and training grounds for boxers, and was indirectly responsible for large contributions to charitable or public purposes. A million dollars worth of U.S. bonds were bought at the hotel during World War II, for example, leading to an Army plane's being named "Grossinger."

Grossinger's hosted many celebrities, and Jennie Grossinger, the hotel's mother figure as well as supreme manager, was known for her ease with all. This anecdote has come down to illustrate the flow of celebrities through what was once a humble Catskills boardinghouse:

Paul Grossinger, Jennie's son and, at the time, general manager of the hotel, reportedly called her and said, "Rocky just phoned. He's landing at the airport in an hour. He wanted to know if he could stop in and see you. Remember how he liked the egg rolls last time he was here?"

"Egg rolls?" said Jennie skeptically. "Rocky's been to my house a dozen times; he's never asked for egg rolls. What do you mean, he's landing at the airport in an hour? Where's he been? I saw him in the dining room last night, talking to Ingemar."

"Not Rocky Marciano," corrected Paul, "Governor Rockefeller!"

Envy at Grossinger's

Somebody would tell chief Grossinger bellboy Benny Rheingold, "Benny, gimme a sentence with the word envy in it."

He would respond, with monotonous regularity: "I vent to a vedding last night envy had fish, envy had kreplach, envy had chicken, envy had strudel!"

A Simple Question

It was a very different thing to be encased in the largely Jewish world of New York or several other large cities than to be out in the heart of America, a small and mysterious minority.

Reminders of medieval European prejudices did not come every day, but as late as 1928, in the upstate New York town of Massena, when a four-year-old girl was reported missing shortly before Yom Kippur, the town's rabbi was brought to police headquarters for questioning "as to whether your people in the old country offer human sacrifices."

The next day the girl, who had fallen asleep in the woods, was found. The rabbi, Berel Brennglass, and his Congregation Adath Israel, were understandably outraged despite extensive apologies from the town's mayor and state trooper. A New York rabbi, after hearing of the incident, suggested Jews issue standing invitations to Gentile friends to visit their synagogues and homes on ritual occasions.

A Rabbi's Market

It was so hard to get rabbis to come serve small Jewish communities in the interior that congregations would often hold on to the one they had whatever the cost. One true story from a town in the Canadian North Woods around the turn of the century told of a young man who responded to the town's ad for a rabbi in a Toronto paper and was hired. Not long into his tenure, word got around that the new rabbi was bootlegging to supplement his income.

Abe Weisman, a congregational leader, went to see the rabbi, who promised he would give up moonlighting on moonshine. Then another congregant advised Weisman that their *rav* had set up a girl in a rented room after she had recently been run out of town by police. Weisman went again to see the rabbi, who got rid of the girl.

Congregants preferred this solution to discharging the rabbi because (1) where would they get another rabbi in the North Woods? and (2) if they fired him, there might be talk all over the province about how the Jewish rabbi is a bootlegger and a pimp.

But sadly, this solution didn't last. A prominent rabbi from Toronto came to the town for some occasion and, after meeting with the local spiritual leader, informed Weisman he was a fake. The "rabbi" soon left for Texas, where he became a cowboy.

Galveston, Oh Galveston

Considerable thought was given to what port of entry would be best for those immigrants to be diverted into the American interior under a plan financed largely by German-Jewish financer and philanthropist Jacob Schiff. This plan, the theory went, would take some of the pressure for absorbing millions of impoverished Russian-Jewish immigrants off New York City and help Americanize the newcomers more rapidly by distributing them more evenly throughout the country.

The Germans, after all, had spread themselves across America, carving out niches in the West, the South, the Great Lakes. The Russians, German thinking went, seemed perversely insistent on preserving their wretched medieval way of life and, to that end, continued flocking overwhelmingly into the same horribly crowded slums of New York and a few other nearby cities.

The Galveston Plan began operating in 1907, aiming to funnel new Jewish immigrants into the interior. Galveston's Mayor Landes visited the Jewish Immigrants Information Bureau the summer afternoon the first group of immigrants arrived and greeted the new arrivals. Rabbi Henry Cohen brought the group together and, in Yiddish, praised the democratic country where they had landed. He then introduced Landes and translated the mayor's remarks into Yiddish for the newcomers.

"You have come to a great country," Landes said. "With industry and economy all of you will meet with success. Obey the laws and try to make good citizens." The mayor then shook hands with each immigrant. One of the group, who had been a schoolteacher in southern Russia, responded for the group in halting English, assisted by Rabbi Cohen:

We are overwhelmed that the ruler of the city should greet us. We have never been spoken to by the officials of our country except in terms of harshness, and although we have heard of the great land of freedom, it is very hard to realize that we are permitted to grasp the hand of the great man. We will do all we can to make good citizens.

※

A number of Galveston immigrants quickly got "lost" in Middle America, troubles described at length and in often sensational language in letters that sometimes made it to the offices of Yiddish newspapers in New York. The following is a translation of an excerpt from one immigrant's adventures in the new land, from a letter to his parents:

. . . I was sent away from Memphis to a country place, Wedley, and there to a village, where we were told we should have to dig earth and raise a terrace for a railway. There we saw three of our people working very hard knee deep in water and we heard from them that they were earning nothing but their food. To our observation that this was hardly worth-while, they replied: "We are sold into slavery. We have signed a contract presented to us, and we must not run away after such an agreement." To our question, how they could be such fools, they replied: "We have signed it under threats of being shot down." To our further question as to where they were boarded, they replied, pointing to a man: "With that Christian." On hearing this, I and my two companions, who came from Warsaw, wanted to leave immediately, but we were threatened with being shot down, to which we intimated by mute signs: "Fire away, then!!" . . . After having wandered about for seven hours, we discovered a house at a distance. We went to it, and found there a couple of blacks, husband and wife, who gave us bread which we ate with onions. Then he put his horse to his cart and took us to the town of Wedley, where we found a Jew, who gave us a dollar and a half each, and sent us off to Memphis. Now we are thanking and praising our dear God for having saved us from evil hands.

※

One of the few things the Galveston Plan had going for it was Galveston's Rabbi Henry Cohen, who acted as host to the new arrivals, smoothing their transition to the New World. Cohen saw that each boatload of immigrants was met, that they were taught some English and directed to communities where their skills could be used. Cohen was known for his dedication to the immigrants, and his generosity didn't stop with Jews alone.

Once a man named Lemchuk, a Ukrainian immigrant who had settled in Galveston, was ordered deported for illegal entry. Rabbi Cohen felt that if this man were sent back, he'd face a firing squad. He rushed to Washington and told Galveston's congressman he needed an audience with President Taft promptly, that it was a matter of life and death.

Though Taft agreed to see the rabbi, he told him the case was under the Department of Labor's jurisdiction and that the decision had been made. "But allow me to say," the President added, "that I certainly admire the way you Jews help each other—traveling all the way up here from Galveston when a member of your faith is in trouble!"

"Mr. President," the rabbi noted, "this man is not a Jew; he's a Greek Catholic."

Taft was quite taken aback, his usually placid, mustachioed face flushed with surprise. "You traveled all the way up here at your own expense to help out a Greek Catholic?"

The rabbi reiterated that the man would be deported on the next ship, which would carry him to the firing squad, unless something were done. "He's a human being," he told Taft. "A human life is at stake; that's the way I see it."

Taft was so impressed he immediately dictated a telegram to the chief immigration inspector at Galveston, ordering him to hold Lemchuk and release him to the rabbi's custody on Cohen's return.

Another Jewish Holiday

A traveling Midwestern salesman had his hands full trying to collect overdue payments from Jewish merchants. He visited one hard-pressed Cincinnati Jewish storekeeper who improvised that he could not pay just this day for shipments received weeks before because it was a special Jewish holiday on which Jews were forbidden to pay debts. Not having heard of such a holiday, the salesman asked its name and was told, "*Erev Mechulah* (the Eve of Bankruptcy)." The salesman sighed and said he would be back another time.

The next day the salesman approached another overdue account, also Jewish, in Columbus, Ohio, and this merchant also claimed he could not pay because of a Jewish holiday. "Don't you try telling me this is *Erev Mechulah*," warned the frustrated salesman. The wholesaler, quick on the trigger, said yes, as a matter of fact, that's just what it was, *Erev Mechulah,* on which Jews could not repay debts.

The salesman smelled a rat and said so. "I don't believe you; yesterday I was told *that* was *Erev Mechulah.* Today you're telling me *today* is *Erev Mechulah.*" The merchant wanted to know who'd told him the day before was the holiday. "Dorfman in Cincinnati."

"Oh, Dorfman," the Columbus merchant replied understandingly. "You see—those Cincinnati Reform Jews only observe our holidays for one day; but here in Columbus, we're more traditional—we keep them for two days!"

✶

Rothstein, no longer a peddler but now a lingerie salesman based in New York, still went on the road a few times a year. Once he found himself in a small Mississippi town. Tired, hungry, and unable to find a restaurant, he went into a general store.

"What can I do for you, sir?" asked the man behind the counter.

"You handle maybe fertilizer?" asked Rothstein.

"Sure do," the man replied amiably.

"Good," said Rothstein. "So wash your hands good and go make me a tuna fish sandwich."

14

THE OLD WORLD
IN THE NEW:
YIDDISH IN AMERICA

Yiddish-Englishisms in American-Jewish Folklore

In learning English, Yiddish-speaking immigrants inevitably Yiddishized the English they were learning at the same time they Englishized the Yiddish they already knew. Some English words fit the Yiddish vernacular so well they were virtually incorporated into Yiddish as spoken in America and assumed a quasi-Yiddish quality. By the same token, some Yiddish words fit the American environment so well they were co-opted by American English and assumed a quasi-English quality.

American-born Jews, children of the immigrants, maintained certain Yiddish words and phrases in their English speech, and these were increasingly incorporated into the larger language. These words and phrases fall into specific groupings: traditional Yiddish or Hebrew expressions like shalom, mazel tov and kosher; food words like bagel, gefilte fish, *matzoh* and *shtikl*; words defining relationships like *bubbeh* and *zeydeh*; and vulgarisms like *yentz, toches* and *shyss*.

Bilingualisms

Perhaps the simplest bilingualisms are those that contain two words, one English and one Yiddish. These include:

1. Food allusions

   a. Matzoh Ball (Spring dance)
   b. Bagel Brigade (KP duty)
   c. Love and Knishes (cookbook title)

2. Religious activities

   a. Mitzvah Corps (Young people organized to perform good deeds)

   b. Shmad Squad (Group organized to resist efforts to convert
      Jews to Christianity—*shmad* mean "convert")
   c. Lake Tvillin (Put on phylacteries. A nonexistent place)

3. Nonsense names

   a. Professor Dreykopf (teacher who makes you dizzy with
      his/her talking)
   b. Doctor Krankheit (Dr. Sickness)

4. Place names

   a. Kosher Canyon (said of Fairfax Avenue in Los Angeles)
   b. Garden of Yidn ("Jews") (any vacation place that many Jews
      frequent)
   c. Borscht Belt (the summer resort area of the Catskill Moun-
      tains of New York—borscht is a beet soup, common fare at
      Jewish meals in earlier times)
   d. Derma Road (derma is stuffed chicken or duck neck or
      entrails, a delicacy served in the Borscht Belt. Thus Derma
      Road is New York State Highway, 17—from New York City
      to the Catskill Mountains)
   e. Kentocus (not Kentucky but any place far from New York
      that therefore deserves to be disparaged)
   f. Yarmulke Heights (Brooklyn)
   g. Bagel Heights (Cleveland, New York, etc.)
   h. Shimini (Shmin) Atzeres, Alabama

5. Punning Christian names

   a. Jesus Kratzmich (Jesus Scratchme)
   b. Shvantza Maria (Shvantz is a bed bug. Santa Maria)

6. Miscellaneous

   a. Erev Christmas (Before Christmas—also erev the weekend,
      etc.)
   b. Words constructed with one part Yiddish and one part
      English

      i. Grepsateria (*Greps* is a burp—thus, a place to eat)
      ii. Mikvatorium (*Mikva* is a ritual bath, -torium is the place—
          as natatorium, auditorium)
      iii. Yinglish (Yi—Yiddish, 'nglish—for English)

New Yiddish in America

The following neologisms are samples of words invented to convey equivalents for English words whose concepts were foreign to Eastern European Jews:

Blishtshmaydl ("flash girl") to mean "glamor girl"

Hehr-unn-trehf ("hear-and-guess") for "quiz show"

Kooshvuch ("kiss-week") for "honeymoon"

Ahruppluhntsh ("down-splash") for "splashdown"

Vikltrepp ("winding steps") for "escalator"

Uhmayn-zugger ("amen-sayer") for "yes-man"

Ess-shtehkeleh ("little eat-stick") for "chopstick"

How Yiddish Traveled

The Slavic vocabulary and linguistic patterns gave Yiddish such ornaments as the *-nik* suffix in such words as *kibbutznik, moshavnik,* and most notably *nudnik,* a bore who carries his passion to extremes.

Words that traveled from Slavic through Yiddish to English and became part of the American vernacular: beatnik, peacenik.

From Slavic to Yiddish to English and back to Yiddish: *allrightnik.*

Bilingual Jests, Puns, Sayings, and Graffiti

"It was a shotgun wedding. It was arranged by a shot g'n (*shadkhn*)."

One woman meets another and says to her, "I hear your Rosie is a prostitutke." The second answers, "It's not true. Whatever a tutke is, my daughter is the best, so she couldn't be a *proste* (common) tutke."

Jewish Indians:

> Chief Potchintoches ("pat on the rear")
>
> Chief Hakachynik ("bang a teakettle")
>
> Shmohawk Indians

Various bilingual riddles exist, such as the following:

> "Why can't they keep Jews in jail?"
> "Because they eat lox (smoked salmon)."

> "What do you call someone who comes from the state of Michigan?"
> "A *mishugener*." ("a crazy person")

> "What is the name of the flagship of the Israeli navy?"
> "The '*Ess, Ess, Mein Kind.*'" (Eat, eat, my child.)

"What is the plural of *yenta*?" *Yenta* in its cruder form is a coarse and vulgar woman. In its less crude form a *yenta* is a know-it-all (e.g., Marcel Proust is a *yenta*). (One old joke among certain Jewish men claimed the plural of *yenta* was Hadassah.)

"What's a bagel?"

"A donut with hardening of the arteries."

"What do you say when General Motors recalls your car?"
"*Oy,* Vega!"

          *   *   *

"What do you call a singer whose voice cracks and crumbles when she sings the high notes?"
"A matzoh soprano."

"Why do they put a railing around the *bimah?*"
"For a safer (Sefer) Torah."

"What do you get when you cross a chicken with a rabbit?"
"Nisht a heen, nisht a hare." ("not there, not here")

Passover-related bilingual puns:

Afikomen round the mountain when I come . . .

Matza Do About Nothing (Pesach play by Shakespeare)

"What is the name of Santa Claus's wife?" "Mary Kratzmich."

Several bilingualisms that served as greetings had a Jewish-Catholic component, but were used by Jews with each other in a jocular way:

"Good morning, boy, how's the goy?" (Non-Jew)

"Good morning, Pius, what's ny-ess?" (What's the news?) or "What's ny-ess, Pius?"

"Gut yontiff, Pontiff." (Happy holiday, Pope)

Manishewitz and Christian Brothers merged. They called their product Manisheygetz wine. (A *sheygetz* is a Gentile male)

Pope John XXIII: Pacem in Terres becomes Pacem in Toches

A pox on your lox;
I'll inveigle
A bagel

Other simple bilingualisms recorded in Los Angeles in the 1950s and
'60s are:
"What's the password?"
"Matzohs."
"O.K., Pass-over."

This joke using Yiddish suggests the ubiquity of the Jews:
An American Jewish tourist in Madrid wants to watch a bullfight but
finds the tickets are sold out. As he stands wistfully near the entrance to
the ring he sees a man go up to the gatekeeper and announce himself:
"Picador"; whereupon the gatekeeper waves him in. *"Adalante, adalante!"*
(Come in, come in!) In a few minutes he sees a second man approach and
present himself, "Matador", and he too is waved in with *"Adalante,
adalante!"* Still a third man appears at the gate and announces, "Torea-
dor"; and the gatekeeper again waves him in with *"Adalante, adalante!"*
The tourist then walks over to the attendant and proclaims: "Isadore."
The response is, *"Kum shoin arein!"* (Come right in!)

She works up a sweat because she works by a Shvitz Bo'd (switch-
board—steam bath). She answers the telephone by a Shvitz Bo'd.

Stay away from him—he smokes *"Yenem's"* (Someone else's).
Or:
"What brand of cigarettes do you smoke?"
"Yenem's."

American-Jewish children played a game called "Tap on the Ice Box"
in Cleveland. In this game the child who was "It" leaned against a lamp
pole. Another child formed a circle with his thumb and forefinger on the
"It" child while a third tapped him through this circle. The "It" child tried
to guess who tapped him. If he did, the other child became "It." If he did
not guess he had to count to a number while the others ran and hid; and
he then attempted to find them. The procedure of forming the circle on
the "It" child's back was called "To make a *shimi lechel* in the old man's
back." *Lechel* means hole in Yiddish—the hole through which the "It"
child was tapped.

Bilingual graffiti containing Yiddish words frequently appeared on
buttons:

"All bosses are schmucks"

"Matzoh balls, not bombs"

"Jesus was raised in a kosher home"

"Marcel Proust is a *yente*"

"Franz Kafka is a *kvetch*"

"*Shvartze* is beautiful"

"Spinoza eats bagels"

During the time of the hipster joke fad, bilingual hipster jokes also appeared:

The hipster looks at the Statue of Liberty and says, "Dig that crazy *Yahrzeit licht.*" (memorial candle)

The hipster sees an ermine stole and says, "Dig that crazy *tallis.*" (prayer shawl)

The hipster sees a donut and says, "Dig that crazy bagel."

The hipster sees a cross and says, "Dig that flying *mezzuzah.*"

The following bilingualisms are Spanish-Yiddish:

Some American Jewish tourists on their way to Mexico quip they're going to "Chapp-a-pulka" ("Acapulco") and to lie on a "Haise Yenta" ("Hacienda"). "Chapp-a-pulka" translates into "catch a chicken leg" (find a woman). "Haise yenta" is "hot yenta."

Aqui est una mesa? (Yiddish punning in Spanish): *"A qui"* (a cow) *est* (eats) *una mesa* ("without a knife")

The following are French-Yiddish, demonstrating the similarity of sounds of "ah voo" in both languages:

Kinsman Road is the main street of what was once one of the major Jewish neighborhoods in Cleveland. An elderly Jewish woman who needed help in Yiddish did not know how to get it. She was downtown and needed to catch the Kinsman streetcar to get home. She approached various people on the street and asked, "You speak French?" All said no. Then she found one man who said, "Yes, I speak French." She asked him, eagerly, *"Ahvoo chapt men* a Kinsman streetcar *ahvoo?"* (Yiddish for "Where does one catch a Kinsman streetcar, oh where?")

Children studying French in high school were asked, "Ahvoo tute dir vay, ahvoo?" ("Where does it hurt you, oh where?")

Bilingual Vulgarisms

Many scatalogical jokes were based on bilingual puns:

An old Jew is sitting on the subway train and muttering to himself: "*Tzores, oy tzores.*" ("Trouble, oh trouble.")

A straphanger standing over him hears him muttering to himself and says, "If you've got a sore ass why don't you stand up and let a lady sit down?"

On the Lower East Side, a teacher asked an immigrant boy to use the word *cactus* in a sentence. The boy replied, "We have a dog at home, and *oy cactus!*" (pronounced "kahktus," it meaning "he does defecate")

A new immigrant asked his friends how to get someplace. They told him to take the subway. He asked them how the subway driver would know that he was there under the ground waiting for a train. They told him that when he got on the subway platform to shout, "Car come on, car come on!"

The next day he went to get a subway train. He shouted out, "Car come on, car come on!" Sure enough, a train came right away but it was an express train and went right past him. He began shouting, "*Kahk 'em ohn, kahk 'em ohn*" ("Defecate on him!")

Bilingual phrases with sexual allusions:

"No chuppy, no shtuppy" (No wedding canopy, no penetration)

"The telephone is ringing. I think it is Ida. Should I *yentzer* (answer)?" (*Yentz* is Yiddish slang for "screw")

My son is a *yentzn* ("ensign") in the Navy.

This is the story of a man who comes home from work one night and sees his wife standing in a sheer robe with nothing on underneath.

"What do you think you're wearing?"

"It's a hostess gown."

"A hostess gown?"

"Yes. *Zest es, vilst es, hostess.*" ("You see it, you want it, you have it.")

*   *   *

This is about a fellow during the 1930s who was standing in a railroad station holding a baby in one arm with his other arm in the air, as if to dry. His fist was clenched. A passerby raised his eyebrows and asked "Fascist?"

"No," he answered. "*Farpisht.*"

A young American couple asks grandfather to baby-sit so they can go out for the evening. As they are about to leave they remind the older man: "Now remember, we use psychology; we talk to him, we reason with him."

When they come back late at night, the kid is sitting in one corner of the living room pouting and the grandfather on the other side pouting. The couple asks the grandfather, "What happened?" The old man glares at them. "*Tsu an alten Zayde zoggt men* fuck you?" ("To an old grandfather one says, 'F___ you?'")

Disappointed

A man went to the Jewish Division of the New York Public Library with this query: "How do you say 'disappointed' in Yiddish?"

Told there was no Yiddish word for 'disappointed,' he was skeptical. He was positive there was such a word. "Just let me use the phone and I'll find the word," he said.

He called his Yiddish-speaking mother. Before he could put the question to her, she asked him whether he could come that evening to a dinner at which she hoped to have all of her married sons. The man said he just couldn't make it that particular evening.

"*Ich bin azoy* 'disappointed,'" his mother said.

The man then knew that the Jewish Division of the library was right.

Another experience was related from the boyhood of a man whose mother spoke in Yiddish with her friends when they didn't want him to understand their conversation. One day, they were apparently speaking in English but made repeated references to "syphilis" and "gonorrhea." The boy was in high school before he found out these weren't Yiddish words.

Zung Ah Yiddishe Vhurt:
Speak a Jewish Word

In the 1950s, many American Jews still either spoke or, at least, understood Yiddish. Salespeople who dealt with Jewish firms had an advantage if they knew some Yiddish expressions. Recognizing this, the Joseph Jacobs Organization, a public relations and marketing consultant to manufacturers and advertising agencies, published a handbook of familiar Yiddish words and expressions for sales representatives calling on Jewish merchants. "Speak a Jewish word," the foreword advised, "and make an extra sale." Some common Yiddish words and expressions include

Transliteration	Meaning
ahlef bayse	The first two letters of the Hebrew and Yiddish alphabet. A common bilingual expression: "As easy as *ahlef bayse*." Example: "Selling that *shlemiel* is as easy as *ahlef bayse*."
ahle-vye	"It should only be that way."
ahz uhch oon vay	Contraction of a phrase meaning "a sigh and a groan." Connotation: "Terrible."
bahleh busteh	A compliment meaning an "excellent home-maker."
behaymeh	An animal; a cow. "*Oy, iz ehr ah behaymeh!*" Connotation: "Oy, is he stupid!" Example: "He's such a *behaymeh* . . . he can't count up to twenty without taking his shoes off."
behryeh	A "five-star" *bahleh busteh*.
billig	Cheap.
borscht	Beet soup. Also used in expressions such as "*billig vee borscht*," meaning "dirt cheap."

Transliteration	*Meaning*
bibbeh	Grandmother. A baby-sitter you don't have to pay.
bubbeh myseh	Literally "grandmother's story." Connotation: A tall tale.
bubbkehs	Small beans. Connotation: Trifling amounts, meaningless things, as in, "She gets paid *bubbkehs* for what she does."
chahsenneh	Wedding.
chahzer	Pig. Used to describe a greedy or gluttonous person.
challah	Bread baked especially for *Shabbes* (Shabbat) and other Jewish holidays.
chochem	Wise man. Sometimes used sarcastically, as in *"Ah groyser chochem!"*
chochmeh	Wisdom. Used to describe a smart strategy or wise saying, and also used sarcastically.
chuhlem	A dream.
chupah	Wedding canopy.
chusson	Groom.
chutzpah	Nerve, gall. (The classic definition of *chutzpah* is that of the guy who kills his parents, then begs for the mercy of the court on the grounds that he's an orphan.)
draykupp	A scatterbrain.
drusheh	A learned sermon or lecture; also used to describe a long-winded explanation.
efsher	Maybe, perhaps, could be.
fahrblunjet	Go astray; blunder; be confused. *"Vehrt fahrblunjet"* ("Get lost!")
fahrgenigen	Pleasure.
flayshig	Any food made from meat or containing a meat ingredient; also the utensils used for cutting and/or eating such food.
frahsk	A hard slap.
fressen	To eat voraciously, as contrasted with *"essen,"* to eat normally.
gahzlin	A real no-goodnik.

Transliteration	*Meaning*
gelt	Money.
gesheft	Business. Common question: "How's *gesheft*?"
geshmahk	Tasty; delicious.
gezunt	Health. Examples: "*Ahbee gezunt*" ("As long as you're healthy"); "*Zai gezunt*" ("Be well")
glick	Happiness; luck.
golem	A robot or automaton; used disparagingly to describe a foolish person.
gonniff	A thief; crook.
goy	Non-Jewish person. From the Hebrew, originally meaning "nation."
goyim	Plural of "*goy*."
goyishe	Non-Jewish; adjective. Example: "Smart he's not. He has a *goyishe kupp* (head)."
grub	Coarse; gross, rude; also, fat. Example: "He's so *grub*, who would buy from him?"
hahndel	To transact business; used to connote "bargain." Example: "If you *hahndel* long enough, you'll get the order."
hechsher	Certification that a food product is kosher: denotes "approval."
hocken ah chynick	Literally, "chopping a teakettle." Connotation: Talking to the point of annoyance. Example: "He *hocked ah chynick* so long he never made the sale!"
kahbtzen	A poor man, a pauper.
kahpuhreh	A sacrifice, an atonement.
kahsheh	Literally, buckwheat, but also used to denote a "mess" someone has gotten into. (A Yiddish word for "question" is pronounced similarly; example: "On Passover, we hear the *feer kahshes* ['four questions']," otherwise known as "*Mah Nishtahnah?*)
kallah	Bride.
kehpehleh	A little head. Used affectionately, such as in "*Ah gezoont ahf dyne kehpehleh.*"
kind	Child.
kinder	Children.

Transliteration	Meaning
kinderlach	Children, used affectionately.
kishkeh	Stuffed derma; also slang for intestines.
kloog	Smart.
kluhg	A curse, as in the expression, *"Ah kluhg ahf Columbus,"* heard among the early immigrants when they found things here were not as they imagined they would be.
k'naydlach	*Matzoh* balls.
k'nubb'l	Garlic. Used for cures and to get a seat on the subway.
k'nocker	A big shot, as in *"Ah gahntzehr k'nocker."* Defined in various ways: "Someone who does crossword puzzles with a fountain pen"; "One who has 'I' problems in his sales pitch."
koontz	A trick, an accomplishment.
kosher	Something that conforms to dietary laws; also, something that's as it should be, on the up-and-up.
kraynk	A sickness.
krechtz	A groan, moan. Example: "Laugh and the world laughs with you . . . *krechtz* and you *krechtz* alone."
kuhved	Honor, respect.
kupp	A head. Used to indicate either intelligence or stupidity, depending on the inflection in the voice.
kvell	To glow with pride.
kvetch	Complainer or "to complain."
kvitch	A scream, shriek.
landsman	One who originally lived in the same town or section of the "Old World."
leck	Lick, taste. Either a noun or a verb. Noun: "A *leck* or a *shmeck*." Literal translation: "A lick or a smell." Connotation: "Just a little bit." Verb: *"Lecking* your fingers." Meaning: "Getting real pleasure."
lehkach	Honey cake. Goodies.
lignehr	A liar.

Transliteration	*Meaning*
mahch a leben	Make a living.
mahch shnell	Hurry up, speed it up, get going.
mayvin	A connoisseur, expert. Sometimes used sarcastically. Example: "Every person is a *mayvin* in his own eyes."
mazel	Luck, as in one of the most common expressions, "*Mazel tov.*"
megillah	Scroll. Also used to describe a long-winded story: "*Ah gahntze megillah.*"
m'hye-yeh	Something particularly delicious.
mensch	A real human being, in the positive sense.
meshuggah	Crazy.
metzee-eh	A bargain. "A *blinndeh metzee-eh,*" a "blind" *metzee-eh,* is used to connote "a steal, a real bargain."
milchig	Any food made from or containing a dairy ingredient.
mishmahsh	A mess, a confusion.
mishpacha	Family.
moyd	A girl. An "*ahlte moyd*" is an "old maid."
myechel	Delicious food or treat.
myeseh	Tale; story. Often used to describe an obvious yarn, as in "*bubbeh myseh,*" or a long, involved story.
nah!	Here it is; take it; so there!
nahchas	Joy, gratification, usually from children.
nahr	Fool.
nahreshkyte	Foolishness.
nebbich	Expression of pity
neshuhmeh	Soul; spirit.
nishkuhsheh	"Not bad."
nosh	Snack; both noun and verb.
nosher	Nibbler; person with a "sweet tooth."
nu	A word of many meanings, depending on the inflection you give it: So? Well? How about it? What's new?

Stella Adler, the actress-director, once taught a class of drama students. A young New York

Transliteration	*Meaning*
	actor joined her class. He appeared shortly before the first session was to begin and greeted her with "What's *nu*?"
	"Not *nu*," Miss Adler corrected him. "The word is pronounced 'nyou' . . . 'knee-you' said quickly. . . . You should pronounce it 'What's nyou.'"
	"Then," asked the actor, "what does *nu* mean?"
	"*Nu?*" said the actress-director, "is the question you ask when you want to find out 'what's new?'"
nudnick	Nuisance, pest, bore. A classic joke: "A *phudnick* is a *nudnick* with a Ph.D."
oy	Another word with many meanings. If you know how to use *oy* and *nu* properly, you already have a pretty good Yiddish vocabulary. "Oy!" can be used alone but is generally used with other words, either Yiddish or English, most often to express dismay but also surprise, pleasure, and other emotions: "*Oy vay!*" = "Oh woe!" or "Oh no!"; "*Oy vay iz mir!*" = "Oh, woe is me!"; "*Oy gevahlt!*" is a more intense expression, used variously to express anguish, horror, intense surprise, disdain. It is almost a prayer.
pahrnusseh	Sustenance, livelihood, prosperity.
pahrveh	Neither *flayshig* (meat) nor *milchig* (dairy); neutral; bland.
pahskoodnyahk	A nasty or revolting person.
pisk	Unflattering term for "mouth"; "big mouth"; also used to describe an able orator.
plotz	Burst, split, explode; applied mainly to people.
potch	A slap; not as hard as a *frahsk*.
puhnim	Face, countenance.
rahchmuhness	Mercy, compassion.
saychel	Common sense; good judgment.
shah	Be silent, be still; when shouted, "Shut up!"
shahdchen	Matchmaker, marriage broker.
shicker	Drunk; either noun or adjective.

Transliteration	*Meaning*
shlehcht	Bad.
shlemiel	Clumsy, foolish and/or unlucky person.
shlepper	A "drag," someone unkempt, untidy; also used to refer to a sponger.
shlimahzel	Luckless person. Maurice Samuel once defined the difference between a *shlemiel* and a *shlimahzel*: "The *shlemiel* spills the soup—on the *shlimahzel*."
shmahltz	Chicken fat, cooking fat; also used to describe buttering someone up, excessive sentimentality, "corn."
shmeck	Smell.
shmendrick	A fool, a simpleton.
shmotteh	A rag, a piece of junk. A Berkeley, California, magazine calls itself *Shmate*.
shnell	Quick. "Mahch shnell!" means "Make it quick!" "Speed it up!"
schnorrer	Moocher, beggar, compulsive bargain hunter.
shtoltz	Proud, assertive, as in *"Zye shtoltz"* ("Be proud!")
shvehr	Father-in-law; also Yiddish for "heavy."
shviger	Mother-in-law.
shye-tel	Wig worn by Orthodox married women.
simcha	Joyous occasion, holiday.
tahm	Taste, flavor. *"Tahm Gahn Ayden,"* literally, "taste of the Garden of Eden," used to describe a "heavenly" taste.
tokkeh	Depending on the inflection of the voice, can mean either "Is that so?" or "That's so!"
tooml	Noise, confusion. A *toomler* in the Catskills is the one who "makes noises" to get activities going.
totteh	Father.
trayf	Not kosher.
tye-er	Costly, expensive; dear to you.
tzimmes	Literally, "a sweet pudding" of carrots or prunes and potatoes; the word is also used to describe the making of a fuss over nothing; as in *"ah gahntzeh tzimmes."*

tzores	Trouble.
uhngebluhzen	Blown up with too much pride; also used to describe someone who's sulking.
yichus	Background, pedigree, credentials.
yingel	A youth, boy.
yuntiff	A Jewish holiday; a corruption of the Hebrew *yom tov* ("good day").
zaydeh	Grandfather.

Getting Mad in Yiddish

Yiddish is a rich, colorful language from its tender caresses to its blood-curdling curses—*tayteh kluhlos*. Many second-generation American Jews can remember their mothers lulling them to sleep with *"Shluhf, myne kind"* lullabies. They can also remember the seemingly infinite variety of ways Yiddish can be used to express anger, from simple name-calling to figurative banishment of the object of ire from planet Earth.

Name-calling ranges from the mild terms for an ineffectual person, such as

shlemiel

shlimahzel

shloomp

shnook

shmegegge

to the crazy or mixed-up individual—

meshuggener

fahrmisht

draykupp

Moyshe kahpoyer

behaymeh

to the ignoramus, ill-mannered, or blowhard—

ahm hah-ahretz

grubber yoong

shtoonk

trahmbehnik

zhluhb

to the pest, gossip, or busybody—

nudnik

tzootzeppenish

yahchna

Yenta Tellerbendeh

to the crook, bastard, or otherwise horrible person—

gonniff

oysvuhrf

gahzln

momzer

pahskoodnyahk (male)

pahzkoostveh (female)

mahchshayfehteh

On the next rung of the ladder of "getting mad" expressions in Yiddish are those that translate into "go to hell," "the hell with him," "get lost," "stop talking like a fool," "leave me alone," and so on:

gai inn drehrd (sometimes this one is extended—"*gai inn drehrd oond bock bagel*"—"Go to hell and bake bagels.")

gai cocken ahfn yahm

hock mir nit kyne chynick

Then things really begin to warm up:

Zuhlst doo hubben ah killeh in boych. ("You should have a rupture in your stomach.")

Ah halehryeh ahf dir. ("You should get the cholera.")

A curse known in Cleveland during the 1920s: *Zuhlst hengen and brennen vi a chandelier.* ("You should hang and burn like a chandelier.")

The following was used by Mel Brooks on a David Susskind television program: *Zuhlst essen a trolley car and cockn transfers.* ("You should eat a trolley car and defecate transfers.")

Zuhlst doo hubben ah meeseh meshooneh ("May you come to an ugly end.")

Ah shvartz yuhr ahf dir ("May you have a black year.")

And the curses get still more colorful.

Philadelphiah Robert Lasson reported that on one of his trips to the Lower East Side in New York he heard a commotion. A man was being thrown out of a store that sold men's socks. The owner, a stocky fellow, was pushing a little, emaciated guy.

"You *momzer!*" the little guy yelled. "You low life. Your store should burn down, and your house with it. Your family should starve. Your wife should scrub floors for Ukrainians. Your daughters should sell themselves on the street. Your sons should marry *shiksas.* And if you make a dollar, it should go to doctors!"

With that, he separated himself from the fat guy and started to walk away. Then he thought of one more curse, the coup de grace. He turned and shouted: "You should come to me for help—and I shouldn't have what to give you!"

Zuhlst vahkzen vee ah tzibeleh mit'n kupp inn drehrd oond dyne feese inn dee looftn ("May you grow like an onion, with your head in the ground and your feet in the air.")

Gutt zuhl ihm bentchen mit drye menschen: aynehr zuhl ihm hahlten, dehr tzvayter zuhl ihm shpahlten, dehr dritter zuhl ihm bahhahlten ("May God bless him with three people: the first should hold him, the second should split him, the third should hide (bury) him.")

Veefeel yuhr ehr iz gegahngen oyf dee feese zuhl ehr gayen oyf dee hent oond dee ibberickeh zuhl ehr zich sharen oyfen hintin. ("As many years as he went on his feet he should go on his hands, and the remaining years he should push himself on his ass.")

Tzen shiffen mit guld zuhl ehr fahrmogen oond dahs gahntze gelt zuhl ehr fahrkrenken! ("He should own ten shiploads of gold—and spend it all on sickness!")

Hubben zuhl ehr ah groys gesheft: vuhs mee veht fahrlahngehn zuhl ehr nit hubben, oond vuhs ehr veht hubben zuhl mee nit fahrlahngehn ("He should have a large business; what people want to buy he should never have, and what he will have to sell people should never want to buy.")

Hubben zuhl ehr ah hoondert hyzer, oond inn yehden hoyz a hoondert tzimmer, oond inn yehden tzimmer ah hoondert betten, oond dehr kahduches zuhl ihm vahrfen foon bet tzoo bet! ("He should have a hundred houses, and in every house a hundred rooms, and in every room a hundred beds, and the delirium should throw him from bed to bed!")

Perhaps the deadliest Yiddish curse, however, is the one that consists of only two words—*Mach shmo*—erasing a person's name and thereby blotting him or her out of memory.

Continuation of the Yiddish tradition could be seen in the "rank-out" playground insult patterns of third-generation New York Jews (and others) possibly cross-fertilized also by black "doing the dozens" traditions, in such examples as:

"I'll rank you so low you'll have to look up to look down."

"I'll rank you so low your mother will be selling (condoms) on 42nd Street."

Yiddish Sayings and Their Humorous Connotations

One of the favorite indoor sports of the generation of Jews whose parents spoke Yiddish was translation of their expressions. Although it was generally possible to convey some of the sense of the originals in English, the pastime was typically suffused with abiding regret that much of their spirit was "lost in translation." These aphorisms and epigrams made up an important part of the folk wisdom immigrants from Eastern Europe brought with them and transmitted to their children in America.

The following chart, the contribution of the late Samuel Asofsky, presents Yiddish sayings in transliteration, their literal (more or less) translation and their connotations. Many were common expressions in the heyday of Yiddish in America during the first half of the twentieth century, and many have survived to some degree into the present.

The Saying	Literal Translation (more or less)	Connotation
Ahz Gutt vill, sheest a bezem.	If God wills it, even a broomstick can shoot.	There is no miracle God can't perform.
Gutt iz mzahveg.	God arranges matches.	Weddings are arranged in heaven.
Gutt zitst oyben oon pohret oontn.	God sits on high and pairs couples below.	Marriages are made in heaven.
Gutt zitst oyben oon pohrket oontn.	God sits on high and rummages below.	God brings confusion among people.
Gutt, fahrzooch mine klahkpoht oon zeh vuhs fahr ah tahm ess hut.	O God, taste my trouble and see what kind of bad taste it has.	You could only grasp my troubles if you were to experience them yourself.

The Saying	Literal Translation (more or less)	Connotation
Der mensch trahcht oon Gutt lahcht.	Man thinks up plans, and God laughs.	Fortune can make a mockery of plans.
Ah shayner gelechter.	A pretty laughter.	Some joke!
Ah Gutt's strahptsheh.	God's lieutenant.	Holier-than-thou person.
Gemaynt ah moloch, iz gekoomen ah goloch.	Thought it was an angel, instead came a priest.	Was expecting a friend, instead came someone aloof.
Ahfeeloo inn gahn ayden vehrt oych nimus.	Even in Paradise it can become wearisome.	People experiencing only comforts can get bored.
Gekoyft ah kaatz inn ah zaak.	Bought a cat in a sack. (Analogous to middle-American 'pig in a poke.')	Got fooled in the purchase.
Geshikt mit der kaatz shalach monos.	Sent the cat to deliver Purim presents.	Sent a sneak to deliver the goods.
Vee koomt dee kaatz eeberen vahser?	How did the cat get across the water?	How did this person get here?
Men shikt nit de kaatz nuch pooter oon dem hoont nuch flaysh.	You don't send the cat to get butter, nor the dog to fetch meat.	Don't send someone for help you know might take advantage.
Nit dee moys iz der gonif nuhr de luch (iz der gonif).	The mouse is not the thief (of your food), but the hole (in the wall) is (the thief).	The thief finds his target not because he is smart, but because the security is weak.
Ah fahrshtupteh kupp.	A plugged-up head.	A dunce.
Fahrshtayt ah krenk.	Understands an illness.	Comprehends little.

The Saying	*Literal Translation (more or less)*	*Connotation*
Ah chochem, ah yid.	A wise one, a Jew.	A clever person.
Ah chochem foon der Mah Nishtanah.	A wise one from the "Four Questions."	Not such a smart person.
Nit kine groyser chochem oon nit kine klayner nahr.	Not a great wise person and not a small fool.	Quite a fool.
Ah Yid ah chochem geet zich an aytzeh.	A Jew, a wise one, counsels with himself.	A smart person will find his own solution.
Ess shtayt geshriben.	It is written.	There is written authority for it (e.g., in the Bible, Talmud, etc.)
Ahvoo shtayt ess geshriben?	Where is it written?	Who says?; Where is the authority for it?
Ahz der rebbe zogt . . .	If the rabbi says . . . (then it's so)	Follow the leader (without question).
Mitn rebens ko-och.	With the rabbi's (leader's) power.	Our *rebbe* (leader) can perform miracles.
Der olem iz ah golem.	The world is a golem (i.e., a robot).	The mass is an ass.
Ah tzig hut oych ah bord oon iz furt ah tzig.	A goat also has a beard, but is nevertheless still a goat.	One can have the appearance of wisdom (or other good qualities) without being wise (or whatever).
Koolo Torah oyf ayn foos.	All Torah (i.e., learning, while standing) on one foot.	An immediate account of all knowledge (of a subject).

The Saying	Literal Translation (more or less)	Connotation
Geyen azoy vee ah rohv mit ah rebbetzin.	Walking like a rabbi with his wife.	The partner is always trailing behind.
Oyfn gonnif brent dee hittel.	On the thief('s) [head], his hat is afire.	A dishonest person always worries about getting caught.
Ah hahlber em-es iz ah gahntze leegn.	A half-truth is a total lie.	A statement is either true or false; it can't be both.
Ahfeeloo oyb ess iz nit em-es iz dus oych ah shayneh myseh.	Even if it's not true, it's still a nice story.	Stories have their value independent of their literal accuracy.
Oyf ah myseh fregt men nit kine kahshes.	Of a story, one doesn't raise questions.	Incidents or sequences in fiction don't have to be true to life.
Dee myseh hut shoyn ah bord.	This story has a beard from long ago.	That's an old one.
Ah myseh foon toyzent mit ayn nacht.	It's (like) a story out of "A Thousand and One Nights."	A strange story.
Oyfn himmel a yahrid.	A fair in heaven.	It's a complete invention (said of a story or incident).
Feert oyf ah vahnt mit ah vahnt.	Brings together a wall with a wall.	Tries to match unmatchables.
Ah myseh ohn ahn ek.	A tale without end.	
Est vee ah faygl.	Eats like a bird.	Not a big eater.
Groys vee ah gehnetz.	As big as a yawn.	A small person.

The Saying	Literal Translation (more or less)	Connotation
Ahz men laygt ahryne inn dee tzaynehr, hut men inn dee bayner.	If you put (food) through the teeth, you will have something on your bones.	You have to eat to stay well.
Der bester mychel iz ah shtickel flaysh.	The best food is a piece of meat.	The best food is what one likes.
Ess shlept zich noch der shtickl broyt.	The piece of bread is dragging behind.	Just about getting along.
Ven est der ohremon hoon? Uhder ven ehr iz krahnk, uhder ven de hoon iz krahnk.	When does a poor person eat chicken? Either when he is sick, or when the chicken is sick.	If one needs something desperately, he can get it, even if he can't afford it.
Ah gooter yid voynt vyter.	A good (i.e., charitable) Jew lives further (down the street).	We don't give any charity here.
Ven frayt zich der ohremon? Ven ehr fahrleert oon gefint.	When is the poor man happy? When he loses something and then finds it.	Recovery of a loss brings new happiness.
Frayt zich ahzoy vee ahn ohremon mit ah ny-ehr tahrbeh.	Is as happy as a poor man (i.e., a beggar) with a new (found) sack.	Acquiring a new article brings joy.
Nayt zich ah bytel.	Sews oneself a purse.	Expects a great find.
Lachn iz gezunt.	Laughing is healthy.	Good cheer maintains good health.
Billig vee borsht.	As cheap as beet soup.	Dirt cheap.

The Saying	Literal Translation (more or less)	Connotation
Vee bye ah yohven ah tzookehr lehkech	(It's as much worth) as a ginger bread for a Russian soldier.	Far from satisfying.
Ahzoy vee ah hoont inn dee nyne tehg.	Like a dog in the nine days (before Tisha B'Av, the period of fasting).	Very hungry.
Kookt oys ahzoy vee ah shmid fahr tug.	Has the appearance of a blacksmith at dawn.	Looks pale.
Eez ahzoy vee ah shaygetz uhn ah fyful.	Is like a Gentile (shepherd) boy without his whistle (horn).	Handicapped without his tools.
Ahz ess zynen neetuh kine maydlech tahntst men mit shiksas.	If there are no Jewish girls (around), then one dances with Gentile girls.	People make do.
Ahz der rohv gayt ahroys foon shool meg zich itlicher zetsen oyf zyne shtool.	When the rabbi leaves the synagogue, anyone can sit in his chair.	Occupying a distinguished individual's place doesn't lend real distinction.
Alleh Yidn vohlten gehvohlt zyne hazzanim, nuhr dus rove zynen zay hayzerig.	All Jews would like to be cantors, but mostly they are hoarse.	Desire alone doesn't bring attainment.
Gahdloos ligt oyfn mist vehr es vill krigt es fahr oomzist.	Arrogance lies (is to be found) in the dung-heap; whoever wants can get it free.	Arrogance is no accomplishment.
Drayt ah kupp.	Turns a head.	Tries to confuse.

The Saying	*Literal Translation (more or less)*	*Connotation*
Fahrdrayen dee kupp.	Turns the head around.	Completely confuses.
Saychel is ahn aydehleh zahch.	Wisdom is a delicate matter.	Wisdom is not something everyone has.
Inn dehr velt ahryne.	Right into the world.	A wild guess.
Gehtruhfen ahzoy vee ah blindeh fehrd.	Hit it (the goal) like a blind horse.	Missed the mark; didn't give the answer right.
Gehmacht foon dem ah tzimmes.	Created a vegetable stew out of it.	Made a big deal of it.
Achtzen vuchen fahr tuhg.	Eighteen weeks at dawn.	Early in the morning.
Ah frahsk fahr tuhg.	A slap at dawn.	Early in the morning.
Ven Gutt ahlayn shluft noch.	When God Himself is still asleep.	Early in the morning.
Shvitst vee ah beever.	Sweats like a beaver.	Works very hard.
Ah Yid oon ah vuhlf gayen nit ahroom laydig.	A Jew and a wolf don't go around idle.	A Jew always finds a way to keep busy.
Der bubbeh's yerusha.	Grandma's inheritance.	Very little.
Ry-ech vee Kayrach.	Rich as Korach.	A very wealthy man.
Ah Pinsker gehvier.	A rich man from Pinsk.	Seems like a rich man.
Uhngehshtupt mit guhld.	Stuffed full of gold.	Filthy rich.
Ahless inn ayneem iz nitoh bye kaynem.	No one can possess everything.	No one is perfect.

The Saying	Literal Translation (more or less)	Connotation
Nitoh vuhs tzoo dygen.	Nothing to worry about.	Forget it.
Gehkayleht dee kapuhteh.	Slew the gabardine coat.	Not such a great insult.
Ahruhpgechapt dee hittel.	Grabbed the hat (from the head).	Insulted.
Fahrfuhrn inn der bord.	Arrived in the beard.	Landed a sock in the jaw.
Ah poteh inn Goot Shabbos.	A slap in (while greeting) "Good Sabbath."	An unexpected insult.
Gehmahcht ah gehvahld.	Raised an alarm.	
Ahz dee bubbeh vuhlt gehaht ah bord vuhlt zee gevehn ah zaydeh.	If the grandmother had a beard she would be a grandpa.	Some things can't be changed.
Ahz dee bubbeh vuhlt gehaht ah bord vuhlt zee gemehgt dahvinen byme ohmed.	If the grandmother had a beard she would be eligible to lead the prayers.	Some things can't be changed.
Glaht inn der vehlt ahryne.	Smooth into the world.	A wild guess.
Ahz men fregt ah shyleh iz trayf.	When one asks a question (i.e., if something is kosher or not), then it is not kosher.	Something questionable is better dropped.
Frehg mir beherem.	Ask me something wild.	I don't have the slightest notion.

The Saying	*Literal Translation (more or less)*	*Connotation*
S'eez ah fahryureeger shnay.	Like last year's snow (fall).	A dim memory.
S'eez ah nechteeger tug.	It's yesterday's day. (Similar to current American, 'it's history.')	It's gone.
Ah klahp fahrgayt, uhber ah vort bahshtayt.	(The effect of) a blow passes, but (the effect of) a word (remark) endures.	Verbal hurt lasts longer than physical pain.
Vuhs iz oyfn loong iz oyfn tzoong.	What's on the lung is on the tongue.	Can't keep a secret; speaks one's mind without restraint.
Gezogt der tuchter, uhber gemaynt dee shnoor.	Said to (i.e., upbraided) the daughter, but meant for the daughter-in-law.	An apparent chiding of someone, really intended for the overhearing bystander.
Rehd tzoo der vahnt.	Talk to the wall.	Talking to a stubborn person.
Drayt zich ahroom ahzoy vee ah hoon mit ahn aye.	Turns around like a chicken with an egg (ready to lay).	Distraught.
Truhgt zich dehrmit ahroom ahzoy vee Avraham mit der meelah.	Carries it around like Abraham with the foreskin.	Can't make up one's mind what to do with something.
Ahleh yevuhnim (oon ahleh rahbuhnim) hubn ayn puhnim.	All Russian soldiers (and all rabbis) have one face.	Those who are different from one look similar to each other.
Ah yeengl oon ah maydl zynen ah glycher shidduch.	A boy and a girl are the correct couple for marriage.	A good match.

The Saying	Literal Translation (more or less)	Connotation
Ah kosherer tuhp mit ah kosherer lehfl.	A kosher pot with a kosher spoon (i.e., ladle).	A prude.
Een tzvayen iz shtarker.	Double is stronger.	In union is strength.
Fahrfahlen dee koo mit dehr shtrickel.	Lost (i.e., disappeared) is the cow with its tether.	The whole thing has vanished.
Ah gahst in shtetl.	A guest (i.e., an arrival) in the town.	Look who's here!
Foon dyne moyl inn Gutt's ayveren.	From your mouth to God's ears.	Hope it happens. God should grant your wish.
Dem fehrd's bytsh's shtehkehleh.	The horse's whip's stick.	A distant relative.
Dem fehrd's foos pohdkuhvehs ahn aynikl.	The horse's foot's horseshoe's grandchild.	A very distant relative.
Zuhl Gutt shomayr oomahtzel zyne.	God should guard and save.	God should help.
Sholom Aleichem, ah yid.	Peace be with you, (fellow) Jew.	How are you?
Vohs macht ah yid?	How does a Jew fare?	How are you?
Oyf vytehr nit ehrger; besser hut kyne shee-oor nit.	From here on, it shouldn't be worse; better (i.e., improvement) has no limit.	Things could be better. (There is always room for improvement.)
Ahn ahm hah-ahretz.	A peasant.	An ignoramus.
Ah groyser ahm hah-ahretz.	A big peasant.	A big ignoramus.

The Saying	Literal Translation (more or less)	Connotation
Ah gruhber yoong.	A fat youth (i.e., guy).	An uncouth character.
Zitzt vee ah puhretz.	Sits like a Polish landowner (i.e., like a lord).	Sits very comfortably.
Shtrashet dee genz.	Threatening the geese.	Making vain threats.
Trahcht foon vahnen ah gahnz pisht.	Thinking about from what part of its body does a goose urinate.	Absorbed in thought; a philosopher (said sarcastically).
Gai shrye "chai v' kye-yum!"	Go shout "The living and eternal One!"	Don't expect help from Heaven.
Gai zye ah nuhvee.	Go be a prophet.	How could anyone predict that?
Veht vehren ah rohv mit a yohr shpehter.	Will become ordained a rabbi a year later.	What's the rush for? There's plenty of time.
Ich mit'n rebben ken; dehr rebbe uhn mir ken oych; ubber ich uhn dem rebben ken nit.	When I'm with my teacher I know (i.e., the lesson); my teacher without me also knows the lesson; but when I'm not with my teacher, I don't know it.	I need help.
Ahn ahzoos puhnim.	An impudent person.	An insolent guy.
Ah groyser ahzoos puhnim.	A very impudent person.	A most insolent guy.
Gevoynt zibben yuhr bah dehr shvigger inn shtoob oon hut nit gezehn ahz dee kaats iz uhn ahn ek.	Lived in her mother-in-law's house for seven years and never saw (i.e., didn't realize) that the cat had no tail.	Not observant.

Pocahontas, Yiddish Version

Ah muhl iz gevehn drei Indians, Geronovitz, der tatte, Pocayente, der mutter, oond der tuchter Minnie-Horowitz. Ain tug iz Minnie-Horowitz gekoommen oond gezuhkt tsu Pocayente, "Mame, ich vil hayreten."

Zuckt Pocayente, "Goot, siz shayn tzeit, du bist yetzt ahn ahlte moyd, sexteen yuhr ahlt. Vehr iz dehr bucher?"

Zuckt Minnie-Horowitz, "Oy, Mame, huhb getruhffen mit a bucher! Ahzay heldische, ahzay shayn, alzay shtark!"

"Oond vuhs iz zyne nummen?"

"Ehr haist zich Sittin' Bullvan."

"Oond vuhs fahr ah yiches hut ehr?"

"Oy, ehr hut a groyser yiches, zyne tatte, Meshuggene Fehrd, is dee gahntzer macher foon ahlle dee Shvartz-foos lyteh."

Zuckt Pocayente, "Goot, mir vellen hubben ah groyseh chahsenneh— Oy vay iz mir!"

"Vuhs is dehr mehr?"

"Mir hubben ain tzoreh."

"Vuhs is der tzoreh?"

"Dee tzeepee iz nit groyse genoog tzu halten ahlleh dee gasten foon dehr chahsenneh, ahlleh dee Shvartz-foos oond dee Shmohawks oond dee gahntze mishpachah."

Shryte Pocayente tzu Geronovitz, "Geronovitz, shtait ooff foon dem tuches oond gay kriggen far mir a buffalo."

Zuckt Geronovitz, "Far vuhs vilst du a buffalo?"

"Mit der flaysh fun dee buffalo ken ich machen a goot gedemte buffalo tzimmes, oond mit dehr peltz ken ich machen groyser der tzeepee, oond mir vellen kennen einleiden der gahntze velt tzum chahsenneh."

Arois iz gegahngen Geronovitz. Ain tug hut pahsiert, tzvey tehg, drei tehg, oond nit kyne Geronovitz. A vuch mehr, koomt ahaym Geronovitz mit gurnisht in dee hent.

"Shlemiel! Voo is mein buffalo?" shryte tzu ihm Pocayente.

"Doo und dyne buffalo tzimmes, ich hub eich baider in bud."

"Far vus? Vus iz dehr mehr?"

"Dee ersht tug hub ich gezehn ah buffalo, nisht goot genoog fahr dee tzimmes, nisht groyse genoog fahr dee tzepee. Dee tzvayte tug hub ich gezehn ahn arnderer buffalo, groyse genoog ubber mit a farfeilte peltz, ahzei meeskyte foon ah buffalo hub ich kyne muhl nisht gezehn. A puhr mehr tehg hub ich gefoonen ah buffalo, shayn, shmaltzedek, groyse—a perfect buffalo."

"Un nu? Vu den?"

"Vu den? Ich hub gegahngen tzoo shochten dem buffalo, ich hub gekookt in myne tahsch, und doo vaist vuhs? Nahr vuhs ich bin, ich hub genoomen mit mir dehr milchedicke tomahawk."

Translation

Once there were three Indians, Geronovitz the father, Pocayente the mother, and the daughter, Minnie-Horowitz. One day Minnie-Horowitz came to Pocayente and said, "Momma, I am getting married."

Pocayente said, "Good! It's about time, you're an old maid, sixteen years old. Who is the boy?"

Said Minnie-Horowitz, "Oy, Momma, have I found me a boy! So brave, so handsome, so strong!"

"And what is his name?"

"Sitting Bullvan."

"And what kind of credentials does he have?"

"Oy, he has great credentials. His father, Crazy Horse, is the big wheel of all the Blackfoot people."

Said Pocayente, "Good! We'll have a big wedding—Oy, woe is me!"

"What is the matter?"

"We have one problem."

"What is the problem?"

"The tepee isn't big enough to hold all of the guests at the wedding, all of the Blackfoot people and the Shmohawks and the whole mishpachah."

Pocayente shouted to Geronovitz, "Geronovitz, get off your ass and go get me a buffalo."

Said Geronovitz, "What do you want a buffalo for?"

"With the meat of the buffalo I can make a good buffalo tzimmes, and with its hide I can make the tepee bigger, and we will be able to invite the whole world to the wedding."

Geronovitz went out. One day passed, two days, three days, and no Geronovitz. After another week, Geronovitz came home, with nothing in his hands.

"Shlemiel! Where is my buffalo?" shouted Pocayente.

"Your and your buffalo tzimmes. . . ."

"Why? What is the matter?"

"The first day I saw a buffalo that wasn't good enough for the tzimmes nor big enough for the tepee. The second day I saw another buffalo that was big enough but had a worn-out hide. I've never seen such an ugly buffalo. A few more days passed, and I found a buffalo— beautiful, full of shmaltz, big—a perfect buffalo."

"Well? What next?"

"What next? I went to kill the buffalo kosher. I looked in my pocket. And you know what? Fool that I am, I had taken with me the dairy tomahawk."

All I Got Was Words

The immigrants worked long and hard, typically at tedious work for little money. It lightened their burden to feel they were doing it *"fahr dehr kinder"*—for their children and their children's children. Most couldn't give them much of material things but they did manage to pass on some philosophy, as reflected in the following verse by an anonymous second-generation *mensch*:

When I was young and fancy free
My folks had no fine clothes for me
    All I got—was words:
        Gutt tzu dahnken
        Gutt vet gebben
        Zuhl mehn lehben oon zyne gezunt
When I was wont to travel far
They didn't provide me with a car
    All I got was words:
        Gai gezunt
        Gai pahmehlech
        Hub ah glicklicheh ryzeh
I wanted to increase my knowledge
But they couldn't send me to college
    All I got was words:

Hub saychel
Zye nicht kyne nahr
Torah iz dee besteh sichoreh
The years have flown; the world has turned;
Things I've forgotten; things I've learned
Yet I remember:

Zug dem emehss   ("Tell the truth")
Gib tzeduka   ("Give Tzedaka")
Hub rahchmunuhss   ("Have mercy")
Zye ah mensch   ("Be a mensch")
All I got was words

Traditional Folk Beliefs and Superstitions

Jewish immigrants to America brought with them from Europe superstitions and folk beliefs they transmitted to their children. Some of these persist to some extent to this day in various forms like the avoidance of the "evil eye." Many of these have no explanation or they have been lost. Some superstitions led to customs that became as binding to many as Jewish law. At times, parents would "invent" superstitions to keep their children "in line."

Belief in the magic of the evil eye is common in the folklore of many people. The Jewish conception is different in that the evil eye is never attributed to God as being jealous of His creatures.

Fear of the Evil Eye

The *ayin hara*—"evil eye"—is as much to be feared as the devil himself; it may, in fact, be the devil. The fear is based on the folk belief that certain persons have the power to cause people harm just by looking at them. Even from afar, the "evil eye" can cause trouble. Here are some specific traditional beliefs:

Praise of a child's beauty may invite the evil eye.

Parents should not divulge intimate facts and knowledge about the child, such as height, weight, and the like, lest this information be used to put the child under the influence of the evil eye.

A *royte bendle*—a red ribbon—placed somewhere on or hanging over a newborn baby, or pinned or tied on the crib or carriage, can protect the baby, and also its mother, from the evil eye. Another way is to place a knife under the mother's pillow. In America, some Jewish buyers of new cars put red ribbons on them to protect them from harm at least until the "newness" has worn off.

An adult may avert the evil eye by making a "fig" (thumb gesture) or by wearing red.

"Uptzoo sprechen ahn ayin hara" ("to avoid the evil eye"), parents and grandparents often recited the following whenever their children were complimented:

Pooh! Pooh! Pooh! *Drye alte vyber huhben gezessehn ahf ah shtayn. Dee ehrshteh huht gezuhgt, 'Yah'. Dee tzvayteh huht gezuhgt, 'Nyne.' Dee dritteh huht gezuhgt, 'Foon vahnit huht ess gekoomen, duhrten zuhl ess gayehn.'* Pooh! Pooh! Pooh!" Translation, in between the "Pooh! Pooh! Poohs": "Three old wives sat on a stone. The first said, 'Yes.' The second said, 'No.' The third said, 'Wherever it came from, there should it go.'"

The fear has generated the expression *kine ayin hara* or *kennehora*—"no evil eye."

Domestic Practices

If two glasses are broken during the course of a day, a third one must be shattered, in order to break an evil spell.

During her menstrual period, a woman should not ferment wine or make pickles.

Using a broom to brush the crumbs from a table will cause poverty.

Mending a garment or sewing on a button while the garment is being worn is taboo.

If the person wearing a garment that is being mended doesn't chew on a piece of thread, his brains will be sewed up.

Needles or pins must not be given directly to someone; if you take a needle from someone, there will be a fight.

If someone drops a hairpin, she (or he) must not pick it up.

Anyone putting on a garment inside out will have bad luck all day.

Shoes placed upside down will cause an argument (Sephardic).

Never mend anything that a mouse has chewed up.

Bread, salt, and sugar (or sweets) are the first things to bring in moving to a new house to ensure good luck.

A kitten walking into a house also brings good luck.

Someone giving a wallet or purse as a present should insert some money to ensure good luck.

Someone who gives something sharp should make sure that he or she gets a penny in exchange so the recipient of the gift isn't cursed.

One brings sweets to a house of mourning to offset sadness, and one brings sweets to a new home to ensure a life of happiness.

Cutlery falling to the floor means that someone will visit, a fork indicating a man, and a spoon a woman (Sephardic).

If an extra place is set at the table unintentionally, a hungry guest will arrive.

Itching of the right eye foretells good news, and of the left, bad.

On setting out on a trip, one should be sure to step on the right foot first.

One should not strip the bedding in the guest room while guests are still in one's house.

A bed should not face the door, as this will result in disaster. One explanation has to do with being carried out feet first.

Dreams

A dream of death will add years to one's life.

To dream of fish is good luck, but it is bad luck to dream specifically of trout.

A dream of silver is good luck, and a dream of paper money, bad.

Folk Medical Beliefs

Having one's ears pierced will cause better eyesight.

Bleeding of the nose can be stopped by dropping keys down the person's back.

Leaving eggshells in the sink will cause a headache.

Love, Courtship, Marriage

If girls want a tall husband, they should hold the Havdalah candle up high.

When your eyebrow itches, your sweetheart is talking about you.

If some food drops from your plate, your lover is hungry.

Girls who sweep the floor and sing at the same time will marry a husband who stammers.

Girls who do not pick up everything while they are sweeping will marry a bald man.

Parents who are marrying off their last child should be placed in the center of a circle formed by the wedding guests, who sing and dance around the parents and place garlands on their heads.

The wedding ring must not be engraved in any way, nor should it contain precious stones.

Once you have left your home on your wedding day, do not return or else you will have bad luck.

If either of the parties to marriage is unfaithful, the complaining mate should go to a rabbi, who will fire a brick to red-hot intensity and intone a prayer over it in order to bring the erring mate back with renewed ardor.

Birth, Infancy, Childhood

If a pregnant woman steps over nails, she will lose her baby.

Persons should not buy or in any other way get clothes, furniture, toys, or anything else for a child before birth.

If you throw a rope at a pregnant woman, it will strangle her child.

If a pregnant woman looks at anything frightening, it will scare the child and make him or her a half-wit.

If a pregnant woman sees a nut and doesn't eat it, but scratches herself, the baby will be marked at that spot.

If a person fails to grant a pregnant woman her wish, mice will eat up his or her clothes.

The newborn child should be wrapped in swaddling clothes to keep it from becoming a cripple.

The sex of an unborn child may be determined in this way: The pregnant woman goes out of the room. A fork is placed on one chair, and a spoon on the other. Both chairs are covered. The woman is called back into the room and asked to choose a chair. If she chooses the chair with the fork, she will have a boy; if she chooses the chair with the spoon, she will have a girl.

Care of Children

If you step over a child, it will not grow.

When a child sneezes, if you pull its right ear, you will stunt its growth.

If a baby is allowed to see itself in a mirror, its teething will be impaired.

If a child is slow in learning to walk, draw a line in front of him or her, and that will speed the child up.

If you slap a baby's face, you will stop it from talking at an early age.

It is considered bad luck to name a child after a living person or after a person who has died young.

To avoid using the expression, "Cross my heart and hope to die," Jewish children in New York used to employ the sign of the Star of David in this way: They touched their chest six times with their forefingers, at the points of the Star of David, according to the following diagram:

Sabbath and Jewish Holidays

To avoid debtors, one should push back the tablecloth on the Havdalah table.

Sewing on Saturday nights brings bad luck.

Nuts should not be eaten between Rosh Hashanah and Hoshanah Rabbah (Seventh day of Sukkat).

To look three times in succession at *Kohanim* when they are blessing the congregation will cause blindness.

Lighting a candle in the synagogue before Yom Kippur begins is supposed to bring atonement to the soul.

In some synagogues those who have both parents living leave during Yizkor.

15

OUT IN THE WORLD: CHANGING NAMES, FITTING IN, MOVING OUT

That Explains It

A man called excitedly to another at a street corner on the Lower East Side many years ago. "Goldberg, Goldberg!" he shouted, approaching him and looking him over, still enthusiastic but a bit dubious. "You've changed so much! The last time I saw you, you were short," he said, shaking his head in bewilderment, "now you're tall! The last time I saw you, you had brown hair," gesticulating excitedly, "now you have red hair! You've changed so much, Goldberg, it's incredible; what's happened to you?"

The second man, taken aback, shrugged and stammered, "But—my name isn't Goldberg!"

"So," the first man snorted, now genuinely enraged, "you've changed your name, too!"

Don't Ask

On first appearances, it seemed everything in the new land depended on money, so when Jewish businessmen had done what they could and succeeded on America's terms, giving up much of their past in the process, they often felt betrayed when they found social acceptance still eluded them. They were still easily set apart by their speech, style and manners.

A number of different jokes have been told about the wealthy Jew who enrolls his son in an exclusive New England WASP prep school, so that he, at least, will fit in where his parents could not. "Please, you being sure titch him right," the father tells the headmaster anxiously. "I'm wanting you should make my son speak with poifect English."

"My good man," the headmaster reassures him, "after a year's association with our boys and our highly trained teachers, your young David will be a master of the language. Of that I am sure. You need not have the slightest worry. When you return at semester's end, you will be unable to distinguish your son's pronunciation from my own!"

Satisfied, the father returns home. At the end of the year, when he comes to pick up the boy, he first visits the headmaster. "Und how is my boy doink?" he wants to know.

"Dun't esk!" says the headmaster.

Name Changes

There are a seemingly infinite number of stories about Jewish names and the changes they have gone through. When Jews from Eastern Europe arrived in America and had to give their names to the immigration authorities, quite often the latter couldn't understand them and gave the new Americans names that approximated the sounds they heard. Here are a few stories of how some Jewish immigrants got their new American names:

The man comes before the judge to have his name changed. The judge asks him what his name is now.

"Smith."

"Your name is Smith. And what do you want to change it to?"

"Wilson."

The judge looks confused. "You want to change your name from Smith to Wilson? What reason do you have?"

"Well," said the man, "listen—every time I go somewhere and say my name is Smith, they always ask me, what was it before you changed it? And then I have to say it was Rabinovitch! Now, I'll say my name is Wilson, and they'll ask me what was it before you had it changed—and I'll be able to say Smith!"

Two men ran into each other in midtown Manhattan, "Shmuel Davidovich," shouted one, "I haven't seen you in four years!"

"Shah," said the other, shaking the first man's hand, "that's not my name any more. Too old country. Now," he said, "It's C. D. Rivington."

"How'd you think of that?" asked the first man.

"Well, you know I used to *schlep* fruit on Rivington Street."

"But where did the C. D. come from?"

"Corner Delancey!"

Namesakes

Four traveling salesmen were riding in the same train compartment.

"Let's introduce ourselves," said one man. "My name's Cole."

"I'm Carleton," said the second man.

"Kent," said the third.

"Also Cohen," said the fourth.

A *hasidic* rabbi, dressed in traditional fur hat, long black robe, long beard and sideburns, traveled to an Alabama city to raise funds for a *yeshiva*. Small children notice him at the train station, follow him curiously through the street, and begin teasing him. The rabbi turns to the kids and shouts:

"Whatsa matter, you kids never seen a Yenkee before?"

Some Orthodox Jewish families groomed their sons from childhood to be rabbis. One young boy was sent to study Talmud with a learned rabbi in a larger city. When he was older, he was sent to a *yeshiva*. He grew a beard and long sideburns, dressed in a long black frock and black hat. He came home for Passover.

When his father opened the door and looked at his son, he shouted, "Rivke, come quick! Look who's here: Joe Collitch!"

A New England Jewish family named Kabakoff petitioned to have its name changed to Cabot, which led to a lawsuit by the old Cabot family. The following rhyme commemorated the controversy:

And this is good old Boston
The home of the bean and the cod
Where the Lowells speak only to Cabots
And the Cabots speak Yiddish—by God!

Another version was:

Boston, land of the bean and the cod,
Where the Lowells speak only to Cabots,
And the Cabots speak only Yiddish.

Bilingual Name Games

What's your name, little boy?
My name is Lemmy (an Anglicized form of the Yiddish name, Leml).
Lemmy, what?
Lemmy kiss you.

"Do you know the Kite sisters?"
"No, who are they?"
"Kran Kite (sickness) and Mie-es Kite (uglyness)."

"Do you know the Fishl brothers?"
"No, who are they?"
"Arty Fishl and Benny Fishl."

"Do you know Mrs. McKenzie?"
"Mrs. McKensie who?"
"McKensie Tappen." (*Mee ken* [One can] *zee tappen* [feel her])

"Kim Aher (come here)."
"Sarah Toga (what a [disagreeable] day)."

How the Jews Became Fergusons

A guy meets up with his buddy from Vilna in New York for the first time
and finds he is no longer Mordecai Schulowitski but now Ichabod
Ferguson. How did he get such a name? "When they asked me my name

on the boat at Ellis Island, I was so excited I couldn't even talk. So I said, *'Ich hob fergessen.'* ('I have forgotten.')."

*   *   *

A Jewish immigrant entered America at Ellis Island and was processed according to standard procedures. These were very confusing to him; he was overwhelmed by the noise and bustle. When one of the officials asked him, "What is your name?" he replied, "*Shayn fergessen.*" (I've already forgotten.) The official then recorded his name as "Shane Ferguson."

Yankele

A jobber went into a store owned by John Kelly. He could tell the man was no born Kelly. He asked him, "How come?"

"Well, you see," the store owner answered, "when I came to America, they asked me my name. So I told them the truth: 'Yankele.' So they wrote down 'John Kelly.' What did I know? So now I'm John Kelly."

No Christian Name

When a pushcart peddler was called into court in New York and asked his name, he answered, "Yainkuf Rabinowski." The judge, apparently thinking this was the man's family name, asked him what his Christian name was. This infuriated Yainkuf, who had nothing 'Christian' about him. "Front name" soon replaced "Christian name" in that particular courthouse.

Nice American-Jewish Names

Immigration officials had their favorites among Jewish names—straightforward, pronounceable ones like Shapiro and Liebman. Confronted by an immigrant whose name they could not handle, they would often suggest he or she take a "nice American-Jewish name" such as one of these. And many times the newcomer would happily oblige.

A Jew Named Kennedy

One immigrant thought he was being asked where he came from. When he said "Canada" the official heard "Kenneda" and put the man's name down as "Kennedy."

Max Backward?

Two Waxman brothers, one Kiva, the other Malech, came to America. Malech, the first to come, was given the name Max. When Kiva came a few years later, he was somehow also given the name Max by immigration. The younger Max, in deference to his older brother, then changed his own name to Sam.

No Good

Despite the long-intensifying alarm in the organized Jewish community over the rising rate of intermarriage (estimated at close to 50 percent by the 1990s), another kind of alarm has been occasioned by the fact that often, a non-Jewish spouse who converts to Judaism became more serious about religious observance than Jewish partners, who had neglected the traditions.

This has led to the story of the Jewish man who complains to his parents that his new wife, a convert, is bothering him by dragging him to the synagogue every *Shabbes*, keeping kosher, and demanding they observe the holidays.

"Don't blame us," shouts his mother. "We told you no good would come from marrying a *shiksa!*"

Joe Jew

And this supposedly true story was the subject of a feature article by Abraham Cahan, originally published in New York's *Commercial Advertiser.*

A Jewish girl on the Lower East Side married an Italian barber on the condition that he convert to Judaism. She insisted also that he observe at least certain practices in an Orthodox manner. She watched him like the proverbial hawk each day to see that he put on his *t'fillin* and said the morning prayers.

Years later, the barber suddenly realizes that their teenaged son, Joe, never performs this ritual and nothing is ever said. "How come?" he asks his wife.

"Because," she says, "Joe is a Jew."

A Yew, Not a Yentile

Mormons used to regard themselves as closer to Jews and especially to the ancient Israelites than to non-Mormon Christians. When Democrat (and Jew) Simon Bamberger ran for governor of heavily Mormon Utah in 1916, he came to a remote town for a campaign address. A delegation met him at the railroad station. Its spokesman, a brawny Norwegian and convert to Mormonism, confronted Bamberger.

"If you tink we let any damn Yentile speak in our meeting house, you're mistaken," he said. "You might yust as vell go right back vere you come from."

Bamberger replied, "As a Jew I have been called many a bad name but this is the first time in my life I have been called a damn Gentile!"

The husky Mormon embraced Bamberger and shouted: "You a Yew, an Israelite. Hear him, man, he's not a Yentile, he's a Yew, an Israelite!"

Bamberger won the election, becoming the fifth governor of the state of Utah and the second Jew elected a governor in the United States.

Conversion Benefit

Louis Sloss, of the San Francisco–based Alaska Commercial Company, was to negotiate at one point in the mid-1800s with a Russian czarist official who had been born a Jew. They were trying to agree on the name of a Russian government representative to be included, for official purposes, in the firm's management of certain Alaskan islands. When he'd come to know the official a while, Sloss asked him why he had converted.

"When I was a Jew, I suffered for my God," replied the bureaucrat. "Now, I have a God who suffered for me."

A Reason

When Henry Morgenthau Sr. was appointed ambassador to Turkey, he confronted Secretary of State William Jennings Bryan, who had offered him the post. After thanking him for the position, he said, "But isn't it a little strange that Jews are only appointed to the Turkish Embassy?"

"There's a reason for that," Bryan responded amiably. "We want a Jew to help us convert the Turks to Christianity."

Religious Preferences

In late nineteenth-century New Orleans, a nun and a married Jewish woman, both teachers at the same fancy private school, became close friends. After some time, they were able to talk about anything together, and each began indulging her curiosity about the other's way of life.

One day the nun asked the Jewish woman whether she had ever eaten ham.

"Yes," she replied, "once when I was in college; I was very curious to know what it would taste like, so I took one bite."

The Jewish woman then asked the nun if she'd ever made love with a man. The nun blushed and replied a bit hesitantly, that, yes, she had once, "long before I took my vows."

"Better than ham, wasn't it?" asked the Jewish woman.

Church Visit

Two poor and elderly Jewish men, seeking a warm place on a cold day, found themselves in a Catholic church. They sat in the last row in the back and looked in wonderment at the ornate fixtures. In front, a hundred white-robed nuns were being inducted into an order.

Noting the unexpected visitors, a priest came over to the men.

"Excuse me, gentlemen," he said, "but what brings you here today?"

"Not to worry," said one of the Jews, "we're from the groom's side."

※

"JESUS SAVES" "But Moses invests"

Hank Greenberg

We shall miss him in the infield
and we shall miss him at the bat
But he's true to his religion
and I honor him for that.

So wrote popular poet Edgar Guest when, during the heated American League pennant race of 1934, it looked like star Detroit Tiger Hank Greenberg would sit out games that fell on the Jewish High Holidays.

The question was heatedly debated throughout the country and nowhere more heatedly than in Detroit. The Tigers hadn't won a pennant in twenty-five years. It was young Hank's second season with the team and his first at first base. The infield had played all season without a single substitution.

One rabbi told Greenberg he must decide for himself. Another found a Talmudic reference to boys playing ball in the streets of Jerusalem. On Rosh Hashanah, Greenburg solved his dilemma by attending holiday services in the morning and playing in the afternoon, hitting two home runs to drive the team to victory. On Yom Kippur, he wouldn't play and the team lost, but the Tigers went on to win the pennant. During the World Series, the rival St. Louis Cardinals derisively called Hank "pants presser Greenberg."

Born in the Bronx on New Year's Day 1911 to Orthodox Romanian-Jewish parents, Greenberg played baseball for James Monroe High School, where he attracted big-league attention. A Yankee scout called at the Greenberg home on a Friday evening and offered Hank's father a contract for the boy, who was still a minor. The elder Greenberg, outraged by what he considered a Sabbath desecration, refused to discuss the matter. Hank would turn down the Yankees and the Senators before signing with the Tigers, who offered to let him attend college first and play pro ball later.

Greenberg used to tell the story of how his father had waited three hours to see manager John McGraw of the then New York Giants to urge him to sign his son. McGraw, apparently hoping to build Giant support among New York's burgeoning Jewish population, had offered $100,000 for a Jewish ballplayer. But after the long wait, McGraw told Greenberg senior that the Giants just weren't interested; his scouts felt Hank wasn't major league material.

Greenberg played in the minors before being called up to the Tigers in 1933. Awkward as a fielder at first, he overcame this weakness by long hours of practice before and after games and by dancing lessons to help make his feet behave.

Greenberg became one of the game's top players. He had a career batting average of .313 and hit 331 home runs. He was twice voted the American League's most valuable player and was paid a salary of $100,000 a season, at that time one of the highest in the sport. In 1956, he became the first Jew named to Baseball's Hall of Fame.

In 1938, he almost beat Babe Ruth's record of sixty home runs in a season. After he hit his fifty-eighth, with five games left in the season, his mother offered to make him sixty-one baseball-shaped gefilte fish portions if he broke the record. But he didn't hit another. In the season's final game, he hit three singles before the game was called due to darkness in the seventh inning. "It's just as well," Greenberg said later. "There was no way I could have eaten all that gefilte fish."

During World War II, Greenberg served four years in the Army Air Force in Asia, taking part in the first land-based bombing of Japan. In later years, he was general manager of the Cleveland Indians and part-owner of the Chicago White Sox.

Mixed Children

Groucho Marx once applied for membership in a California athletic club but was turned down because the club didn't admit Jews. He then followed up with a request that his children, who, he argued, were only half-Jewish, be granted "a special permit to enable them to go into the pool up to their navels."

✺

An Irish-American broadcaster, after launching his own Irish radio show in Philadelphia in the 1930s, managed to charter his own station and was assigned the call letters YJMJ. JMJ was a well-known acronym used by parochial school children to dedicate their service to Jesus, Mary, and Joseph.

When an insistent Jewish civil libertarian repeatedly attacked the broadcaster for what he called religious abuse of the public airways, an irate Irish lawyer told the Jew: "You know what those letters JMJ really stand for? It's Jews and More Jews!"

Ginsburg

Ginsburg became a legendary figure on the naval ship on which Chaplain Ernest M. Lorge served in World War II. He came on board with $10, and through a continuous streak of good luck in gambling and other at-sea business dealings amassed a fortune.

This was when German U-Boats were menacing Allied ships, and the ship was part of a convoy formation that zigzagged across the Atlantic. After fourteen days of tedious voyage, it neared the British Isles, and the chaplain suggested to his congregation that in gratitude for their safety, they might want to make contributions to the United Jewish Appeal. They responded generously. Several of the men asked the chaplain, "Did you get the money from Ginsburg?"

"Ginsburg?" he responded. "I still have to meet the man. Thus far he is only a name and a rumor to me."

The men insisted Ginsburg had made a contribution of $1,000 to the UJA that was to be delivered to Chaplain Lorge. The chaplain asked two of the men to accompany him on a visit to Ginsburg. They found him down in the deepest hole of the ship.

"I just wanted to clear up a misunderstanding," the chaplain told

Ginsburg. "Rumor has it that I received some money from you, and you know that is not the case."

"Didn't you get the thousand dollars?"

"Come, come, Ginsburg, you must know I never received any money from you."

Ginsburg seemed genuinely surprised and called to one of his cohorts: "Tony, didn't you give the money to the chaplain?"

"Of course I did. Ask Father Quinn."

To Ginsburg, "the Chaplain" was Rabbi Lorge. To Tony, it couldn't have meant anyone but Father Quinn.

Lorge assured Ginsburg that there was nothing to worry about because he knew Chaplain Quinn and himself would straighten the matter out amicably and equitably.

"Oh, no," said Ginsburg, "let Tony's Padre keep the money and here is my part to Jewish charity."

With this he pulled out the biggest roll of U.S. currency Chaplain Lorge had ever seen and counted out another thousand dollars for the UJA.

Horses at Shavuos

"Shavuos starts tomorrow," the Kentuckian wired his son at Princeton.

The son promptly wired back: "What are the odds?"

Shavuos is the season in Louisville to celebrate not only the giving of the Torah at Mount Sinai but the thundering rhythm of hoofbeats at Churchill Downs. Happy family reunions take place all over town. Bar/bat mitzvah parties, wedding festivities, anniversary get-togethers, and birthday celebrations are held off to "the Sunday after," when many a *l'chayim* is said over mint juleps.

Colonel Matt Winn's Jewish friends are credited with persuading him to take over Churchill Downs and make the Kentucky Derby one of America's great sporting events. Winn liked to tell the story of a Jewish friend who phoned to tell him that he intended to place a lot of money on a Derby horse. "I hope I break even," quivered the voice on the phone. "I need the money."

Two of the top horse trainers were Jewish—Max Hirsch and Hirsch

Jacobs. Max Hirsch trained Assault, the winner of the Triple Crown (Derby, Preakness, and Belmont Stakes) in 1946.

Some race horses have had traditional "Jewish" names—Hatikvah, Kibbuz, Mit Glick, and Shaigetz among them.

A story that made the rounds was about a Christian clergyman who entered a horse in the Derby. Confronted by his board of trustees to explain his action, he pled guilty. "It is true that Jack Krantz and I own Deuteronomy. Jack trains and enters the horse at his own expense. I have never set my eyes on the horse. I get half of his earnings because I allow my half of the horse to run when Jack's half runs. If you will provide a way for my half to remain in the stable while Jack runs his in the Derby, I am perfectly willing to abide by your recommendations."

Greenhorns

The Shapiros were passing through New Mexico. An Indian tried to sell them a rug. Shapiro and the Indian haggled over the price but they couldn't come to terms.

Later, Mrs. Shapiro said, "That was a beautiful rug. Sorry we didn't buy it."

"You saw that we couldn't get together," her husband said. "I couldn't understand his language and he couldn't understand mine."

"Yes, that's right," Mrs. Shapiro said. "I guess he hasn't been in this country too long."

Under protest, the rabbi took off his yarmulke, and the judge later dismissed the charge. The rabbi filed formal complaints over his treatment in the courtroom and the judge eventually apologized.

"When I insisted upon the removal of your headcover, I had no idea of the implications thereof nor intended an affront to the Jewish religion," Hitchings said. "In fact, I did not know you were a rabbi or a Jew."

Onward, Hum-hum Soldiers

A dilemma young Jews across America have faced in their efforts to fit in while staying loyal to their identity as Jews has come from the singing in public schools of vaguely to blatantly Christian hymns, prayers and Christmas carols. The virtual requirement they sing along—or stand out awkwardly in environments with few Jews—has brought internal conflict and soul-searching few who have gone through it will forget. Often children would (and still do, with carols) compromise by omitting the most distinctly Christian verses or changing Christian words to something more "kosher" to forestall a sense they were cowards or betraying their people.

Eli Evans is one of those who wrote of such crises in his book on Southern Jewish life, *The Provincials*. Growing up in the 1940s and 50s in Durham, North Carolina, where his father was a prominent retailer and, for many years, mayor, Evans' family was both distinctly Jewish and highly integrated into the general life of their overwhelmingly, and militantly, Christian community. Evans faced special yet very recognizable strains as a highly visible young Jew in a Southern environment he called not just Christian but "Christ-haunted."

In a time when assembly each morning began with the Lord's Prayer, Evans relates how he'd never close his eyes, fearing that would be "real praying." Instead he'd look downward, bowing his head so no one could see his open eyes, making hissing sounds as the rest recited: "And forgive us our trespasses as we forgive those who trespass against us." This subterfuge was useless for hymns, when all eyes were open and people could tell if one wasn't singing. Evans would sing all the words but "Christian" and "Jesus," stopping or humming on those, or replacing Jesus with Moses. The terms of Evans' separate peace were such that he led his sixth-grade class into its graduation ceremony, marching in, "shoulders back and head erect," singing proudly to the assembled community:

Onward, hum-hum soldiers
Marching as to war
With the cross of Moses
Standing at the fore.

Ikak, Reb Yid

Many Jews, particularly storekeepers, in the South and elsewhere, had normal and profitable business relationships with known Ku Klux Klan members. In Birmingham, Alabama, a major Klan center for many years, a pawnshop owner known as "Cousin" Joe sold pistols and sheets, among other things, to Klansmen. Birmingham Klansmen, though aware of Joe's committed and distinctive Jewishness, would give him the Klan handshake and say "Ikak" (I am a Klansman) on coming to the store. "Cousin Joe" would respond "Iyak." He recalled, with that difficult blend of feelings that often characterized the Jew's ambiguous position in southern society: "All of them were friends of mine."

*   *   *

A Jew and a hunchback were passing a synagogue. The Jew said, "I used to be a Jew." Then the hunchback said, "I used to be a hunchback."

Return Home

A young Talmudic scholar left his home in Pinsk, in White Russia, and came to New York. After many years in America, he returned to the old country for a visit. When he knocked at his parents' door, his elderly mother could barely recognize him; he was dressed in the most modern American fashion and looked like a creature from another world. "Where's your beard?" were the first words from her quivering lips.

"Nobody wears a beard in America, Mama," he replied.

"But at least you keep the Sabbath?" she ventured.

"Everybody works on the Sabbath in America." His mother sighed painfully.

"So how is it with the food?"

By now, the man was apologetic. "Ah, Mama," he said, "it's so much trouble to be kosher in America."

The old woman hesitated for a moment. Then she gripped her son's arm and, in a confidential tone, whispered, "Tell your old mom—you're still circumcised?"

16

GIVING IT AWAY/ TAKING IT BACK: FUND-RAISING AND PHILANTHROPY

Zionist leader Meyer Weisgall was known as a master fund-raiser, someone who really knew how to talk to the rich. Once, it is said, he invited an extremely wealthy man out to lunch. After eating, the man took out his checkbook and wrote a check for $50,000.

"Thanks a lot," said Weisgall, tearing up the check with a look of disgust, "but the meal has already been paid for!"

Peace Unto You

One successful fund-raiser, knowing from experience the level of contention within Jewish communities, would urge "peace in the community" wherever and whenever he appeared. Invariably, leading local figures would approach him later and say, "It's amazing! Positively amazing!"

"What's amazing?" the fund-raiser would ask.

"How'd you know we had a fight?"

A Satisfied Check

May Weisser Hartman was born to Russian-Jewish immigrant parents in New York in 1900. At fourteen, she went to work for an orphan asylum and began a distinguished career as an administrator of Jewish institutions for homeless children, which responded to a problem then far more prevalent in the Jewish community than it is today.

Fund-raising is, of course, a crucial part of administration of any charitable institution, and Ms. Hartman related a number of her early experiences with fund-raising in her autobiography, *I Gave My Heart*. Once, when the orphanage couldn't meet its mortgage payment, the finance chairman sent her, then fifteen, to ask more time from the renowned rabbi from whom the building had been bought. Rabbi Klein received her warmly but, when told her mission, asked: "How come they send a child to ask me this?"

"I suppose they were too embarrassed to come themselves," she responded off the top of her head. The rabbi smiled and agreed to wait until the orphanage had the funds.

Another time she was asked to perform a similar errand, but this time with the president of the Bank of the United States when a note held by that bank fell due and the orphanage couldn't pay. Again, the president was courteous and asked why the directors had sent a young girl on such a crucial mission. Prepared this time, she gave the banker the same answer she'd given the rabbi. It worked again, with the banker, though not as well. He agreed to extend the note for three months.

On another occasion, a lodge secretary gave her a check for a deposit on a purchase. He told her she should go over to the bank and have them "satisfy this check."

She didn't understand the request and said, "What shall I ask?"

He repeated, "To satisfy this check." When she asked again, he was already annoyed and she was feeling stupid.

She went to the bank, cautiously approached the teller, and, in a weak voice, said, "I'd like to have this check satisfied."

"What?"

She repeated herself.

The teller went over to a bank officer, then came back with a smile on his face and said, "Here's your satisfied, I mean *certified* check."

She blushed in embarrassment, and when she returned to her office she said to the secretary, "Here's your certified check," and hissed, "not *satisfied!*"

He shrugged and reiterated: "When that stamp is on a check, everybody is satisfied."

"If Mr. Rosenwald Had Six Dozen Eggs . . ."

Julius Rosenwald, the onetime head of Sears, Roebuck and Co., gave away $63 million during his lifetime and $12 million more in bequests in his will. He was responsible for the construction of 5,367 schools, in addition to shops, homes, libraries, health clinics and YMCAs for blacks in 883 counties in fifteen Southern states. In his far-reaching efforts to improve the condition of Southern blacks, he braved bitter prejudices. His Southern competitors spread the rumor that Rosenwald was really a black masquerading as a Jew.

His helping hand made Rosenwald an object of hero worship among many Southern blacks of his day who celebrated his birthday and hung his photograph alongside those of Lincoln and Booker T. Washington in homes and schools. In one black school of that time, a teacher taught arithmetic this way: "If Mr. Rosenwald had six dozen eggs and if Mr. Rosenwald bought four more eggs, how many eggs would Mr. Rosenwald have?"

During World War I, General John Pershing gave a reception for his top brass to which the "dollar-a-year" men who had military status were invited. Rosenwald appeared—dressed in a general's uniform. The reception began with each officer announcing his full name and title. After the generals had sounded off, one after the other, the mail-order king announced himself: "Julius Rosenwald, General Merchandise."

Despite his great generosity, Rosenwald was legendary for his dislike of waste and extravagance. One day Rosenwald's valet was sent to buy some razor blades for the personal use of the Sears, Roebuck president. He returned with a dollar's worth of blades. After all, he figured, a rich man like his employer would want more than a few blades at a time.

The multimillionaire sharply reproved his valet.

"Why buy so many blades?" he demanded. "They might go down in price. Perhaps later we could have bought the blades cheaper!"

Rosenwald always pooh-poohed the idea that there are geniuses in business. He asserted that the chief element in accumulating a fortune, including his own, was sheer luck. "By luck a man stumbles into an unusual opportunity and by more luck he holds on to it," Rosenwald said. He bought into Sears himself only because of his brother-in-law, who found out about the possibility of buying the stock but didn't want to risk it alone. To illustrate his point, he loved to tell the following story from Jewish folklore:

"Once there was a man who awoke one morning to find himself the winner of a fortune in a lottery. 'How did you do it?' his friends asked. 'It was this way,' he explained. 'One night I dreamt the number 9, and the following night I dreamt of the number 8, so I used my brains, multiplied the two numbers together, got 68 and bet on the number!"

Rosenwald made his fortune by helping transform Sears, Roebuck from a small mail-order house into the world's largest retailer. In his twenties, Rosenwald said his aim was to have a $15,000 annual income: $5,000 for personal expenses, $5,000 for saving, and $5,000 for charity. In 1895, the year Roebuck sold out to Sears, Rosenwald, then a clothing supplier, bought a 25 percent share in the company. His brother-in-law, who wouldn't last long in the business, bought another 25 percent. Rosenwald organized the business while Sears wrote the ad copy. Tension grew between the two. Rosenwald felt Sears promoted cheap merchandise of questionable quality. Rosenwald argued for "truth in advertising" and emphasized customer satisfaction. In 1908, after a dispute between them, Sears resigned as company president and Rosenwald replaced him.

Sears, Roebuck became an institution dear to small-town America's heart as few have. When Eugene Talmadge ran for re-election to the Senate, he told Georgia farmers they had only three true friends: "Jesus Christ, Sears Roebuck and Gene Talmadge." President Franklin Roosevelt once suggested the way to show Russians the superiority of the American way of life was to bombard the Soviet Union by air with millions of Sears catalogues.

Many Sears fans were not so taken with Rosenwald's philanthropy toward blacks. Ironically, the company he once headed faced government legal action in the 1970s and 1980s for alleged discriminatory employment practices though Sears struck back with a class-action countersuit against ten federal agencies, saying the government's anti-discrimination regulations were contradictory, confused and unfair.

Rosenwald's philosophy of philanthropy emphasized stimulating self-help and spending in the present rather than laying in store perpetual trust funds. Much of his donations were in the form of matching funds; "a spur," as he put it, "not a crutch." For example, although the 5,000-plus "Rosenwald" schools cost some $28 million to build, more of the total money actually came both from taxes and from black contributions than from the Rosenwald Fund.

On the second point, Rosenwald argued that no one was able to foresee the needs of the future and mandated that his fund be spent in full within twenty-five years of his death.

"Our immediate needs," he said, "are too plain and too urgent to allow us to do the work of future generations." Rosenwald may have been naive at times about the ability of money to solve all problems, as when he reportedly offered a large sum to F. L. Smith, an objectionable Illinois Senate candidate, to quit the race.

Louis Pizitz of Birmingham

Louis Pizitz of Birmingham, peddler, department store owner, and philanthropist, became known as "the godfather of merchandising in Birmingham" and acted as a virtual government in "promoting the general welfare" in a day before governments in this country saw that as their responsibility.

When Alabama coal mines closed and miners were faced with starvation in 1909 and again during the Great Depression of the 1930s, Pizitz bought out mines to offer work and then sold the mined coal at the cost of production. In 1914, when the price of Alabama cotton plummeted to 11 cents a pound, Pizitz went around buying it up at 15 cents a pound and storing it. He promised that whatever he got for the cotton over and above that price would go back to the farmers; when World War I broke out later that year and the price of cotton soared, he was as good as his word.

During the Depression, Pizitz started a tradition of opening his huge department store on Thanksgiving Day as a free restaurant to anyone in need, giving away thousands of free turkey dinners. When banks closed in the Depression and teachers couldn't cash their paychecks, Pizitz cashed them himself, supplementing the teachers' salaries with donations of his goods. (The State of Alabama reimbursed him for the checks in 1933, though at the time it was not clear that they would.) He regularly distributed truckloads of foods for Christmas feasts for prisoners. He gave liberally to Jewish, black and general causes.

Born in Poland in 1868, Pizitz came to America in 1889 and became a peddler in Georgia. In 1892 he opened his own store in the Georgia town of Swainsboro, and six years later moved to Birmingham, where he started a larger store. In 1919 he began building the seven-story Louis Pizitz Dry Goods Co. department store.

Numerous anecdotes grew up around Pizitz. Employees recalled how he used to circulate among them Saturday nights, and, like a father distributing Hanukah *gelt*, visit with each of them personally and count out their week's pay in silver dollars drawn from his huge pockets. It was said he knew each employee and his salary without keeping any books.

Pizitz was known for retaining the Russian custom of grabbing people he liked and kissing them on both cheeks. As Pizitz's circle grew to include prominent WASPs from more restrained backgrounds, some took this better than others. When Oscar Underwood, newly elected to the U.S. Senate, showed up at a Pizitz birthday party and got this customary greeting, he was described as "nearly shocked out of his pants."

Minnie's Music

For more than forty years, Minnie Guggenheimer was fund-raiser and impresario for Stadium Concerts, Inc., which sponsored open-air summer concerts at City College's Lewisohn Stadium in upper Manhattan. Fine music was brought to millions of people for virtually nothing (as little as a quarter a ticket into the early 1960s). Minnie worked full-time in the unpaid position, arranging concerts and raising money to cover the program's tremendous deficits.

But she was perhaps best known for her intermission stage style and way with words, as maybe a younger and feminine incarnation of the same spirit that animated movie mogul Sam Goldwyn. It was said that, great as the music was, nearly as many people came to City College to hear her intermission appeals and announcements.

Minnie introduced such musical greats as Marian Anderson, an unknown young black woman chosen as winner of the 1925 citywide talent search, persuaded George Gershwin to play his "Rhapsody in Blue" publicly for the first time in 1927, and brought Van Cliburn to the campus in 1958 to play the same piano concert with which he'd just won Moscow's International Tchaikovsky Competition.

She may be even longer remembered for times like the season opener of 1948, when after Mayor O'Dwyer's announcement that a new stage would be built for the next season, she asked all subscribers to take part in the groundbreaking ceremonies. "We'll all go down there and lie—lay," she started, and then corrected herself, "I mean, we'll do something with spades!"

Or the time she began a detailed written introduction for a prominent politico. At the last minute, she dropped the lengthy intro and told the audience instead: "I can only tell that his *Who's Who* is six inches long!"

Or the time Mayor LaGuardia came to a concert to present a city award to the evening's featured performer. "The mayor's going to decorate our soloist," she said, "—that is, if he can find a place where she isn't already decorated!"

Or the time she brought the crown prince of Sweden to the stage snapping her fingers and calling, "Here, Prince! Prince!"

Or the times she announced *H.M.S. Pinafore* as everybody's favorite by Gilbert and Solomon, that Jan Peerce would sing the role of Aida, and that Roger Hammerstein personally would conduct a song from *South Pacific*.

Or the time, supposedly to express thanks for sponsorship of a concert by Rheingold beer, she exulted to several hundred Rheingold workers and distributors about how much she'd always loved Budweiser, especially for setting her hair.

Or the time in 1947 when she said she would announce the forthcoming appearance of "one of the best-known names in the musical world," then hesitated, pulled out a crumpled check from her pocketbook, and reading her notes with evident difficulty, announced the name, "Ezio Pinza, baaas."

"Oh dear, that can't be right," she said, "a bass is a kind of fish!"

Or the time she announced a last-minute change with, "We won't be able to have that thing by Smetana tonight, but I don't think it matters very much. Smetana is some kind of mustard or sour cream, isn't it?"

Or the time, waiting for three of the Metropolitan Opera's most prominent stars to resume their performance, she underlined her intermission appeal with the earnest pledge: "If I get enough money, I'll be able to give you better artists in the future!"

※

Kaskowitz, skiing in the Alps for the first time, loses his way. A rescue team is dispatched to look for him. On the third day, alone and freezing, he hears a megaphoned voice booming over the mountains, "Kaskowitz! Kaskowitz! Where are you?"

A feeble voice reaches the search party: "If this is the UJA (United Jewish Appeal), I gave at the office!"

Albert Greenfield of Philadelphia

Albert Greenfield, the Philadelphia real estate and banking tycoon, was also known as a powerhouse fund-raiser for Jewish and other causes. He was considered a master of the technique of inviting wealthy men to a luncheon and embarrassing them into pledging more than they wanted to. "Fifteen thousand?" he would scream from the dais. "On thus-and-such deal alone, you made thirty thousand. On that deal with me you made forty thousand!"

Religious Acts

Two engines on an airplane crossing the Atlantic suddenly caught fire and the plane quickly lost altitude. The pilot got on the public address system, briefly explained the situation, and suggested each passenger perform a religious act in accordance with his beliefs. The Moslems got up and bowed toward Mecca. A Protestant group began singing hymns. Catholics prayed over their rosaries. A Jewish couple started walking up and down the aisle, requesting contributions for research to prevent future airplane engine fires.

No Shame

A wealthy man was accustomed to giving $1,000 gifts to his local Federation. He always gave anonymously. One year, he was finally prevailed upon by vigorous fund-raisers to give $10,000. He was asked if he wished, as usual, to make his gift anonymous.

"Of course not," he said, taken aback. "What do I have to be ashamed of now?"

Ends and Means

While it is generally acknowledged that Jewish fund-raising is in a league by itself, the United Jewish Appeal broke through to new heights in its search for the ultimate donor with its Israel Education Fund. Donations below $100,000 were politely refused and redirected to UJA. The funds went to building schools (feeding the legendary "edifice complex" of wealthy donors) that combined academics and vocational training. While a large part of the attraction of giving to the fund was doubtless its snob appeal, the stated purpose of the schools was: "Education to break down social barriers."

Fund-Raising Tips

Fund-raising, experts have said, is part art, part science. Paul Zuckerman, a Detroit businessman who has chaired UJA and headed the Jewish

Agency, Israel's fund-raising arm, gave these tips to a convention of Federations in the 1970s:

> It is important to rate to get the most.
>
> In every city, there are men who have always been the pacesetters in terms of giving and working; they are not giving as much as they can. We must have the courage to take a look at what they are really worth and ask for that amount.
>
> It is an accepted principle that one man should never go alone to solicit a major gift. It is too easy to say no to one man, especially if he is a friend or neighbor. When two or more go, it is no longer one Jew asking another for a gift—it is the entire community, it is the Jewish people.
>
> When a national leader, an Israeli, and a respected local leader call on a man, then quite literally the world Jewish community is calling on him.
>
> If we honor a man, give him a position of leadership, then I sincerely believe he has a responsibility to live up to it.

The 1967 War

Despite the understandable focus fund-raisers place on the rich, Jewish charitable endeavors have historically, of course, had an extremely broad base of support. When American Jews feared for Israel's survival in the 1967 and 1973 wars, this trend was particularly notable. Some contributions reportedly received during the 1973 war included $13 in savings from a child's piggy bank, a year's worth of reparations money contributed by a former German citizen, $160 in tips sent by a group of youngsters parking cars at World Series games, a $1,000 check dropped into a collection box across from the New York Stock Exchange, a mass of traveler's checks sent by a woman going off on vacation who cancelled her trip so she could donate them instead, and $30.69—all her savings—sent by one elderly woman.

During the 1973 Arab-Israeli war a crack pro-Syrian guerrilla unit was said to have broken into the Bank of Tel Aviv and escaped with U.S. $20 million—in pledges.

Pledging and Squeezing

Once, in Chicago, a group of men were at a bar. A burly Texas cowboy type got up, squeezed a half orange on his plate and offered $500 to anybody who could get one more drop of juice from the rind he'd left on the table.

A short, pale, frail-looking man with heavy horn-rimmed glasses got up and walked over to the cowboy's seat. Several of the men suppressed snickers at first. But the little guy squeezed and squeezed, and to their amazement, managed to get half a glass of juice from the shreds in front of him.

"That's amazing, man," said the humbled Texan, pulling out his billfold. "How'd you do it?"

"Easy," said the little guy with a smile. "I'm a fund-raiser for the UJA."

※

A wealthy New Yorker pledged a million dollars to the UJA but then refused to pay up despite innumerable requests to do so. Exasperated, a wealthy contributor asked him over lunch: "If you had no intention of paying, why did you pledge in the first place—and a million at that?"

"Simple," the man answered. "When I pledge, *I pledge!*"

17

THE SYNAGOGUE IN TRANSITION

Not Today

An old *shammes* (sexton) stood outside a little *shul* on the East Side trying to pull in a *minyan*. With an experienced eye, he guessed who was Jewish and who was not. He buttonholed one man with a portfolio under his arm.

"Please, *reb yid*. We need a *minyan*. Come in for a while."

"Oh, I'm sorry. Not today."

"And why not today, *reb yid*?"

"Well, I'll tell you. When I have a big deal on I don't *daven*, and I've always had good luck."

"And what happens when you do *daven*?"

"Frankly," said the man, a bit apologetic, "this I never tried."

Stages

The following were described as the three stages in the life of a freethinker by a prominent one, *Forward* editor Abraham Cahan, in 1902:

1. When he passes a synagogue and gnashes his teeth;
2. When he passes a synagogue and smiles;
3. When he passes a synagogue and, though inclined to sigh because the world is still in such a state of ignorance, nevertheless finds himself taking an interest in such moments as these, when men stand together immersed in a feeling that has nothing to do with the egoistic life.

Without Grape Juice,
There Is No Joy

During the early years of Prohibition, the exemption granted rabbis for the sale of sacramental wine became a touchy subject in most Jewish communities and a new source of contention between Orthodox and Reform movements. A majority of American Jews at this time were recent arrivals, born in Europe, and their children. Although unenthusiastic about Prohibition, they did not want to appear to be seeking special favors under the law. The more established German Reform Jews were even more anxious to avoid threats to their recently growing sense of security as Americans. The phenomenon of pseudo-congregations employing pseudo-rabbis to get wine caused widespread outrage. "If you want to drink booze, you'll have to join the Hebrew church," was an expression of the time reported in Los Angeles.

On the other hand, wine had long been central to Jewish traditional observance. Reform Jews argued that the "fruit of the vine" could just as well be grape juice and that fermented wine was unnecessary, but the Orthodox disagreed. Conservative talmudic scholar Rabbi Louis Ginzburg also held in a 1922 responsum that grape juice could substitute for wine for ritual purposes, although many continued to reject this view. With time, the issuance of wine licenses seemed under better control and the issue gradually faded from public attention.

"No Praying!"

The American system of selling High Holiday tickets—both to raise funds for synagogues, and to accommodate the massive increase in synagogue attendance on those days—has led to a variety of jokes. One of the most famous is this:

One Yom Kippur, a burly Gentile ticket-taker at a Bronx synagogue was confronted by a ticketless Jew who begged stubbornly to be allowed in. "No ticket, no admission," the guard insisted.

"I've got to talk to my partner, Shulman, in the tenth row," the man explained. "It's very urgent."

"Look, buddy, for the last time," the guard said, "I'm telling you, you can't get into this synagogue without a ticket!"

"But it's a matter of business," the man persisted, "I'll just be a minute—I swear to you."

"Well," said the guard, hesitating, "maybe if it's just a business matter, I'll let you in for a minute. But remember," he warned the Jew, "no praying!"

New Aesthetic

Samson Benderly, a young Palestinian Jew studying medicine in Beirut in 1898, met a visiting American-Jewish doctor and accepted his invitation to come to Baltimore. After finishing his medical studies in America, Benderly astounded his friends by suddenly deciding on a career in Jewish education. He soon became principal of a small Hebrew school operated by the Hebrew Education Society in Baltimore.

Benderly was known as a pioneer and innovator. One of his ideas was to insist on what was considered an unusual level of cleanliness for a traditional *cheder* (Hebrew school). In this quest he negotiated value differences between traditional teachers and the new land. He feared children who went to the bright public schools during the day would be depressed by the frequently dingy aura of the *cheder*. In one anecdote Benderly related, he had located in one *cheder* an especially fine teacher he wanted to engage for his school. As politely as he could, he asked the young man, "Could you manage to wear a clean collar and clean your fingernails?"

The man, though not insulted, gave Benderly a one-word answer: "Why?"

"It might be more aesthetic, don't you agree?"

"Aesthetic?" asked the teacher. "I'm not sure what that has to do with education. Beauty does not enter into my philosophy of life." Benderly, however, didn't give up. Despite this early culture clash, he prevailed and brought the man into his school.

Raffling Off the Torah

Besides being religious institutions, synagogues throughout the New World were independent financial entities typically without the security of support they had enjoyed in the *shtetl*.

Like many other synagogues across America, Oakland's Temple Sinai (First Hebrew Congregation) had its troubles balancing the books. There was chronic tension between the bulk of Jews who attended services, most of them only a few times a year, and the handful of men of wealth and standing who primarily bankrolled the congregation and tried to keep it on a path of ambitious growth.

In 1927, President Albert Lavenson, of a prominent department store family, scolded the congregation in his annual message. He was unhappy that $2,000 for a part-time cantor couldn't be raised and that nearly three-quarters of the congregants paid only minimum dues of $30 yearly. This, he noted, was "not consistent with the array of automobiles crowding the neighborhood of the temple on High Holidays." Non-members were even worse of course; perhaps 150 families wouldn't join and pay dues though their children were enrolled in Sunday school or their wives in the Sisterhood. Lavenson, a retired vice-president of Emporium Capwell's, argued:

> Religion is in one respect like any trade commodity; if it means anything
> to us, we must pay adequately for it . . .

And he raised a new slogan: Give the synagogue as much as you pay for gasoline!

Noting the congregation's feeble Sabbath attendance, he explained for those who may have "misunderstood" its role that the board of directors could "not be expected to worship as proxies for the general membership."

Just as the Reform First Hebrew Congregation suffered from debt after buying a new building, Oakland's Conservative Beth Abraham also had troubles from its new structures, finished in the pivotal year 1929. During the 1930s, religious school teachers went unpaid and utilities were cut off one weekend due to unpaid bills. At one point, county sheriffs padlocked the synagogue doors, but enough money to keep the congregation afloat was raised through an emergency sale of lifetime seats.

But the most severe money troubles may have been those of Beth Jacob, the city's small, mostly first-generation, Orthodox *shul*. A February 1925 directive included an order that "a new *pushke* (poor-box) should be bought, with a good lock, that no one can tamper with." Rabbi B. M. Paper, ordained in Lithuania, was able to supplement his income during Prohibition by the sale of sacramental wine. A gallon would go for $6.50 and the synagogue would get 12 percent of the proceeds. In the early 1930s, Paper was selling some 200 gallons a month, ostensibly for religious purposes, although the congregation had a membership of only about seventy families.

Paper, however, was small potatoes, compared with other Orthodox "wine rabbis," writes historian Fred Rosenbaum in his book *Free to Choose*. One of these made deliveries from a horse-drawn van that looked like a laundry wagon but was packed inside with port, sherry and vermouth.

The 1933 repeal of Prohibition in fact caused a profound fiscal crisis for Beth Jacob. The synagogue—which then charged 50 cents a month dues—had not paid the rabbi a salary since the economy turned down, and now he was without an alternative income source. The congregation owed both rabbi and cantor thousands of dollars in back pay and had no plan to raise it. Paper proposed the *shul* pay him back by buying a Torah and raffling it off. So it was done; 1,700 one-dollar tickets were sold, a Torah acquired for $190 and $1,500 in debt satisfied in December 1934. Other ambitious money-raising schemes followed. A sale of inscriptions in a Golden Book in 1935 netted $630 and a "Memorial Services System" in 1936 apparently proved profitable. By the spring of 1937, Rabbi Paper was proposing an electric memorial tablet "guaranteed to bring in considerable money."

Half a Loaf

A rabbi came home from services one *Shabbat* looking tired and depressed.

"What's wrong?" his wife asked.

"I tried to persuade the congregation to give more to *tzedakah* (charity) and do more for the poor. I spoke for almost an hour. I used all the persuasive powers I have. I showed them as convincingly as I possibly could that it's the duty of the rich to help the poor."

"And—you don't think they believed you, is that what's wrong?"

"Well, I wouldn't say none of them believed me," the rabbi allowed. "I think I convinced the poor."

Crown of the Torah

A rabbinical student at New York's Jewish Theological Seminary was hired in 1943 to serve as "weekend rabbi" for a new Jewish center in a suburb in New Jersey.

After the High Holidays, it was impossible to get together a *minyan*—the traditional ten men necessary for a service. One, two, three, Sabbath mornings passed, waiting in vain. Some Saturdays no more than four people showed up. At the end of the month, the "rabbi," Stuart Rosenberg, put out an alarm to congregational leaders that they needed to start coming Saturday mornings or there could be no synagogue.

That next Saturday morning there were ten men—and all were honored with an *aliyah*, being called up to say blessings over the Torah. Most of the men hadn't been to the synagogue since their *bar mitzvah*. The congregational president was called up as *golel* (to dress the Torah after reading) and given the *keter Torah*, or crown of the Torah, by Rabbi Rosenberg. Not knowing what to do with it and apparently, as president, too embarrassed to ask, he placed the object gingerly on his own head. "Everyone guffawed," recalled Rosenberg, "even those who were not exactly sure why they were laughing."

Handwriting on the Wall

Visits to Sunday School rest rooms with careful attention to wall scrawlings can add to our picture of how new generations of children blend their American and Jewish heritages. A handful of inscriptions noted over the years include:

"Shep Nachas and His Rippling Rhythm"
"You Bet Your Tallis"
"I'm Schechita the Banana and I'm Here to Say . . ."
"Give me a little knish, will you, huh?
What are ya gonna mish, tell me, huh?"
"You must remember this,
A knish is just a knish,
That no one can deny."
"Deck the halls with loaves of challah . . ."

Our Little Secret

A rabbi became friendly with a minister who took a strong and sincere interest in Judaism. One day they were talking and the minister asked, in a very earnest tone, "You know, I have observed something about your synagogue that's made me very curious. This one thing has me stumped; I've never found anything in my reading on it. Tell me, rabbi, what is the special ceremonial practice Jews have that requires them to stand *outside* the synagogue?"

You'd Never Believe

"What did you learn in Hebrew School today, Danny?" a California Jewish mother asked her young son.

"Our teacher told the story of the Israelites crossing the Red Sea."

"What did she tell you?"

"Well," Danny began, "it was like this, Ma. The Israelites were all camped out by the Red Sea, exhausted after their long train ride from Egypt. Just when they were about to go to sleep, one of their spy helicopters reported that Pharaoh had left Egypt with four divisions and a hundred tanks and was coming after them. Moses told the people not to worry, everything would be okay, that he had a Mastermind helping them with their strategic decisions and he could handle *anything*.

"The next morning, the scouts saw a giant dust cloud approaching from the west. Moses heard from the Mastermind telling him to have his chemical warfare division put down a smokescreen between the Israelites and the Egyptians and have his engineers build a pontoon bridge across the Sea. The bridge was built and the Israelites got across just as the Egyptians arrived. Then Pharaoh ordered the Egyptians to cross the bridge and follow the Israelites.

"When the Egyptian soldiers were all on the bridge, the Mastermind told Moses to send the Israeli Air Force out to drop bombs all the way up and down the bridge. The bridge was destroyed, the Egyptians were drowned. So it was like this that Moses, with the help of the Mastermind, saved the Israelites from Pharaoh and the Egyptians."

The mother eyed Danny quizzically for several seconds. "Is that *really* the story your teacher told you?"

The boy sighed apologetically. "Well, no, Ma, it's not. But if I told you the way the teacher told it, you'd just never believe it!"

Christmas Stories

The Jewish family settled in a small Midwestern town and, in the course of years, became quite assimilated. They maintained a few irregular elements of Jewish identity but in most ways couldn't be distinguished from their Christian neighbors. At Christmas they had a tree and their little boy enjoyed it as much as anyone in town.

One Christmas, when the boy was six, he was asked to a party given by a Christian school chum. When he got home from the party, he was filled with curiosity. "Tell me, Daddy," he asked his father, "do Gentiles, too, believe in Christmas?"

Putting the *Ch* Back

One modern Jewish father, determined to "put the *Ch* back in Chanukah" and distract his young boy's attention from all the commotion about Christmas, was apparently successful in getting his four-year-old to love the Chanukah story. He was profoundly gratified to see the boy taking an active and sincere interest in the Festival of Lights and insisting on lighting the menorah each night. On the last night, the father took the boy aside and explained that there would be no more Chanukah lights until the next year. "There are no more candles, Daddy?"

"No, son," the father answered gently.

"You mean Chanukah is all over?"

The father said it was.

"Oh, boy," said the young Jew. "Now comes Christmas, right, Daddy?"

May He Rest

Jews long assumed a special language they could use with each other, partly Hebrew, partly Yiddish, partly a matter of inflection and tone, not needing explanation when conveyed to another Jew. But in our times, these messages may not always be clearly understood, especially between generations.

One pious older Hebrew teacher, for example, who had spent many years in Israel, would always reminisce about "my father, *alava shalom*."

Her eight-year-old Alef class students and even her older Daled class students hadn't grown up with this phrase, Hebrew for "may he rest in peace." Over years, they heard over and over about "my father, *alava shalom*, this" and "my father, *alava shalom*, that." One day, for some reason, the teacher showed the Daled class an old newspaper clipping with her father's picture, and underneath it the name Irving Greenberg.

"Gee," some of the kids said, "how'd they get his name wrong?"

"Oh, let me look," said the teacher, but she looked, smiled and, said "no, that's his name: Irving Greenberg."

The kids looked at each other funny and then, almost as one voice, shouted, "But *you* always called him Oliver Shalom!"

Another gap in bringing the old world into the new comes when the father says he is tired and headachey and is going up to bed, and his daughter, just home from Hebrew school, consoles him absently with: "May you rest in peace."

Transformation of the Bar Mitzvah

First-generation American Jews used to bring their thirteen-year-old sons to *shul*, often on a Thursday, for their bar mitzvahs. The boy would be called up to the Torah reading with the father and grandfather beside him. After the ceremony, *lekach* (honey cake) and wine were served, and typically that was that.

Charles Angoff, in his *When I Was a Boy in Boston*, wrote that on the Thursday he was to become a bar mitzvah his father woke him up at 6:30 A.M. and took him to *shul*. He was called to the Torah for the first time, some congregants wished him *mazel tov*, his father put his arm around him, congratulated him, and then went off to work. That was

Angoff's bar mitzvah. (His mother, sensing his feeling of emptiness, did subsequently invite relatives and friends to a small reception on Saturday night.)

Compare that with the following scenes of actual bar mitzvah ceremonies:

> On a football field in Miami, five hundred spectators witness a marching band, preceded by a bevy of cheerleaders in costume, usher in a young, downy-chinned lad driven onto the field on a float bearing a replica of the Torah scroll.

> In New York City, the three hundred guests who made the scene will long remember the bar mitzvah that took place in the Electric Circus on St. Mark's Place. There was a psychedelic light show and a musical happening by Cat Mother and The All-Night Newsboys. The women appeared in everything from micro-minis to evening pajamas, and the men's attire ranged from sloppy hippy to foppish mod. The guests joined in the bugaloo, the horse and various other tribal dances throughout the afternoon.

> Immediately following the religious service, the friends and family adjourned to the social hall. From the ceiling hung a large cage, in which were two hundred of the brightest plumaged, loudest screeching parakeets ever assembled under one temple roof. Opening the cage was the highlight of the bar mitzvah reception.

No Cause for Alarm

There is a story that in the late 1950s, the Hollywood mogul Michael Silverstone determined to give his son a bar mitzvah to end bar mitzvahs. He called in his ace director and ordered him to stage the project, a bar mitzvah the like of which had never been seen.

The director arranged for a bar mitzvah safari to Tanganyika (now, Tanzania, in southeast Africa). Six C-47s would fly the guests to Mombasa, Kenya. From there the party would proceed to Mount Kilimanjaro, the highest point on the African continent. Snow covers Kilimanjaro's peak although it is near the Equator, and at its base, the climate is tropical. At the foot of this great mountain, the bar mitzvah would take place.

The planes arrived on schedule in Mombasa. A local tourist agency provided an English-speaking guide, 72 elephants, 200 native elephant keepers and pack-bearers, a chef trained at the Waldorf Astoria, and a rabbi. The caravan journeyed for several days to reach the famed mountain. Finally, drained from days of riding plodding elephants, the celebrants approached the bar mitzvah site. The guide informed them that after another mile they would break out of the jungle and reach the clearing at the foot of the mountain.

Just as they neared the clearing, they heard the sounds of a strange chant. The guide became confused; the voices were not singing any native language with which he was familiar. Maybe it was some unfriendly tribe from another area. He asked the celebrants to halt; he would go ahead to scout out the situation.

Fifteen minutes later he returned, grinning broadly. "There is no cause for alarm, Mr. Silverstone," he reassured the proud father. "It's just that there is another bar mitzvah being held at the foot of the mountain. In an hour or so, we will be able to proceed."

The movement toward gender equality, establishment of the State of Israel and the plight of (formerly) Soviet Jewry all had major impacts on this Jewish tradition in America. The bat mitzvah for girls is an American invention, initially the brainchild of Rabbi Mordecai M. Kaplan, founder of Reconstructionism (whose daughter, Judith Kaplan Eisenstein, who died in 1996, is believed to have had the first bat mitzvah in 1922.) Some parents take their sons to Israel for their bar mitzvah ceremonies at the Western Wall or at an Israeli synagogue. A later development was the "twinning" in the ceremony of the bar mitzvah boy or the bat mitzvah girl with a Soviet Jewish counterpart.

Another American Jewish innovation is the adult bar mitzvah and bat mitzvah for those who never celebrated the rite in their youth. Often these are group events that take place after a period of intense study.

The American *Shadchan*

The *shadchan*—matchmaker—was an entrenched institution among Eastern European Jews who arranged marriages for their sons and daughters. He was most typically pictured as a figure dressed in black gabardine, running from house to house, black notebook in hand, exaggerating his clients' positive qualities while ignoring or downplaying their less attractive ones, cajoling and bargaining for dowries.

America was the death of the old-style *shadchan*. In the United States, though, the European *shadchan* realized the business possibilities of the "profession" and the marriage broker agency was born. For many individuals, young and old, who patronized the matrimonial bureaus, the *shadchan* was no joke, and often their only salvation.

Not all *shadchanim* were professional. Many Jewish women used to "make matches" as a hobby. Ida, daughter of the Ramaz, one of the most famous rabbis in the world, was one. Ida was obsessed with matchmaking—she herself called it a "disease." She looked down on professional *shadchanim* and, being proud of her amateur standing, never took out a license.

No one was safe from Ida. She had many "offices"—the benches on upper Broadway, in the parks, and above all, the lobbies of apartment buildings. At the time she died in 1946, her family discovered she had had an official position she had never told them about. After the funeral, an old lady said to her children, "All the club members were at your mother's funeral."

"I didn't know that Mama belonged to a club," one of the daughters said.

"Oh, yes," the lady said. "It was the club of all the women who sit on the benches of Broadway. Your mother was the president."

Wherever she was, Ida used to "ply her trade." When she lived in Worcester, Massachusetts, she indulged her avocation as well as she could in a city short of benches. One day, when her husband Harry was in Fitchburg peddling notions, he chanced upon a "fashionable restaurant," whose owner was a widow with a daughter named Felice.

When the widow found out that Harry was the husband of "the daughter of the Ramaz," whose matchmaking proclivities she was well aware of, she pressed into his hand a photograph of Felice for Ida's gallery. When Ida saw Felice's picture, she melted, because Felice was such *ah shayneh maidel* (pretty girl), but, being rushed at the time, did nothing about her.

Years passed and Felice's mother died. Harry implored Ida to find a husband for her. Ida agreed, but said she must go to New York to do it. A few evenings on the bench in the lobby of the Ramaz's apartment building or on one along upper Broadway, and Felice's destiny would be happily sealed. This plan seemed too informal to Harry. "In that case," said Ida, "I will go to see Levine, the professional *shadchan* from the Bronx, and come right back."

Ida took Felice's photograph with her, and when Levine saw it, he was so impressed "he right away melted also." He was at that very moment writing to a young man in Atlanta, a furrier, who by the bye had an automobile. He sent Felice's photograph to Atlanta, along with vital statistics, and waited for results.

They came. The young man was ecstatic. Arrangements were made for him to come to Worcester to meet Felice in person. The meeting was set for a Sunday. On Thursday, Ida's son, then nine, woke up too ill to go to school. He demanded an apple. He said that an apple was the only thing that could cure him. Ida couldn't find an apple. The boy started to howl. Ida was frantic.

At this moment, a special delivery letter arrived. It was from Levine. He said that, along with Felice's photograph, he had also sent a photograph of one of his Bronx clients. The Bronx girl did not appeal to the Atlantan as much as Felice did, but the Bronx girl had a mother who was "well fixed." Mother and daughter took a trip South, stopped off in Atlanta, met the "eligible" one, and bought some furs from him. Before too long, the Bronx girl and the furrier were engaged.

Ida threw the letter to the floor. To toy with an orphan girl's destiny! The treachery of sending off another girl's photograph! All the time Ida was stewing, her little darling screamed for an apple. At that moment Ida heard a peddler crying in the street, "Apples! Golden Apples!" Ida called down to the peddler, whose name was Ginsburg, to bring up some apples. She ran to her son's bedroom with an apple. When she came back to the living room, Ginsburg was staring, enraptured, at Felice's photograph. Ida went to work.

"Are you married?" she asked.

"I was. My wife died."

"Do you want to get married again?"

Unable to answer, Ginsburg stared at the photograph, his hand trembling.

Ida extolled Felice's virtues. She could see Ginsburg melt.

"A girl like this I would marry even in the dark."

"She has no money, Ginsburg. All she has is what you see in the picture."

"Even if she has half, I'll marry her."

"She's yours," Ida said.

New Matchmakers

Isaac Bashevis Singer said, "For thousands of years, Jews had matchmakers. Today, if you suggest a matchmaker the girl is offended, so you suggest a computer and she thinks it's all right."

Computer dating and matchmaking services have proliferated. What's more, the classified ads sections of English-Jewish newspapers now teem with personals from people looking for mates and companions. Below are a few samples:

KISS NO MORE FROGS. Meet sincere, good-looking, professional Jewish man, 29, 5' 10", 155, nicely built, I seek a relationship with cuddly Koala bear. 21–29. Send phone number; photo appreciated but not necessary.

Voluptuous, buxom woman wanted who is attractive, educated, Jewish, pleasant, nonaggressive, submissive, warm, giving, loving and sweet, 5' 3" to 5' 10", age 27 to 44, for very successful attorney in his 40s. Recent photo please.

BATHSHEBA WANTS DAVID. Classy college professor early 30s, petite, pretty, warm, witty, seeks sincere adventurous man for friendship and romance in NYC.

Jewish Prince, in late 20s seeks sincere Jewish Princess who is affectionate, nonsmoker, enjoys movies, dining, and a good sense of humor.
FAT WOMAN PREFERRED. Attractive, masculine, SWJM, 29, mature, 6', 200 lbs., would like to meet large woman with personality. Don't be shy, write.

If You Will It, It is not a dream. Let's live the Jewish dream in Israel together. Attractive, personable woman with a sense of humor, love of Yiddishkeit, fellow Jews, and Israel seeks to meet man with the resources (emotional and financial) to make aliyah and live a productive life in Israel.

I HAVE A VERY special sister, who is looking for a very special guy. She is 25, 5' 6", stunning, slim, M.S. in education, artistic, warm, sensitive, personality; she is health-minded and dynamic. Enjoys dancing, languages, photography and genuine zest for life and living. We are a loving educated Jewish family. P.S. She doesn't know I am doing this, it's her Hanukah present.

18

CLASSIC AMERICAN-JEWISH HUMOR

Second Chances

Levine comes to see the treasurer of his burial society. "I'm here because my wife has died," Levine says sadly, "and I have to make arrangements for her funeral."

"Your wife?" says the treasurer. "But we buried your wife two years ago."

"No, no," says Levine, "that was my first wife. This was my second."

"Oh, really?" says the treasurer, leaping to his feet and shaking Levine's hand enthusiastically. "I had no idea you got married again! *Mazel tov!*"

Am I Thirsty

It was his first night in a strange town and the young man fretted in the room he had rented in the rooming house. He was far from home. The room was stuffy. But the worst thing was he couldn't get to sleep. His room was next to that of an old Jew who kept whining, in a hoarse, grating voice, "Oy, am I thirsty!"

He was about to doze off after one or two minutes, but the man would again break the night silence. "Oy, am I thirsty!"

For over an hour this went on. It was past midnight. He needed to get up at six. He pulled a cup out of his satchel, rushed down the hall to the sink, filled it with water, and brought it to the old man's room. The old man was surprised and grateful. At last, the young man thought, we'll get to sleep.

He was drifting away finally in blessed quiet a couple of minutes later when again he heard the old man's plaintive wail.

"Oy, vas I thirsty!"

Unsatisfied

Esther Levy went to Coney Island with her three-year-old grandson. She'd just bought the boy a cute sailor suit and hat, and she watched happily as he played with his toys near the water.

Without warning, a huge wave crashed into the shore and pulled the boy into the ocean. Esther was hysterical. "I've never been religious," she shouted, "But, God, please save that boy! I'll do anything! I'll never ask anything of you again!"

The boy disappeared from view, with Esther crying passionately. The boy appeared briefly, then went under a second time. She was shaking and screaming. He went under for the third time and she shouted still louder, begging God to save her grandson's life.

The ocean suddenly spat the child back on the beach. Esther's final prayer was answered. He was shaken but conscious. Esther picked him up and put him down next to her on a blanket, far from the water. She looked him over up and down for a moment, and then she turned toward the sky and said, "But he had a *hat*, too!"

Special Order

A man went to a baker and asked him to bake a cake shaped in the letter Z. The baker said he'd need a week for this special order. The customer agreed and returned a week later. With some pride, the baker showed him the cake.

"Ach," said the man sadly, "you misunderstood me. You made it a script letter; I wanted it a block letter."

"Well, if you give me another week, I'll make it for you in a block letter," said the dutiful baker.

But when the customer returned the following week, he told the baker he'd wanted it with blue icing and not in red.

The baker apologized and said he could redo it in another week.

A week later the customer returned, and was happy. "Just what I wanted," he said.

"You want to take it with you," asked the relieved baker, "or should I have it delivered?"

"Don't bother," said the man, "I'll eat it right here."

Wherever You Go

In the 1940s, a refugee couple, only months out of a concentration camp and safe in the United States, go to a supermarket in Miami Beach to buy oranges and the clerk asks, "Juice?"

The man nods cautiously. "Yeah." So the clerk puts some little juice oranges in a bag and hands it to him.

When he gets home, he tells his wife, "It's the same as it was in Germany. The first thing he asks is are we Jews. Then he gives me the smallest oranges."

❋

The afternoon get-together was winding down and one of the ladies wanted to compliment the hostess, Mrs. Siegel, on her cookies. "They were so wonderful I ate five of them!" she exulted.

"You had six," Mrs. Siegel noted, "but who's counting?"

❋

The older Jew had vowed to himself that if he ever made money, he'd treat himself to a trip around the world. Through decades of hard work and self-denial, he achieved his goal and finally he was off, traveling the Earth. At one point he found himself trudging through the Sahara, clad only in bathing trunks. After miles of walking across the hot barren sand, he encountered another man.

"Hey," the man says to him, "what are you doing with a bathing suit? There's no water for thousands of miles in every direction!"

"That's true," said the Jew, looking around in awe, "but you got to admit—it's a beautiful beach!"

Test

A woman goes to a kosher butcher to buy a chicken. After rejecting several just on their appearance, she settles on one for careful examination. She lifts a wing and sniffs under it; then she lifts the other and smells. Then she spreads the chicken's legs apart and smells again. She shakes her head with obvious dissatisfaction.

"This chicken's no good," she says to the butcher, "give me another."

"Gimme a break, lady," says the butcher. "Could you pass a test like that?"

Final Wishes

On her eightieth birthday, a Jewish woman makes out her last will and testament and goes to her rabbi to discuss some details. In addition to the monetary bequests, she tells the rabbi she has two final wishes. The first is that she be cremated. The rabbi tries to dissuade her, explaining that it is against Jewish law, but the woman refuses to budge. Finally abandoning what seems a useless argument, he says, "So what's your second request?"

"I want my ashes scattered over Bloomingdale's!"

"Bloomingdale's! Bloomingdale's? Why Bloomingdale's?"

"That way, I'll be sure my daughters will visit me twice a week!"

In the early 1940s, an elderly New York Jew resolved to surprise his wife with a gift of underthings for her birthday. He went to Macy's and began looking through the lingerie section. He finally settled on a brassiere display.

"May I help you, sir?" a young salesgirl asked, but the old man was so embarrassed he could barely speak.

"Do you know your wife's size?" she asked. The man shook his head nervously.

"Well," she said softly, "can you tell me this—are they big?"

"Hoo, boy, are they!", the man replied, turning toward her with a sense of relief. "Hitler should have 'em for tonsils!"

When Max and Manny, two widowers, retired from the clothing business they ran together, they went on a safari to central Africa. One evening, separated from their party, they suddenly heard a terrifying roar.

"Max," said Manny.

"I heard."

"Be quiet! Look behind me! What is it—a lion? a tiger? a cheetah?"

"How do I know?" cried Max, "What am I? a furrier?"

Waiter Jokes

An older woman rushed into an unfamiliar but obviously Jewish restaurant downtown to escape a driving rainstorm. She was exhausted and depressed and looked weighed down by her tremendous shopping bag, which seemed about to give way under its load.

"Waiter—ah—what a day—it's been so awful," she said to a waiter even before he'd made it to her table. "The crowds—the pushing, shoving rude people! The subway! The filth! And then the rain! I could just die. Tell me—could you give me a bowl of chicken soup with some *kreplach*, and a kind word for an old visitor?"

The waiter promptly brought her bowl of soup, placed it on the table in front of her and began to leave.

"Waiter!" she cried, "Please! What about my kind word?"

The waiter regarded her severely, then bent down and whispered confidentially in her ear, "Don't eat the *kreplach*."

Yossel, a popular waiter at the local delicatessen, passes away, and several of his customers engage a spiritualist to try to communicate with him.

"Knock on the table as you did when he was with you," says the medium, "and he will appear."

The old customers knock, and knock some more, but there is no sign of Yossel. They knock louder and louder, and finally they call his name, louder and louder. After this has gone on for ten minutes, Yossel finally appears, cloth over his arm, dignified and unhurried.

"What happened, Yossel?" says one of the group, "Why didn't you come when we knocked?"

"It wasn't my table," says Yossel.

The Jewish tourist in the downtown New York deli asked the waiter what kind of sandwich he had on his plate.

"Corned beef on rye, just like you ordered."

"But I haven't hit any corned beef yet."

"Take another bite."

The tourist did and shook his head. "Still no corned beef."

The waiter looked at him ruefully. "You must have gone right past it."

A customer at Ratner's, the famous kosher dairy restaurant in Manhattan, was concerned he would be late for the theater. Waving at a passing waiter, the diner asked, "Excuse me, do you have the time?" Lifting his eyebrows slightly, the waiter replied in a low voice, "Not my table."

Halpern visits a Chinese kosher restaurant on the Lower East Side. To his amazement, his Chinese waiter speaks to him in Yiddish.

On his way out, Halpern compliments the owner on the meal and remarks, "What an incredible gimmick you've got there—a Chinese waiter who speaks Yiddish!"

"Not so loud," whispers the proprietor. "He thinks we're teaching him English."

A Martian dropped into a Manhattan Jewish bakery. "Excuse me, sir," he began cautiously, tapping on the counter, "but what are these little wheels?"

The counterman regarded the alien indulgently. "They're not wheels; they're bagels. Here, have one." He looked again at the strange individual with a catlike head and long green limbs, who by now was lustily devouring the bagel. "Hey, you from out of town, or what?"

An ethereal smile passed across the Martian's face as he licked his thin lips. "You know," he said, pointing to the bagel, "these would go great with lox!"

A gorilla walked into a Manhattan kosher delicatessen and asked for a corned beef sandwich on rye, pickle on the side, to go. The proprietor put together the corned beef sandwich and told the gorilla it would be seven dollars. He realized he was staring at the animal as he paid, and excused himself. "I'm—I'm really, really sorry," he stammered, "but you know, I've never seen a gorilla in here before."

"And if you keep charging seven dollars for a corned beef sandwich," replied the ape, grabbing his bag and heading for the door, "you never will again!"

Not So Good

"So, Hana," one middle-aged woman commiserated with another, "I hear you've had a hard time."

"Had? You think things are so good now?"

"So what's happened?"

"Ah. In April, we had a fire in the kitchen. In May, my youngest, Joey, was hit by a car. In June, my oldest says she's getting a divorce. In July, my husband, may he rest in peace, died of a heart attack. And next week—" she sighed, near tears, "the painters are coming!"

*   *   *

A beautiful young woman arrives at a dinner party with a crusty little old man. At dinner, the woman to her left remarks about the diamond the young woman is wearing. "I think it's the most beautiful diamond I've ever seen," she says.

"Thank you," says the young woman. "This is the Plotnick diamond."

"Oh? The Plotnick diamond? Is there a story to it?"

"Oh, yes. This diamond comes with a curse, a terrible curse."

"Oh, my," says the lady, "a curse? What's the curse?"

The young woman whispers confidentially in the other's ear, "Plotnick."

A to B

Dorothy Parker claimed the only thing she learned in school was "if you spit on a pencil eraser, you can erase ink."

A well-known short story writer, satirist and critic, she could close a show with her brief reviews in such magazines as *The New Yorker* and *Vanity Fair.* She once wrote of an actress, "She ran the gamut of emotions from A to B," and of an author, "The only 'ism' he believes in is plagiarism." She may have done more than any other individual to inspire the development of contact lenses with her famous quip, "Men seldom make passes at girls who wear glasses." Before her death in 1967, she suggested for her epitaph: "Excuse My Dust."

A & Q

Although the writer and critic Gertrude Stein did not strongly identify as a Jew and her lifelong companion Alice B. Toklas actually converted late in life to Catholicism, these two literary women were responsible for what might be considered an all-time great Jewish deathbed scene. As Ms. Toklas recalled the last conversation of Ms. Stein's life in her memoir, *What Is Remembered*:

> I sat next to her, and she said to me early in the afternoon. "What is the answer?"
> I was silent.
> "In that case," she said, "what is the question?"

Are You Jewish?

A lady approached a very dignified-looking man on the New York subway many years ago and said, "Pardon me for asking, but are you Jewish?"
"No, I'm not."
"Are you sure you're not Jewish?"
"Yes, I'm sure."
"Are you absolutely sure you're not Jewish?"
"All right, all right—if it will make you stop asking, I'm Jewish."
"You know, that's funny," she said. "You don't look Jewish."

Wrong Numbers

Joe Holtzman answered the phone with a brusque "hello."
  "Hello; is this MU 7–4248?"
  "No, lady; you've got the wrong number."
  "Are you sure?"
  "Have I ever lied to you before?"

*   *   *

An older Jewish woman in New York answers the phone.
  "Ma?"
  "Barbara darling, what's the problem?"
  "Don't ask, ma. The kids are sick, the dishwasher's broken, the toilet's backed up and flooding the bathroom. At one o'clock I'm having four friends over for lunch. What can I do?"
  "Barbara dear, don't worry. I'll get a bus and come to the city. Then I'll take the train out to New Jersey. I'll walk the mile and a half to your house. I'll take care of the kids, I'll cook a nice lunch for your ladies, and I'll even make dinner for Jerry."
  "Jerry? Jerry?—who's Jerry?"
  "Your husband, Jerry!"
  "But Ma, my husband's name is David," and she paused. "Is this 898-5066?"
  "No, it's 898–5056."
  There is a long pause and then a gasp on the line. "Does this mean you're not coming?"

Humor with the Yiddish Still In

An older woman, a survivor of Nazi concentration camps, came in the late 1940s to Worcester, Massachusetts, to live with grandchildren. Her big problem, shared with many other new American arrivals throughout this country's history: She couldn't speak English.

One day she went to the supermarket to get a chicken. To make herself understood, she got the butcher's attention, then flapped her arms in the air, and then, for good measure, emitted a sharp cock-a-doodle-do, so powerful it reverberated throughout the large store. The butcher smiled indulgently and spoke quietly to her in Yiddish, telling her in a kind voice that she could merely tell him what she wanted.

"*Baruch ha-shem!*" shouted the old lady, "*Ir redt Edish!*" ("You speak Yiddish!") to him and she smiled. "*Yetzl ken ich upholten reden tzu dir in* English!" (I can stop talking to you in English!)

At a *bris*, the young couple argued violently over the naming of their baby. Each insisted the child be named after their respective deceased father. The *mohel* turned to the mother and asked, "What was your father's name?"

"Berel," she said.

"And your father's name?" he asked the red-faced husband.

"Berel" was the answer.

Taken aback, the *mohel* asked, "Well, what are you arguing about? If both of your fathers were called Berel, then name the boy Berel."

"Ah, no," cried the young mother. "My father, *alav hasholom*, was an *ehrlicher yid* (refined Jew) but my husband's father was a *fehrd gonnif* (horse thief)."

With Solomonic wisdom, the *mohel* turned to both and said, "Very well, call him Berel anyway. If he turns out to be an *ehrlicher yid*, he'll be named after your father. If he grows up to be a horse thief, it will clearly show that he's named after your husband's father!"

After the meeting of the lodge, the men went to a little coffee shop nearby for some pound cake and tea.

"By the way, Nat," Abe said. "I understand you have a *mazel tov* coming, with your brand new son-in-law."

"It's not much of a *mazel tov*," Nat said, with a *ziftz*.

"Why? What's wrong?"

"I've got *takeh tzores* from my new son-in-law. He can't drink and he can't play cards."

"This is *takeh tzores*?"

"Sure. He can't drink, and he drinks. He can't play cards, and he plays!"

*   *   *

Meyer was just finishing the dessert when Ethel said, *"Ich hub epes fahr du tzu zehen."* ("I have something for you to see.")

Said Meyer: *"Vos eez?"* ("What is?")

Ethel brought in a new hat, with all the trimmings—birds, feathers, flowers, the works.

"Nu, how do you like it?" she said, in translation.

"It's all right," Meyer said, cautiously and noncommittally. "And tell me—how much did it cost?"

"A little less than sixty dollars," Ethel said, triumphantly. "Fifty-nine ninety-eight!" ·

"Fifty-nine ninety-eight? It's a sin to spend that much for a hat!"

"Nu-nu, shrei nit. Die averah eez auf mein kupp!" ("Now, now, don't holler. Let the sin be on my head!")

Two friends meet.

"Have you seen Moe lately?"

"Ye-es, I've seen him. He isn't so good."

"Vat seems to be the trouble?"

"I don't know. He said he vent to see a doctor, und the doctor says he's got cancer."

"Cencer shmencer," says the other, *"abei gezunt."* (As long as he's healthy.)

"Milchig" and "Flayshig" Jokes

"Milchig" (dairy) and *"flayshig"* (meat) may not be eaten together, according to Jewish *Kashrut* dietary laws. What's more, utensils and plates used to eat meat foods may not be used to eat dairy foods. This has been the grist for a number of American-Jewish jokes. The following is a sampling.

This story goes back to the days when doctors made house calls. An old Jewish man was very sick, and the doctor made a home visit. He took the man's temperature, checked his pulse, listened to his heart, looked into his eyes. Then he looked around in his bag but couldn't find what he wanted. He said to his patient's wife, "I have to examine your husband's throat, but I don't have a wooden tongue depressor. Please give me a spoon."

The woman asked the doctor, "Do you want one that's *milchig* or one that's *flayshig*?"

A husband and wife were having a terrible argument. They cursed each other at the top of their lungs. The wife slapped her husband. He went berserk. He went to the drawer where she kept her kitchen utensils, grabbed a knife, and came threateningly at her. She cried out, "Jake, Jake, stop, you took a *milchig messer!*"

One woman always threatened to commit suicide. When she made these threats, she would grab a knife and point it to her breast. She would say that if the other family members didn't do what she wanted, she would kill herself. Everyone in the family was cowed by her dramatic threats except her elderly father. When they asked him why he wasn't alarmed, he replied, "Don't you see—she always grabs a *milchig messer?*"

I Don't Believe

It was nearing Christmas. A Jewish mother decided to take her seven-year-old son on a tour of the brilliantly lit and busy stores.

Winding their way through the toy section of a large department store, they were greeted by the ubiquitous Santa Claus.

"Hello, sonny!" said Santa, in a ho-ho-ho voice. "I'm Santa Claus. Tell me what you want for Christmas."

"I don't believe in Santa Claus," said the youngster.

"Don't you believe in Christmas?"

"No, I don't," said the youngster defiantly.

"Well, what *do* you believe in?"

"I believe in Hanukkah, that's what!"

"*Oy,*" Santa exclaimed, "*ah gezunt ahf dein keppeleh!*" (A blessing of health on your head.)

Another Jew

An old Jew was jaywalking across a New York street. A policeman saw him and started to write out a ticket for him. The old man either didn't understand or pretended not to understand and started to make a disturbance. So the officer took him to the jail. Because he was so old they didn't want to keep him in jail so they took him right to the judge, who wasn't Jewish.

The judge saw this was an old man, and that there really wasn't anything to punish him for. So he asked the man, "What do you do for a living?"

The man answered, "I'm a *minyan* man."

The judge never heard of this before so he asked him, "What's a *minyan* man?"

The old man replied, "Well, by my people, when you go to pray you need ten men. My job is wherever there are nine men, I join them to make ten men."

The judge didn't understand this. He said, "So? When I join nine other men I make it ten men too."

The old man smiled broadly and said, "Ah, *frynt* Judge, *bisst eychet a Yid!*" (Friend Judge, you're also a Jew!)

※

Teacher (in socialist Sunday school): Here is your Yiddish essay. It couldn't be worse. I can't understand how one person could possibly make this many mistakes.
Student: Please excuse me, teacher, but I did not do this alone; my father helped me.

※

A man in a theater taps a fellow on the shoulder.
"Do you speak Yiddish?"
"No."
He taps another man.

"Speak Yiddish?"
"No."
He taps a third fellow.
"Speak Yiddish?"
"Yeah, I do."
"Please, vat time is it?"

Generations

In America, the children bring up the parents.

The Jewish mother gave her young son two new shirts for his birthday. The boy rushed to his room, tore off the shirt he was wearing, changed into one his mother had given him, admired it in the mirror, and rushed back, shouting, "Ma, isn't it beautiful?"

"Whatsa matter?" asked his mother sadly. "You don't like the other one?"

Just One Question

The rabbinical student was understandably fearful before leaving his lifelong home in a Polish *shtetl* for a position in America. On his last day at home, he goes to his rabbi, a great talmudic scholar, who offers him an adage that, he tells the younger man, will give him the strength he needs for the struggles ahead. "Life," the rebbe tells him, "is like a cup of tea."

The young rabbi is profoundly impressed by his teacher's remarks and departs for America spiritually uplifted. He has a successful career in the New World and, thirty years later, hearing his rebbe is dying, returns to Europe at great trouble and expense to see him one last time.

After sitting with the old man for an hour, the rabbi says, "Rabbi, I have just one question. For thirty years, every time I've been confused or depressed I've thought of what you said to me that day I left for

America. It's helped me through the worst times. But—to be perfectly honest, you know, rabbi, I never fully understood its real meaning. And now, now that you are about to go on to the next world, perhaps, Rabbi, perhaps you would be so kind as to tell me just what those words mean. Please, Rabbi, tell me, why, why, why is life like a cup of tea?"

The old man looked wearily but deeply into the younger man's eyes for a moment. Finally he shrugged slightly and replied in his weak, raspy voice, "All right, so it's *not* like a cup of tea!"

He Meant Well

An older Jewish woman in the Bronx, a member of the immigrant generation, had a son who went to Hollywood and became a famous and wealthy producer. He would visit her every year but she wouldn't come out to California even though he, of course, offered to pay for her visits. Sometimes he would get conscience-stricken at leaving her behind in New York and try to ease his feelings by getting her expensive presents. One week he called her on the phone and said, "Ma, I'm sending you two presents: a Picasso and a Jaguar."

The next week he called her again, as usual. "Mama, you get the presents?"

"I got one of them!" she replied, near tears. "Which one? Who knows?"

Helping Hand

Comedian Sam Levenson used to say that on his fifth birthday, his father put his hand on his shoulder and told him: "Remember, my son, if you ever need a helping hand, you'll find one, right at the end of your arm."

Hitler's Punishment

During the Second World War, an American soldiers' magazine sponsored a contest for the best answer to the question: What would be the best punishment for Hitler when he was captured?

The competition was actually won by a Jewish soldier with the American army in Italy, who said: "He should live with my in-laws in the Bronx."

Instructions

Bluma gave her granddaughter a sewing kit for her wedding.

"Ah, Grandma, thanks so much for the present! It's beautiful!"

"So enjoy."

"Ah, who wouldn't; everything you've given me, scissors, thimble, thread—but Grandma, just one thing, where's the instructions?"

Pictures

Mrs. Fishman was happily wheeling her new grandson down the street when a neighbor stopped her, looked in the pram, and exulted, "What a beautiful baby!"

"Ah, it's nothing," shrugged Mrs. Fishman. "You think *he's* beautiful? Wait till you see his *pictures!*"

The Venerable Young

When one Jewish couple in their thirties had their first child, the grandmother remarked: "I've been waiting for this baby so long I thought he'd have a beard!"

Mixed News

A Jewish man nearing thirty decided it was time for a heart-to-heart talk with his parents. "Look, Mom, Dad, I've got some good news and some bad news," he said. "The bad news is—I'm gay."

"*Gay*? My God! *Gay*?" screamed his mother. "After that—what could be *good* news?"

"My boyfriend's a doctor," the man replied.

That's a Business?

Four mah-jongg players were discussing their respective sons.

"My son," said the first, "is a lawyer. He makes $170,000 a year. He has a nice home, nice car. He dresses his family in fine clothes. He does all right."

The next woman spoke up. "My son is a psychiatrist. He'll never have to worry, believe me. Two couches he's got! I don't know exactly how much he makes, but it must be $100,000, easy."

"That's very nice," the third woman smiled. "My son deals in stocks and bonds. I can't tell you what he makes, but it's in the high six figures. He has a large house in White Plains, a summer home in Nyack, two cars. He sends his children to private school. His wife has everything she wants. What more could I ask for?"

"My son," said the fourth, "is a rabbi. He makes $20,000 a year but his congregation gives him a three-room apartment."

"A rabbi!" the first woman gasped. "What kind of business is *that* for a Jewish boy?"

Baseball

Grandpa Weber wanted desperately to be closer to his grandson Dave, but the boy was a baseball nut while the older man couldn't make head or tail of the game. One night, when the boy was at a party, the older man watched a key game between the Dodgers and the Giants from beginning to end.

"Davey!" shouted Grandpa when the boy came in, "you know what I did? I watched the big game between San Francisco and Los Angeles—the whole game!"

"Great, Grandpa; what was the score?"

"It was an incredible game—the score was nine to eleven!"

"Who won?"

"Who won?" Grandpa repeated, shrugging. "Eleven!"

Einstein Jokes

Sammy's grandpa, a gray-bearded patriarch from Russia, was confused by the commentary in the papers about Albert Einstein and his new theory of relativity.

"Could you tell me, Sammy," he asked the young man one day, "who's this Einstein and what's this relativity business about?"

"Well, Grandpa, Einstein's the greatest scientist in the world," Sammy began, and then realized his own confusion about the subject. "Well—relativity—it's a little hard to explain. Suppose we put it this way—

ah—okay—if a guy's girlfriend sits on his lap, well—maybe, an hour—it feels just like a minute. But, say, on the other hand, if the same guy sits on a hot stove, a minute would feel like an hour. Yeah. I guess—that's relativity!"

Grandpa looked more confused than ever. For a moment he kept his own counsel, musing, a strange expression of disbelief in his eyes. Then he looked at Sammy. "Tell me, Sammy," he asked, incredulous, "from *this* your Einstein makes a living?"

The Einsteins once visited the Mount Wilson observatory in California. "What's that one for?" Mrs. Einstein asked, pointing to a particularly complex-looking piece of machinery. The guide told her the machine was used to determine the shape of the universe. "Oh, really," Mrs. Einstein is reported to have replied, "my husband does that on the back of an old envelope!"

Reprieve

An astronomy professor from the university was finishing his lecture to a joint meeting of the synagogue's sisterhood and men's club.

"Some of my colleagues," he said, "believe our own sun will probably die out within the next four or five billion years."

"*How* many years did you say?" shouted out Mrs. Ehrlich in a worried tone from way in the back.

"Four or five billion," the scientist replied.

"*Whew!*" said Mrs. Ehrlich. "I thought you said *million!*"

Light Bulbs and J.A.P.s

How many Jewish mothers does it take to change a light bulb?
None. "It's all right—I'll sit in the dark!"

*   *   *

How many Jewish-American Princesses (J.A.P.s) does it take to change a light bulb?
Two. One to pour the Tab, one to call Daddy.

How many Zionists does it take to change a light bulb?
Four. One to stay home and convince someone else to do it, a second to donate the bulb, the third to screw it in, and the fourth to proclaim that the entire Jewish people stands behind their actions.

Q. What does a J.A.P. make for dinner?
A. Reservations.

Q. What's a J.A.P's idea of natural childbirth?
A. No makeup.

*   *   *

A midrash on Sinai from twentieth-century America:
When Moses came down from the mountain after seven long weeks and met the anxious multitude, he told them:
"I have some good news and some bad news.
"First—the good news. He's got His list down to ten."
The people cheered. "And what, Moshe, is the bad news?"
Moshe frowned. "Adultery is still on it."

How the Jews Got the Commandments

God was looking around to see which nation would bring his command-ments to the world. He went to the Italians and asked: "Would you receive my commandments?"
"What's one of them?" the Italians asked.
"Thou shalt not steal," said God. The Italians weren't sure they could live with that, so God went nearby to the Germans.
"Would you accept the burden of my commandments?" asked God.

"What's one of them?" asked the Germans.

"Thou shalt not kill," said God. The Germans weren't sure they could live with that, so God offered His commandments next to the French.

"Would you be the nation to bring my commandments into the world?" God asked the French.

"Well, what's one of them?" they asked.

"Thou shalt not commit adultery." The French weren't sure they could live with that, so next God ran into Moses, of the Jews.

"Moses," He said, by now a little frustrated. "Will Israel be the nation to receive my commandments?"

"How much do they cost?" Moses asked.

"They're free," God said.

"We'll take ten!"

Questions

Why does a Jew always answer a question with another question?

Why *shouldn't* a Jew always answer a question with another question?

Why do Jews have short necks?

(Questioner shrugs.)

Don't Depend on Me

An old man, less than five feet tall and wearing a black yarmulke, hobbled in with a cane to NASA headquarters in Washington. He strode up to the receptionist and, brandishing a piece of paper in her face, asked, "Who do I talk to about this ad?"

ASTRONAUT TRAINEES SOUGHT
Ages 21–35, perfect physical health. Advanced degrees in science and engineering required. Air Force experience preferred. Contact NASA.

The receptionist told him the name of the chief of training.

"Tell him I'm here. The name is Tishman, Irving Tishman."

"Well—Mr. Tishman, excuse me, but on whose behalf are you here?"

"On whose behalf? For my own behalf!"

"Well—Mr. Tishman, do you have an advanced degree in science?"

"No. Also I'm not an engineer. I don't know anything about the Air Force. And besides, I am eighty-one years old and not in such good health!" he said, quite satisfied with himself.

"Well—I don't quite understand; why do you want to see Mr. Smith?"

"I just want to let him know," said Tishman, raising his cane slightly, "that on *me*, he should not depend!"

A distraught man was telling his Jewish psychiatrist about his strange dream. "I saw my mother," he said, "but when she turned around to look at me, she had your face. That really scared me, I woke right up, and couldn't get back to sleep. I just lay there in bed, my mind blank, waiting for morning to come, and then I got up, drank a Coke, and came right over here for my appointment. I hoped you'd be able to help explain the meaning of this really scary dream."

The psychiatrist gazed steadily in silence at the man for a full minute before responding: "A *Coke*? Is that a breakfast?"

Faith

Levine was on his first mountain-climbing expedition when a storm broke. A ledge gave way and he fell fifty feet straight down—managing, incredibly, to stop his fall by grabbing onto the thick sturdy branch of a tree.

"Help! God!" he screamed.

An enormous voice came out of the sky. "Levine?"

"Yes! Yes!"

"Do you trust me?"

"Certainly!"

"You have total faith?"

"Yes! Yes!"

"Let go of the branch!"

"What?"

"Let go of the branch!"

Levine was quiet for several seconds. "Excuse me," he finally said in a cracking voice. "Excuse me for asking, but—is anybody else up there?"

"Adam," said Eve, "after we eat the apple, we're going to do *what?*"

19

JEWS AS SEEN
BY OTHERS

Impressions

Jews are members of the human race—worse than that I cannot say of them.
—Mark Twain

They own, you know, the banks in the country, the newspapers. Just look at where the Jewish money is.
—George S. Brown, Chairman, Joint Chiefs of Staff, mid-1970s

The two most important characteristics of the Russian Jews are their short stature and their contracted flat chests.
—Study by American social scientists, 1885

Intellectual avidity . . . intensity of feeling, high imagination . . . the extremest idealism, with an utter disregard of the restraining power of circumstance and conditions . . . a character often full of imagination, aspiration and appreciation.
—James B. Reynolds, head social worker at New York's University Settlement House, on the qualities of the new Jewish immigrants that struck him most

The Jewish children are the delight of their teachers for cleverness at their books, obedience and general good conduct.
—The U.S. Industrial Commission, ca. 1900

The lips were pressed together again and again with a long, deep and almost solemn emotion; such kisses as English-speaking people exchange only at moments of direct tragedy or the most passionate exaltation. These kisses are, I think, peculiar to Russian Jews.

—American newspaper reporter at Jewish
wedding, ca. 1885

Life has always admitted the existence of the "intelligent, intellectual and refined" Jews of whom our correspondent speaks. It sympathizes with them in their suffering from the acts of the great majority of their race. *Life* has never criticized the Jews for their religion, but for their racial characteristics.

—*Life Magazine*, 1901

It will be long before they produce the stoical type who blithely fares forth into the wilderness, portaging his canoe, poling it against the current, wading in torrents, living on bacon [*sic*] and beans, and sleeping on the ground, all for "fun" or "to keep hard."

—Sociologist Edward A. Ross,
The Old World in the New,
1914

The Jews could be put down very plausibly as the most unpleasant race ever heard of. As commonly encountered they lack many of the qualities that mark the civilized man: courage, dignity, incorruptibility, ease, confidence. They have vanity without pride, voluptuousness without taste, and learning without wisdom. Their fortitude, such as it is, is wasted upon puerile objects, and their charity is mainly a form of display.

—H. L. Mencken, 1922

We need oil, not Jews.

—Bumper sticker, 1974

Reflections

Mary Murphy had a crush on the boy who sat next to her in school and spoke of him constantly to her mother.

"What *is* he?" she asked her mother one day.

"What do you mean?" asked her mother quizzically.

"You know, what *is* he?" Mary persisted.

"Why—he's an American, of course, just like you," her mother said.

"Oh, I know *that*," responded Mary, "but what *else* is he?"

"Oh, that," said the mother, "well—he's a Jew."

Mary gazed at the window with a pensive air. "So young," she mused sadly, "and already a Jew."

Ten-year-old Tom Wilson was late to Sunday school and the teacher wanted to know why.

"I had a fight with the Jewboy across the street," said Tom. "I punched him in the nose."

The teacher was shocked and angry. "A Christian doesn't hit anybody, Tom," she moralized. "And a Christian must be *especially* careful in the way he treats a Jew. Don't forget that Jesus was a Jew."

"I don't know about that," said Tom with a defiant air, glancing back at his buddies. "Maybe Jesus was a Jew, but God sure is a Presbyterian!"

This section attempts to provide a suggestive sampling of some ways Jews, as a people, have been viewed in the folklore of other Americans over the past two centuries. As Jews have become progressively more assimilated into American society and, at least in outward appearance, increasingly indistinguishable from their neighbors, it may be difficult to recall the curiosity and concern evoked by Jews in America of a more insular time.

Body and Soul

Folklorist Nathan Hurvitz reports the persistence into the twentieth century in the United States of beliefs that the Jew was somehow physically different from the Christian. A non-Jewish folklorist told Hurvitz that, as a youth, he had been led to believe that Jewish women have a tuft of hair like a cottontail rabbit's tail at the base of the coccyx, or tailbone. Mrs. Hurvitz, as a teenage girl in the 1930s in Cleveland, was asked by a Polish girl if Jewish girls menstruated "just like other girls."

Another young Jewish woman in 1930s Cleveland reported that an Irish girl with whom she worked seemed to be chronically staring at her forehead. When asked about this, the girl explained she was trying to see the scars where the Jewish girl's horns had been amputated. The belief that Jewish children are born with horns that are amputated early in life has been widely reported. Some non-Jews have reported their belief that Jews have a characteristic odor. Southern mountain whites have reported to anthropologists their belief that Jews habitually carry knives.

Other beliefs, also primarily reported from some rural or mountain folk, center around circumcision, which members of some of these relatively isolated groups appear to believe somehow changes a man's sex. One folk expression from 1930s Cleveland reflected awe over the Jews' reputed genital size, saying, "They cut off a piece before they know how long it's going to be."

Who Is a Jew?

I keep a jewelry store in Memphis, and have much dealing with soldiers. Few of those I have come in contact with have ever discovered the fact of my being a Jew. A captain who pretends to have great faith in me came to my store some time ago, and begged me to go with him and look at a certain golden chain which he wanted to purchase, and which the little "Irish Jew" around the corner kept for sale.

"You know," said he, "I can't believe what this Irish Jew tells me and wish you would go with me and look at the chain whether it is good gold or not." . . . I told my friend the captain, however, that he was quite right—that Irish Jews were least of any trusted. I went with him, looked at the chain, and on my recommendation he purchased it.

A chaplain of an Illinois regiment, in speaking to me of two brothers, remarked that one of them was a Jew, and a mean man; and "the other not a Jew and a perfect gentleman!" Some soldiers congregated in my store the other day, got to speaking as the best way of discovering whether a man was a Jew or not. One of them stoutly asserted that every Dutchman was a Jew. . . . But one of them finally capped the climax by asserting that every man who fell on the original price he asked for an article was a Jew!

—*Harper's Magazine*, 1865

The Merchant

Tare and Tret, Gross and net,
Box and hogshead, dry and wet,
Ready made, Of every grade,
Wholesale retail, will you trade?

Goods for sale, Roll or bale,
Ell or quarter, yard or nail,
Every dye, Will you buy?
None can sell as cheap as I!

Thus each day Wears away,
And his hair is turning gray! O'er
his books, Still he looks,
Counts his grain and bolts his locks.

By and by he will die—
But the ledger book on high
Shall unfold How he sold
How he got and used his gold.

—Nevada City *Nevada Journal*

Local Affairs

Circumcision.—We were induced to witness the rite of circumcision at the house of a Jewish friend, on Wednesday. The officiating priest was the Rev. Mr. Laski of San Francisco. The ceremony consisted of first lighting a couple of candles, putting on of hats by the whole company present, procuring a glass or two of wine, and reading a portion of Hebrew. Second, introduction of the child, nipping in the bud, and a short ceremony of reading. Third, partaking of hospitalities, more reading which was all Hebrew to us, and adjournment. Those curious in such matters are advised to obtain further information by seeing for themselves, or consulting a rare old book a part of which is said to have been written by Moses.

—Nevada City *Nevada Journal* (12/11/1857)

The English novel *Harrington*, republished in an American edition in 1818, illustrated how prejudices against the "Jew Peddler" were used and transmitted in the Old World and the New.

One day, the subject, Harrington, a six-year-old boy, stayed up a bit late. He watched from his room as an old, dark-complexioned man with a long white beard slowly approached the house, carrying a lantern and a big bag over his shoulder and crying rhythmically, "Old Clothes! Old Clothes!"

The maid insisted it was time for Harrington to go to bed. When the boy tried to resist her, she said: "I'll call to Simon the Jew," pointing to the peculiar old man, still crying in his strange accent, "and he'll come up and carry you away in his great bag."

For several weeks she kept warning Harrington about "Simon the Jew." When that story grew stale, she told the lad stories of other Jews who found and kidnapped children to crucify and then sacrifice for their secret midnight feasts. She warned the boy to be careful on the streets to be sure the Jews didn't catch him, saying there was no way to know what they might do to him.

The East Side and Its Observers

The Lower East Side of Manhattan in the early years of the twentieth century was widely considered the most crowded place in the world. Close to a million people—three quarters of them Jews—lived at one time in less than one square mile in lower Manhattan. If all Manhattan had been as dense as the predominantly Jewish Eleventh Ward, it could have held 25 million people. And if that density were extended outward, the entire population of the world today could fit into the New York metropolitan area.

Government officials despaired of their ability, to accurately estimate the population of the East Side. A witness testifying before the U.S. Immigration Commission put it this way:

> At the hour of retiring, cots or folded beds and in many instances simply mattresses are spread about the floor, resembling very much a lot of bunks in the steerage of an ocean steamer. . . . The only way to properly determine the census of one of these tenements, would be by a midnight visit, and should this take place between the months of June and September, the roof of the building should not be omitted.

Gentile observers of the Lower East Side used to wonder at the Jew's incredible ability to live in crowded places. Edward Alsworth Ross, a professor of sociology at the University of Wisconsin, provided this scholarly assessment in his 1914 study of immigrants, *The Old World in the New:* "Save the Italians, more Jews will crowd upon a given space than any other nationality."

He explained soberly:

Centuries of enforced Ghetto life seem to have bred in them a herding instinct. No other physiques can so well withstand the toxins of urban congestion. . . . As they prosper, they do not proportionately enlarge their quarters.

More Questions than Answers

A sampling of contemporary magazine articles during the Great Migration:

Are the Jews a Pure Race?

Are the Jews an Inferior Race?

Will the Jews Ever Lose Their Racial Identity?

Is There Room for the Jews?

What It Means to Love a Jew

What It Means to Be a Jew

I Am a Jew

Jews: Nation or People?

Jews Are Not Aliens

Why the Jew Is Too Neurotic

Money and Business:
Jokes on Jews

Miss Cohenstein: Why, Fader, he has moneysch to burn!
Cohenstein: Nonsense, mein schild! You can'd insure moneysch!

—*Puck* (1898)

Son: Fader, dis pook says as moneysch does not pring happiness.
Father: No, mein Sohn, It's der interest vot you gets on der moneysch vot makes you happy.

—*Puck* (1898)

Gilhooly went into Mose Schaumburg's store on Austin Avenue, to buy an umbrella. Mose showed him two kinds of umbrellas, which looked very much alike, one of which was a dollar and the other a dollar and a half.

Gilhooly examined them critically, and asked: "What is the difference between them?"

"Half of a tollar," responded Mose.

—Texas Siftings (1882)

Information

Ikey: Who vos it dot said "peezness is peezness?"
His father: I don't know, Ikey. I would like to know who efer said it vosn't.

—*Puck* (1897)

Mr. Isaacs: Mein Sohn, vich would you radder haf, if some von offeredt to gif it to you, seat in der United States Senate or a seat in der Stocks Exchange?
Isaacs Junior: Vhy, a seat in der Senate, Fader; it gosts more!

—*Puck* (1899)

Mr. Aaron Levy, a gentleman of the Jewish persuasion, was sleeping soundly on board a ship that had become disabled. Suddenly he was awakened by the cry, so welcome to all else on board, of "A sail! a sail!"

Jumping up from his berth, forgetful for the moment of his whereabouts, the ruling passion strong in death exhibited itself in the auctioneers' cry: "A sale! A sale! Where? where? Put it off, whatever you do, until I've got my catalogue ready."

Powerful Saint

Jim Hickey: Are there any saints in the Jewish calendar, Isaacs?
Isaacs: Ja; vun—Ein Gustomer!

—*Puck* (1891)

Abraham: Vere vos you all dis day?
Ikey: Fadder, I vos in de woods, an' I saw a nest full of young burts, and dey did nothin' but sing "Cheap. Cheap!"
Abraham: Mine cracious, Ikey! Get all dem burts you can! I'll hang dem in der frond window and let dem holler 'bout de goots.

—*Life* (1895)

A Good Location

Isaacheimer: How is dot cousin of yours gettin' along?
Cohenstein: Pretty good. He vas doin' business on Broadway.
Isaacheimer: On Broadway? And he's only six months in der country! Vot line is he in?
Cohenstein: Matches, shoe laces undt suspenders.

—*Puck* (1896)

Our Israelite friends have sometimes been accused of lugging the idea of money into every sort of conversation. This is not always the case. In front of a Lexington Avenue residence, one evening this week, a young man said tenderly to his girl: "Well, we are at last enkaget. And it is so sweet that I to not even look at the cost."

—*Judge* (1881)

In a Shipwreck

"Oh, Isaac! ain't it awful"

"Yes; but ain't yer glad now dat we didn't buy first-class tickets, Rachel?"

—*American Wit and Humor* (1907)

A Stock Market View

Ah, Jacob, I fear I hafe not many tays to live.

Nonsense, Fader, you have as much as t'irty years yet pefore you.

Noh, Jacob, no! The Lord isn't going to take me at 100 when he can get me at 70.

—Puck (1889)

Mrs. Ikelstein: Ron mit der doctor, k'vick, Solomon! Ter paby is swallow't a silver tollar!

Mr. I.: Vos it dot von I lefd on der dable?

Mrs. I.: Yes, dot vos id. Hurry mit der doctor.

Mr. I.: Don'd get oxcited, Rachel, it was gounderveid.

Old Sexual Folk Humor on Jews

A Jew advertised twin beds for sale. The ad read: "For sale, twin beds, one hardly used."

A young woman went to confession and told the priest she had broken the Seventh Commandment. "Don't worry," he said, "just put two dollars in the poor box, say an Act of Contrition and you're forgiven."

"But, Father," she said, "you don't understand. There was perversion." The priest said in that case he couldn't forgive her.

So she went to the minister and told him she had broken the Seventh Commandment. He told her not to worry but to put two dollars in the prayer box and he would pray for her. "But you don't understand," she said. "There was perversion involved." The minister said he couldn't help.

Finally she went to the rabbi and told him everything. He said, "I'll pray for your forgiveness."

"But how can you help me when the minister and the priest couldn't?"

"Oh, those *goyim*," he said impatiently, "vat do they know about fency lovink?"

A blacksmith, a woodchopper, and a Jew masquerade in a harem as eunuchs but are found out when they have erections. The blacksmith's penis is mashed; the woodchopper's is chopped off. The Jew is then asked his occupation. "Me? I'm a nobody," he said, "I peddle lollipops."

Told by Jews

Often it is hard to draw the line between jokes told on Jews by others and those told by Jews on themselves, as in the following, more contemporary jokes, recorded among Jewish schoolchildren though probably not originated by them.

Why did the Jews wander for forty years in the desert?
Somebody dropped a quarter.

* * *

Q: What are the three most important Jewish holidays?
A: Yom Kippur, Rosh Hashanah, and September 25.
Q: Why September 25?
A: That's when the new Cadillacs come out.

A similar joke published in a national magazine a century earlier went:

Q: What are the two biggest days in the Jewish calendar?
A: The Feast of Passover and the opening of the dramatic season.

Why do Jews have big noses?
Air is free.

The Case of Leo Frank

"Our little girl—ours by the Eternal God—has been pursued to a hideous death and bloody grave by this filthy perverted Jew of New York. It was determined by rich Jews that no aristocrat of their race should die for the death of a working girl . . . While the Sodomite who took her sweet life basks in the warmth of today, the poor child's dainty flesh has fed the worms . . . When mobs are no longer possible, liberty will be dead!"
                                   —Tom Watson, *The Jeffersonian* (Georgia, 1915)

Nineteen thirteen was the year Mary Antin's *The Promised Land* appeared. America was Antin's Promised Land: a world so different from that which the European Jewish immigrants had left, she argued, as to rightly relegate the fears of their persecuted past to history. Not only, suggested Antin, was anti-Semitism a relic of that soon-to-be-forgotten past, but the immigrants' customs and identities as Jews were perhaps no longer relevant in this new Promised Land.

But 1913 was also the year of the murder trial of Leo Frank, an event that would become legendary in its own time and lead ironically to creation of both the B'nai B'rith's Anti-Defamation League (ADL) and the revived Knights of the Ku Klux Klan. Frank's case both was propelled by powerful folklore images and passed into folklore itself as, in the words of one historian, "perhaps the most lurid manifestation of anti-Semitism in American history." The case came to be probably the most debated in American history up to its time, cited outside Georgia as an example of "trial by newspaper," "trial by mob," and a distinctly American form of anti-Semitism.

Leo Frank was the son of a well-off German-Jewish family who came to Atlanta from New York to manage the factory of the National Pencil Company, in which his uncle was a partner. (Frank was voted president of Atlanta's B'nai B'rith lodge, a position to which he would be re-elected from jail.) Mary Phagan, a fourteen-year-old employee found murdered in that factory, was the daughter of a dispossessed Georgia tenant farm family pushed off their land by economic change, like most of the newcomers to Atlanta who had doubled its population in the previous fifteen years.

In a 1913 Atlanta half of whose population lived on streets without water mains and more than a third in neighborhoods without sewers, those impoverished, displaced, fundamentalist rural people maintained an intense pride and a chronic anger toward the outside forces that seemed to be ruining their way of life. Only their fallen economic position led them to regretfully let their women go to work in what were considered degrading, sinful factories where children worked sixty-six hour weeks for as little as 22 cents. When Mary Phagan's badly beaten body was found in Frank's factory, the city's newspapers pounced on the sensational crime. (*The Georgian*, Atlanta's newly-acquired Hearst paper, tripled its circulation in 1913 to become the best-read paper in the South.) Ten thousand people came to view the girl's body. The corrupt, inefficient Atlanta police hadn't caught up with the city's rapid growth. In the previous two years, for example, eighteen black women had been found murdered and none of the killers brought to justice. For the murder of a white girl, such incompetence was unthinkable; the papers and public screamed for a solution. The Mayor publicly—less than a week after the murder—warned the police: "Find this murderer fast—or be fired!" But the department was no more on top of this crime than anything else; police failed to even look for fingerprints before letting the factory be overrun by curious citizens. Frank was the last person to admit seeing Mary alive. A month after her killing, he was indicted.

Frank had three strikes against him, in the view of white rural-bred Georgians: He was a Northerner, a capitalist and a Jew. Frank's indictment offered an ideal focus for decades of accumulating resentment. The image of a sweet defenseless girl at the mercy of her lustful Yankee Jew industrialist boss seemed to combine the most powerful available images of good and evil.

The only clear evidence against Frank was the testimony of Jim Conley, the factory's black sweeper, the logical suspect himself if not for Frank's indictment. A month before Frank's trial, Atlanta solicitor-general Hugh Dorsey argued for an hour and a half to prevent the city's grand jury from indicting him for the murder. Later, after Conley was sentenced to a year for complicity in the crime, his lawyer claimed that his client had been the true murderer.

Conley had served numerous jail terms for various crimes and would later serve fourteen more years on a chain gang. He gave a variety of stories to police between his arrest and Frank's trial. Finally he claimed to have helped Frank carry Mary's body to the coal cellar where it was found. He testified of confidential knowledge Frank was a "sexual pervert" though the nature of his highly touted perversion was never clarified.

Conley's contradictory statements fit Southern white stereotypes that blacks might lie until they ran out of lies and then fall back in desperation on the truth. A detective told the packed courtroom just how the police had finally "gotten the truth" from Conley: "We pointed out things in his story that were improbable and told him he must do better than that. Anything in his story that looked to be out of place we told him wouldn't do."

The case built into something of a contest between anti-Semitic and anti-black prejudice. Though a habitual drunk and thief, Conley became a folk hero among many poor Atlanta blacks for his assertiveness in fingering his employer. It was rare for any white man in the South to be convicted on the testimony of one black, let alone with a criminal record, especially in a capital case.

Frank and his lawyers in fact used shared white stereotypes about blacks. "No white man killed Mary Phagan," Frank declared shortly after his indictment. "It's a Negro's crime through and through." Frank's chief lawyer called Conley a "dirty, filthy, black, drunken, lying nigger." But Conley's tenacity in standing by his basic story through three days of cross-examination helped convince many of Frank's guilt. A black bootblack was quoted thusly by a reporter:

> Well, boss, dem niggers down on Decatur Street, day ain't talken of nothing but Jim Conley. He got de best of de smartest of 'um. Nobody can fool er nigger like Jim!

Solicitor-General Dorsey had lost several big cases and his political ambitions were sinking. Evidence supporting Frank's innocence was suppressed—for example, tests showing teeth marks on the victim's shoulder didn't match Frank's. After the trial, numerous prosecution witnesses recanted, claiming they had been threatened, bribed or confused by days of unremitting questioning. After a talk with authorities, doubtless reminding them of Georgia's law mandating death for perjury in capital cases, many changed their minds back again. The press meanwhile made a fair trial hard by continually printing rumors and accusations, particularly about Frank's alleged sexual proclivities, fueling public hysteria.

The jury had to pass twice daily through angry crowds shouting anti-Semitic slogans. One then-teenage Jew who attended every day of the month-long summer trial recalled: "The yokels lined the streets yelling at the jury every night when they went to the hotel: 'Hang the Jew!'" The jury, judge and defense attorneys were warned repeatedly they wouldn't leave the courtroom alive were Frank released. Observers felt if the jury acquitted Frank, he would be dragged from the courtroom and lynched then and there. The judge interrupted the lawyers' summations on a Saturday for fear a verdict announced on a Saturday night would cause a bloody riot.

Frank was confident of acquittal and his prominent and respected attorneys over-confident as well in the apparent weakness of the state's case, never seeming to fathom the trial's social nature. They called over 100 witnesses to attest to Frank's character—virtually all Northerners, Jews or Frank's employees—their testimony easily outweighed in the jury's eyes by that of local people who said Frank had an improperly familiar way of talking to young women.

Dorsey charged the defense in his summation with raising the "race question," then told the jury: "They (Jews) rise to heights sublime, but they also sink to the lowest depths of degradation!"

The jury convicted Frank in under four hours and was roundly applauded in front of the courthouse by a mob of thousands that carried Dorsey away on its shoulders. Frank's lawyers brought appeals that dragged on for two years. The trial judge publicly expressed doubt about Frank's guilt but saw no basis for appeal. The state Supreme Court upheld the verdict 4 to 2 and an appeal to the U.S. Supreme Court failed.

Agitation grew nationwide for a new trial. Besides the mob pressure that prejudiced the trial, numerous witnesses had now recanted, Conley's lawyer insisted on his guilt and new evidence emerged. More than a million Americans (including over 10,000 Georgians) signed petitions supporting Frank; many public figures, including one of Georgia's Senators and six state legislators, urged commutation of his sentence. But the furor was widely seen in Georgia as an attack on the Southern way of life and a conspiracy by Jews and Northerners to get one of their own off the hook.

Former Georgia congressman and Populist Party leader Tom Watson, who ran for vice-president with William Jennings Bryan in 1896, was the most prominent voice of anti-Frank feeling. He had a huge following among white rural Georgians through his weekly *Jeffersonian* and other publications, which were the only link many had with the larger outside world. Watson asked his readers if it were possible to punish a Jew for a crime and warned commutation for the "jewpervert" would bring the bloodiest riot in the South's history. Watson ran a picture of Frank retouched with thickened lips and popping eyes, writing

> You could tell Frank is a lascivious pervert . . . by a study of the accompanying picture: look at those bulging satyr eyes, the protruding sensual lips, and also the animal jaw.

Mary Phagan, on the other hand, was the

> little factory girl who held to her innocence . . . a daughter of the people, of the common clay, of the blouse and overall, of those . . . who in so many instances are the chattel slaves of a sordid commercialism that has no milk of human kindness in its heart of stone!

Georgia's popular outgoing Governor John Slaton received more than a thousand death threats during his consideration of the Frank case. Anti-commutation rallies were held regularly across the state and by mid-1915 mass meetings against Frank were actually taking place daily in Atlanta. Under this pressure, Slaton carefully examined evidence, heard the lawyers, visited the crime scene and commuted Frank's sentence to life in prison, issuing a 10,000-word explanation and suggesting to friends a pardon might follow when the public had calmed.

A mob of many thousands armed with guns and dynamite marched in response on Slaton's home outside Atlanta, surging past Atlanta police and turned back only by state militia, who stayed for days while armed men kept trying to attack the mansion through woods surrounding it. Mobs burned the governor in effigy across the state and the next week, when his term expired, Slaton fled and did not return to Georgia for more than three years. Several Georgia communities told Jewish residents to leave town. A boycott of Atlanta's Jewish merchants was organized, coordinated by cards received by thousands of Atlantans reading:

> STOP and THINK! Before you spend your money, shall it go to a fund to PROTECT MURDERERS, to buy Guvernors? . . . Now is the time to show your true colors; to show your true American blood . . . AMERICAN GENTILES, IT IS UP TO YOU.

A few weeks after his commutation, Frank was stabbed in the throat by a fellow inmate who said he had been called "from on high" to kill the

Jew. Frank enjoyed a near-miraculous recovery. But the next month twenty-five men recruited from the "best" people of Mary Phagan's hometown of Marietta outside Atlanta, wearing goggles and hats pulled down low over their faces to disguise their identity, cut the phone lines leading to the Milledgeville Prison Farm, overcame weak security and seized Frank.

The party brought Frank back to Marietta, where his continuing calm, evident sincerity and insistence on his innocence in the face of death actually convinced all but four of the group they could forgo the lynching. But realizing posses were out seeking them across the state and it was too late to return their prisoner, the party went back resignedly to its plan, though at least one of the group refused to take part. Frank was hanged and the men left without waiting for him to die. A participant said the group felt no spirit of vindictiveness. "They felt," he said, "it to be a duty to the state and a duty to the memory of Mary Phagan." An amateur photographer took snapshots of Frank's body, which tourists were soon able to buy for a nickel in half Georgia's rural drugstores. None of the lynchers was prosecuted although their identities were well-known and many even gave newspaper interviews. The group that lynched Frank became the nucleus of the revived Klan. The case stood as a powerful illustration of American anti-Semitism and reduced for many Jews the attractiveness of the South as a place to settle.

Nor were Jews reassured by the political aftermath of the Frank case. Not only had Governor Slaton, once a shoo-in for the Senate, been driven into exile. Hugh Dorsey, Frank's prosecutor, was handily elected Governor in 1916 and Tom Watson Senator in 1920.

❀

A Jewish character was once taken out of a radio soap opera. The sponsor's representative explained to James Thurber of *The New Yorker*, "We don't want to antagonize the anti-Semites."

The Six-Day War

The Six-Day War of 1967, in which Israel defeated several Arab countries almost overnight, led to a distinct strengthening in the Jewish image held by many Americans, most particularly in the South.

*   *   *

During the anxious period directly before the Six-Day War, national
Jewish organizations sought statements from prominent American politicians supporting Israel. A group of well-known Georgia Jews approached then governor Lester Maddox, a noted right-wing and
segregationist militant, for a statement. Maddox agreed quickly and
commented that "everybody ought to be for Israel." Since Maddox was
not known for being close to Jewish interests, curiosity was expressed as
to why he would offer such an opinion. Maddox reportedly winked and
said, "I ain't never seen a camel yet that can outrun a Cadillac."

*   *   *

The following is a joke that made the rounds after the Six-Day War:
An Arab commander is told an Israeli soldier has been spotted in a
certain secluded valley in the desert. He sends ten of his best men to
intercept the Israeli, but he waits a couple of hours and they don't come
back. He sends another platoon to check on them. They don't come back
either. Then he sends out the better part of his regiment. A night and
another day passes; they aren't heard from. After waiting many hours
and conferring with central command, the commander proceeds into the
valley with his entire army. As they trek through the desert, they see in
the distance, first a few men lying on the sand. Soon they are in an
incredible scene of total devastation—thousands of men dying, tanks
destroyed, utter catastrophe around them. Then finally, one of the
wounded men cries out to them in Arabic with his last breath: "Go back!
Go back while you still can! It's an ambush! There's two of them!"

Street Rhymes

Folklorist Nathan Hurvitz observes that a "vehicle which is often
characterized by hostile attitudes and which carries and reinforces such
attitudes is the street rhyme."

As folklorist B. A. Botkin wrote in his *A Treasury of American Folklore*:

One of the most fascinating fields for the students of beliefs and customs as these enter into the vernacular poetry of folk rhymes are the jingles and doggerels of childhood. . . . Like popular jests and sayings in general, play rhymes have their local and contemporary sources or applications, illustrating the principle that "The happiness of a witticism or of a taunt hangs on its relationship to some sort of angle to the customs and notions prevalent in a country."

Botkin points out that when these rhymes are "recited or chanted as a rhymed or rhythmic accompaniment to rope-skipping or ball-bouncing, as a formula for counting out, as a nominy or set speech, as a taunt, quip or crank, they have social and poetic interest apart from their game or pastime usage."

In this section, the rhymes are divided into the following categories: Moses Rhymes; Red, White, and Blue Rhymes; Hostile Rhymes; Bilingual Rhymes; and Miscellaneous Rhymes.

Moses Rhymes

Moses rhymes refer to Moses as "King of the Jews." The following were used as rope-skipping and ball-bouncing rhymes from World War I to about 1925.

Holy Moses, King of the Jews,
Sold his wife for a pair of shoes.
When the shoes began to wear
Holy Moses began to swear.

Holy Moses, King of the Jews,
Sold his wife for a pair of shoes.
When the shoes they did not fit
Holy Moses threw a fit.

Holy Moses, King of the Jews
Say "It" and I'll give you my shoes.

The child saying these rhymes would offer to give his shoes if the hearer would say "It" correctly, but the hearer would be required to give his shoes to the child saying the rhyme if he did not say "It" correctly. The hearer would, of course, repeat the line, "Holy Moses, King of the Jews," and the child saying the rhyme would retort, "You didn't say 'It,' give me your shoes!"

*   *   *

The following rhyme was known in New York City around World
War I:

Where was Moses when the lights went out?
Down in the cellar eating sauerkraut.

Botkin in *A Treasury of New England Folklore* reports two variants of this
rhyme. The first reads:

Where was Moses when the lights went out?
Down in the cellar with his shirt-tail out.

The second was reported as "a dialogue spoken when a light is blown
out by a breeze."

Where was Moses when the lights went out?
He was in the dark with his shirt-tail out.

Red, White, and Blue Rhymes

These rhymes were popular before World War I and through the 1920s.
Some were used by Jewish children exclusively, while others were
popular among both non-Jewish and Jewish children.

Red, white, and blue
Your (my) mother (father) is a Jew.

The following rope-skipping rhyme was known to Hurvitz in Cleveland in 1925.

Red, white, and blue
The color of the Jews.

Some red, white, and blue rhymes were known to non-Jewish
children and then used by Jewish children, while others were known
only to Jewish children.

Red, white, and blue
Your mother is a Jew
Your father is a curlyhead
And so are you.

Red, white, and blue
Your mother is a Jew
Your father is a Chinaman
And so are you.

Red, white, and blue
Your mother is a Jew
Your father is a Dutchman
And so are you.

Red, white, and blue
Your mother is a Jew
Your father is a bagel
And so are you.

This rhyme was known in Boston about 1940 and in Los Angeles in the 1950s.

True blue
She's a Jew.

Hostile Rhymes

These rhymes, which express negative attitudes about Jews, were chanted by Jews as well as non-Jews. In some cases, Jews changed the words around to fit those who were taunting them.

The following rhyme was the parody of a song in the animated cartoon film *Snow White and the Seven Dwarfs*, first released in 1937.

Hi ho, hi ho
I belong to the C.I.O.
I pay my dues
To a bunch of Jews
Hi ho, hi ho.

A variant expresses the same sentiment negatively:

Hi ho, hi ho
Don't join the C.I.O.
Don't pay your dues
To feed the Jews
Hi ho, hi ho.

A derisive attitude toward Jews is in the following rhyme, known in New York City about 1920:

In 1492
Your father was a Jew
He walked on the grass
And fell on his ass
In 1492.

A variant was known in Brooklyn in the 1940s:

In 1492
Columbus was a Jew
He sat on a rock
And hurt his cock
In 1492.

The following rhyme and its variants were sung to an Oriental tune during the 1920s and 1930s:

They don't wear pants
In the hootchie kootchie dance
And the dance they do
Is enough to kill a Jew.

They don't wear pants
In the southern part of France
And the dance they do
Is enough to kill a Jew.

The girls in France
Wear tissue paper pants
And the things they do
Is enough to kill a Jew.

In Detroit, Jews turned the last rhyme around:

The girls in France
Wear tissue paper pants
And the things they do, *oy oy*
Is enough to kill a *goy*.

The following rhyme known in New York during the early 1940s appears to be related to the rhymes sung to the tune of the popular song, "It Ain't Gonna Rain No Mo'," published in 1923.

A rabbi sat on the railroad tracks
saying his *brocus* (prayers)
Along came a choo-choo train
And knocked him in the *tocus* (buttocks).

And some more:

Abie, Abie
King of the Jews
Piss in his pants 'n'
Shit in his shoes.

—Waco, Texas (ca. 1930)

I took a piece of pork and stuck it on a fork,
And gave it to the curly-headed Jew, Jew, Jew.

—Cincinnati (1886)

"A Rogue of a Jew."

Jack sold his egg
To a rogue of a Jew,
Who cheated him out
Of half of his due.

The Jew got his goose,
Which he vowed he would kill,
Resolving at once,
His pockets to fill.

—Mother Goose (pre-1940)

Bilingual Rhymes

These rhymes either start off with letters of the Hebrew and Yiddish
alphabets and rhyme them with English words, or simply combine
English and Yiddish.

Aleph, gimmel, beis.
Hit the teacher in the face.

Aleph, beis, gimmel, dollar
Hit a Jew and make him holler.

Matzohs, matzohs
Two for five
That's what keeps the Jews alive
Now I know their fav'rite dish
Matzohs and gefilte fish.

A rhyme reported in many different places in the 1920s and 1930s is the following:

Amo, amas, amat
A *mame's*, a *tatte's*, a *kind*
(Also: A *mame's*, a *tatte's*, a *zun*).

The rhyme was used by Jewish students in their elementary Latin classes. The second line, in Yiddish, is "A mother's, a father's, a child." (Also: "A mother's, a father's, a son.")

"Hocus-pocus, kiss my *tocus*" found its way into the street expressions of American-Jewish children. This phrase was used in the following rhyme known on the East Side of New York before World War I.

Tammany, Tammany
Hocus-pocus
Kiss my tocus
Tammany!

"*Tocus*" is also used in the following defensive rhyme by Jewish children against Christian teachers, known in Detroit about 1940.

Shakespeare
A kick in the rear
Merry *kratz-mine*-tocus
And a happy new year.

The following was particularly popular in Los Angeles and New York:

A nickle a *shtickle*
Was quite a rhyme
But now the same *shtickle*
Will cost you a dime.

This rhyme, known on the East Side of New York between 1915 and 1920, describes some common problems of those years.

Papa we gotta move uptown,
Cockroaches on the walls they creep,
The mice they play while we sleep,
Papa we gotta move uptown.

Papa we gotta move uptown
On the top floor in the back
Haise vasser nishtoh kein lek
(Hot water there isn't a drop)
Papa we gotta move uptown.

The following gained sufficient popularity to be used by first- and second-generation American Jews. It may be making fun of Jewish immigrant males who rushed to become "Americanized" by cutting off their beards:

Yankee Doodle went to town
A-riding on a *fehrdl* (horse)
Er fohrt arein in barber shop
Un shert zich op dos berdl.
(He rides into the barbershop and has his beard cut off.)

The following rhyme was originally a Christian hymn. Corrupted by generations of Sunday school students, it was further corrupted by Jewish children who may have learned it from non-Jewish friends:

One Sunday morning
In St. Peter's yard
With Moses playing fullback
And Jesus playing guard
The angels on the sidelines
In harmony did yell
When Moses scored a touchdown
And beat the team from Hell.

  Stand by gosh by Jesus
  Hocus-pocus
  Kiss my tocus
  Stand by gosh by Jesus.

Miscellaneous Rhymes

These jingles may have originally been parts of songs or parodies, but they took on a separate existence as street rhymes.

Izzy, Ikey, Jakey, Sam
We're the boys who eat no ham
City College, City College
Rah, rah, rah.

The following is from Brooklyn, 1920–25:

Here comes the bride
All dressed in white
Here comes the groom
Skinny as a broom

Here comes the Jew
All dressed in blue

The following rhyme was known in Los Angeles and was reported by a non-Jew who learned it from her Jewish sister-in-law:

Roses are reddish
Violets are blue-ish
If it weren't for the *goyim*
We'd all be Jewish.

The following rhyme, widely known after 1920, expresses the acceptance of a stereotype:

If you need an operation,
Dr. Cohen is my relation,
I can get it for you wholesale.

A similar rhyme was originally part of a joke. It took on a separate existence and became well known in many communities:

My name is Fink
And what do you think
I press clothes for nothing?

Camp Parodies and Cabin-Tent Songs:

Shul days, *Shul* days
Good old fashioned *shul* days
Matzoh, herring and gefilte fish
We were brought up by a *Yiddishe tish*

I remember when I was a boy
We used to say *oy, oy, oy, oy*
Binst a gonniff un a schmutziker goy
When we were a couple of kids.

—Detroit (1935–40)

We were girls from Fresh Air College
All we do is gather knowledge
Eat gefilte fish and *knaidlach*
Don't you think we're kosher *maidelach*
When we graduate we will marry
Izzy, Ikey, Abie, Harry
Don't you think we're grand
We're the girls from Fresh Air Camp

—Detroit (1939–40)

Alleman, Alleman
Allemane Iago, *Ess* a bagel
Ishkie, *kishkes*
Hit 'im in the *kishkes*
Hokus pokus try and choke us.

—Camp Aliyah, Los Angeles

Give a yell, Give a yell,
Give a good, substantial yell,
and when we yell we yell like Hell,
And this is what we yell:

 Ish kabibble

 Ess a Bagel

 Ishkes, Fishkes, Hit 'em in the *kishkes*

The following are examples of rhymes recorded among Jewish children in the 1960s:

In 1814 we took a little trip
Along with Colonel Jackson on the mighty Mississipp'.
We took a little bacon and we took a little beans
But the bacon wasn't kosher so we had to eat the beans.

—to tune of "Battle of New Orleans,"
sung on Jewish day camp buses,
Queens, N.Y. (ca. 1960)

I went to the doctor,
The doctor done said,
"Rosie's little nosey
Needs short'nin' bad."

—Los Angeles Jewish day camp
(ca. 1967)

Street rhymes have also been one manifestation of the particular
folklores linking blacks and Jews in America (discussed in the following
section). As in other folkloristic expressions, there are rhymes that link
blacks and Jews together from the standpoint of the majority culture, as
well as those by members of each group about the other.

Some rhymes, presumably from a white Christian standpoint, link
blacks and Jews in some way as allies against the majority culture, or in
their common status as "out" groups.

The following doggerel, for example, was reported in northern
Arizona during Franklin D. Roosevelt's fourth presidential campaign in
1944, purporting to be a letter from FDR to his wife Eleanor:

Dear Eleanor:
Roses are red
Violets are blue
You court the niggers
and I'll court the Jews
And we'll stay in the White House
As long as we choose

*   *   *

Sheeny, sheeny
Alley picker
Your father was a Jew
And your mother was a nigger.

—Detroit (1935–40)

The following black rhyme suggests a link between blacks and Jews as
allies against "whites":

Baa Baa Black Sheep, have you any wool?
Yes, sir, yes sir, two bags full.
One for the Black man, one for the Jew
Sorry, Mr. Charlie, but none for you.

The following anti-Semitic street rhymes were reported by black writer Richard Wright in his book *Black Boy* (1945):

Jew, Jew, Jew
    What do you chew?

Jew, Jew,
Two for five
That's what keeps
    Jew alive.

Bloody Christ killers
    Never trust a Jew
Bloody Christ killers
    What won't a Jew do?

Red head
    Jewish bread
Five cents
    A Jewish head.

Red, white, and blue
    Your pa was a Jew
Your ma a dirty dago
    What the hell is you?

A rotten egg
    never fries
A cheating dog
    never thrives.

This one was reported by black writer Nathan Hare:

Akka, Bakka soda cracker,
Akka, Bakka boo
If your daddy chews tobacco
He's a dirty Jew.
Out goes the rat
Out goes the cat
Out goes the lady
With the seesaw hat.

And More

The day was dark and dreary
The rain was falling fast
Lightning struck a bald-headed Jew
And knocked him on his ass.

*   *   *

I hear a rumblin' in de skies,
Jews, screws, de fi dum?
I hear a rumblin' in de skies,
Jews, screws, de fi dum.

—Black ditty, Atlanta (ca. 1875)

Blacks and Jews in American Folkore

Besides the image of the Jew brought over by European settlers, refined in the New World and carried down in white American folkore, a separate, overlapping folklore tradition developed among black Americans.

Blacks and Jews have had a distinct relationship throughout much of American history, and special attitudes, traditions and folklore grew up around it. In the eyes of the white Christian majority, blacks and Jews were long seen as having a special relationship. Jews were outsiders because they were not Christians, blacks because they were not white, and white Christian folklore often implied a link, even an alliance, between the two.

Black religion emphasized the Old Testament; blacks often identified with the ancient Hebrews in the liberation of Israel from slavery in Egypt. Yet in Christian myths they had in common with white neighbors, they also shared traditional European folklore ideas about the Jews and money, and the Jews and the death of Jesus.

From the Jew's early days in America, especially in the South where black slavery was an ever-present fact of life, a conflict arose between two impulses in the American Jew: one, an ethical tradition that commanded him to everywhere fight injustice and predisposed him to see the world in sharply moral terms; the other, the overwhelming desire to become part of America, to commit himself to the New Land and succeed on its terms, which strengthened the tendency to see things increasingly as his American neighbors did. Jews were visible as both abolitionists and slave-dealers. Rabbi Isaac Mayer Wise, a prominent spokesman for increasingly assimilated American Jews of his time, responded to abolitionists who criticized Southern Jews for their silence on the slavery question:

> Go down South and expound your doctrines to the community; and if you dare not do it, why do you expect the Jews there to stand in opposition to the masses of people?

In more recent times, a broadly similar conflict led to Jews taking leading roles in the civil rights movement while often making Southern Jewish communities, wanting to continue living in harmony with white Christian neighbors, acutely uneasy.

Decision

This ambivalence led to the story about the civil rights trial in a Southern state where, by unlikely chance, all twelve jurors turn out to be Jews. The jury deliberates and deliberates for days as the entire state, white and black, waits anxiously. Finally, after two solid weeks of deliberations, the jury re-enters the courtroom. "What's your verdict?" asks the judge.

"Your Honor," says the foreman, "we've decided not to get involved."

🌞

The Jewish immigrant peddler from Europe had no tie to the Southern racial code. From the Jewish standpoint, the white Southern dirt farmer or "redneck" often evoked memories of the violent, ignorant, anti-Semitic peasant of the old country; blacks, on the other hand, were unlike anyone the Jew had ever seen.

To the surprise of both blacks and whites, he would automatically call blacks "Mister" and "Missus," visit their homes, and treat them as respectfully as he did whites. When he got his own store, he would let blacks try clothes on before buying and refund for clothes that had been taken home if they weren't right. He'd run a "one-price" store for all and offer credit to black customers. What to him were the simple imperatives of running a business and treating customers right led to a special friendliness with blacks and a suspiciousness on the part of many Southern whites.

Although Jews were Caucasian racially, they tended to occupy, in the minds of all three groups, a somewhat mysterious third category. Jews certainly weren't like other whites, though they clearly weren't blacks. Many younger Jews have used the term "white" as their ancestors used "goy" to refer to WASPs and other non-Jewish groups. Black writer Claude Brown, in his *Manchild in the Promised Land*, illustrated in unflattering terms one folkloristic black view of the difference between Jews and "crackers":

> Some white people is crackers and some of them is Jews . . . White people is all mean and stingy. If one of them is more stingy than he is mean, he's a Jew; and if he is more mean than he is stingy, then he's a cracker.

The section that follows includes samplings from traditional black folklore stories about Jews, white Christian folklore about blacks and Jews, anecdotes and jokes about blacks and Jews, Jewish adaptations of black folklore, and some more contemporary material.

Some Black Folklore Tales

A white man, a Jew and a Negro all went to Hell.

The devil made a proposition to all the folks who were there, that anybody who would give him five dollars, he would let out. So the whole group started going out, everybody standing in line to give the devil his five dollars.

Finally, the line sort of stopped moving and the people in back started saying, "What's the matter? Why don't you take their five dollars and keep the line moving?"

"It's not me," said the devil. "It's these three men arguing up here. Now, this white man just gave me his five dollars and he can go on out. But the Jew wants me to let him out for $4.98. And the Negro wants me to let him out now, and he says he'll see me Saturday, when he gets his pay."

Sagacious Jew

There was four fellows, a Jew, an Italian, a white man, and a colored man. They was all four buddies. So they were sitting down talking one day, and the colored fellow says, "Let's make a pot; the first one dies gets five dollars apiece to carry him across Jordan." Well, in a couple of months the Italian died. So the colored fellow told them, "Boys, let's go and give our Italian friend his five dollars." The Jew says, "B'jesus, how can we give him the five dollars? He's dead and in the box." So the white fellow says, "Oh, that's easy, just follow me and I'll show you what to do about it."

So they line up and go in. The white fellow takes out his billfold, pulls five dollars out, and drops it in the box. The colored man was next; he takes his billfold out, and drops five dollars in the box. And the Jew he was last. He reaches out and gets the ten dollars was dropped in the box, and writes the Italian a check for fifteen.

One time there was a Jew, an Irishman and a colored man. A man was going to give away a million dollars, and he wanted to see who was the smartest of all. Whoever was the smartest he was going to give the million dollars. So he asked the Irishman, "What would you do if you went to sleep and dreamt that you had a million dollars and woke up and found that you had a million dollars?"

The Irishman, being a wise man, jumped up and said, "I guess I'd invest it. Get me a business of some sort, try to get me another million." So he said, "All right."

He went to the Jew. He asked the Jewish fellow, "Uh, supposing you went to sleep, dreamt about a million dollars, woke up, and found you had a million dollars? What would you do?"

The Jew jumped up all excited. He said, "I'd buy me a couple of meat markets, kosher markets, and so forth, try to get me another million."

He came to the colored guy. He said, "Uh, if you went to bed and dreamt about a million dollars, woke up, and had a million dollars, what would you do?"

The colored guy jumped up and said, "Shit, I'd go back to sleep and try to dream me up another million."

Once a blessing was given out in Heaven. There was a Jew, a white man, and a Negro man there, and God was going to bless 'em all; give 'em all something they could live by. First he asked the white man what he would rather have most in life. He said, "Common knowledge." He asked the colored man what would he want. He told God he wanted all the money he could spend, all the cigars he could smoke, a new Cadillac, and a pretty woman. Last he asked the Jew fellow what he would have. He said, "Just give me Sam's address and I'll get all I need."

What Won't They Do

In the South there was the story of the young black slave who was nowhere to be found the day she was to go to a new mistress, a Jewish woman. Finally, the young woman was found hiding under a bed. "I don't want to go live with Miss Levy," she said, crying and terrified.

"Why not? She's a fine lady, and would be a kind mistress, and you won't have hard work there."

"Oh, no," cried the girl, "but, Miss Lakes, they say Miss Levy is a Jew; and if the Jews kill the Lord and Master of the world, what won't they do to a poor little nigger like me?"

*   *   *

Blacks who bought trinkets from the "Jew peddler" often didn't associate him with the legendary "Children of Israel" who God freed from slavery in Egypt. In another story, one "mammy" told her mistress that since she would surely never reach the Land of Canaan, she would like to see some of the Children of Israel wherever she could. The white woman, hearing of the arrival of a peddler nearby, told her servants where the peddler would be, that she might see a "Child of Abraham." But the black woman soon came back, disappointed and angry.

"Missus," she's supposed to have said, "Dat's no Chillen o' Israel. No, dat's de same ol' Jew Peddler w'at sole me dem pisen, brass yearrings las' 'tracted meetin' time. Sich low down white man as dat, he neva b'long to no Lan' o' Cainyan!"

Jokes and Slurs on Blacks and Jews

In the following folkloristic story of white Christian origin, the Jew is seen as the offspring of a black-Chinese union:

> Mandy had decided to marry and gave her missus notice. "And whom may you be marrying?" asked the missus, just to be polite.
> "A very nice gentleman, Ma'm," Mandy replied. "His name is Sing Lee."
> "Why, that's the Chinese laundryman!" the missus exclaimed with horror, and began painting for Mandy the disadvantages of miscegenation, especially in the matter of children.
> The Negro woman nodded her head understandingly. "Ah just knows they'll be Jews, Ma'am," she agreed. "But Jews ain't so bad."

* * *

Q: What do you get when you cross a Negro with a Jew?
A: You still get a janitor, but now he owns the building.

Sayings

You look sharp as a Jew salesman at a nigger picnic.
Niggers love to ride around like a Jew in a Cadillac.
—Durham, North Carolina (ca. 1950)

A nigger is a Jew turned inside out.
—Cleveland (1930s), North Carolina (1950s), L.A. (1970s)

Peddler Pearlman and the Blacks

The following is a description of the first encounter of David Pearlman,
just arrived in Americus, Georgia in 1884 from Lithuania, with black
people. David is being taught peddling by his cousin Sam.

The boy (David Pearlman) quietly opened the fence gate, tiptoed onto the
front porch, looked back at Sam for assurance, tapped lightly on the door,
half-hoping that no one inside would hear either the knock or his
near-whispered and near-unintelligible, "Meestaah Poodeluh." To his
dismay, he heard a commotion coming from inside the shack. The door
suddenly flew open, yelling children poured out and danced around him
yelling, "It's him. It's him," and he unexpectedly found himself looking
into the eyes of a large, smiling black woman.

The startled boy, never having seen a black person before and momentarily
unable to distinguish between her skin and the darkened background of the
shack's interior, thought he was confronting two bodiless eyes and an empty,
floating dress. He stepped back in fright, screamed, "A *dybbuk*" (evil spirit) and
landed flat on his back pinned by the weight of his pack. . . .

Sam looked down at his young apprentice, laughed, and helped him to
his feet after unstrapping the pack. By this time, the blacks from the other
shacks which Dave had not seen from the road were congregating around
the two peddlers. Dave did not know what to make of the scene. The first
imagery that made sense of what he saw was that of a demon dance he
had heard the superstitious women of Baisagola (Lithuania) describe.
Terrified, he spit in the air all around him, uttered a *kayn-ahora* to ward off
the Evil Eye, and started to turn to run, only to be stopped by a smiling
Sam who had Dave's arm in a vise-like grip.

As he cautiously followed Sam's instructions and spread the goods in the
pack out on the ground, constantly glancing over his shoulder in order not to
be surprised by these "dark strange-looking" people, occasionally spitting in
their direction for good measure, he was equally stunned by what next took
place. The blacks said to his cousin in disunion: "Please, Mr. Sam take it
out . . . Let us hear them words . . . Say somethin' holy. . . . Read to
us . . ." Sam then took out his prayer book and began praying in Hebrew
accompanied by a discordant chorus of "amens" and "hallelujahs."

(Reprinted by permission of the American Jewish Historical Society)

Some Black-Jewish Jokes

Around 1920, four Jewish businessmen shared a private suite on a Pullman car on a cross-country train trip. Every hour on the hour, they would ask the porter for one thing or another—food, drinks, water, soap, soda, towels, cards, paper. They would ask him questions about arrival times, the weather, anything and everything. Not once did they tip the poor fellow a cent. When they arrived in Los Angeles, the porter piled up their luggage and waited for the generous tip he felt he richly deserved. But each one in turn took his luggage and walked off without a word.

The porter stood there stunned—not just disappointed, but genuinely surprised, and as he mused about the exhausting two-day-plus trip, angry. After five minutes, just as the disgusted porter was about to get back on the train, one of the Jews rushed up with an apologetic look, and said, "Porter—please—forgive us—you were so good to us. We were so preoccupied with the deal we're trying to make here it just slipped our minds that we hadn't repaid your kindness." With that, he handed the porter two crisp $20 bills.

The porter was aghast. This was by far the biggest tip he'd ever received. He felt terrible for having misjudged the four Jews and wanted to make amends himself.

"Mister," he said, shaking a little, "thank you. Mister—mister—Now I know they's wrong, that story about you Jews crucifying our Lord. You Jews couldn't have crucified him. Maybe—maybe—I bet you all just worried him to death!"

The story is told of the Southern lady who, during World War II, decided to invite a few soldiers from a nearby base home for Thanksgiving as a patriotic gesture and to provide company for her younger female relations. She called the office of the camp chaplain and explained she would like four dinner guests. Before she hung up, the lady said, "And Chaplain, I would prefer it if none of the soldiers were Jewish."

"I understand," said the chaplain, and he promised it would be done. On Thanksgiving Day, at the appointed time, the lady opened her door to greet four handsome black soldiers. "There must be some mistake," she said, taken aback despite her deeply bred politeness.

One of the soldiers spoke up. "No, ma'am," he said. "No mistake. Captain Goldberg's a real smart man. He don't make no mistakes."

In financial circles in New York, the joke was told of the black messenger who tried to deliver a message personally to J. P. Morgan. The haughty receptionist rebuked the man, saying, "*You* can't go in *there*— that is *J. P. Morgan* of Morgan and Company!"

"That's all right," the messenger replied, tapping his chest. "*I'm* the *coon of Kuhn*, Loeb & Company!"

A black man was reading a Yiddish newspaper on a New York subway train many years ago. At a stop, a Jew standing next to him asked him cautiously, "Excuse me—but—are you Jewish?"

The black man looked up at the Jew mournfully. "Why—" he replied, "don't you think I got enough *tzores* (troubles) being a *schvartzer* (black)?"

Two black men recently arrived in New York some years ago passed a synagogue on Rosh Hashanah when suddenly they heard the long loud blast of the ram's horn.

"What's that?" said one man, startled, to the other.

"Oh, that's just the Jews blowing their *shofar*," said the other.

"Oh, *Jesus!*" said the first man. "It's like I always say, those people *do* know how to treat their help!"

Color Cautious

To avoid possibility of giving offense to anyone who might be listening by referring to "blacks" or "schvartzers" in public, one older Jewish woman always called blacks "bluers."

At least one black man was given the middle name Nevertheless by his mother, who picked it out of the Book of Exodus.

Topping the List

The Anti-Defamation League of B'nai B'rith was one of the many organizations to file an amicus (friend of the court) brief opposing racial segregation in schools with the Supreme Court before the Court's 1954 decision. Since the organizations were listed alphabetically, the ADL came out on top, prompting one Southern Jew to complain to an ADL official. "I don't mind you slipping in a word or two, but why in hell did you have to head the list?"

*   *   *

A Jewish storekeeper in eastern North Carolina mused about a black boycott of white stores in the 1960s. "At first, when we were boycotted, we were bitter," he said, "we had done so much for the Negro here—the only credit store in town, the first to start lay-a-ways, the first to hire Negro clerks.

"But when it actually came," he said, looking at the bright side, "we often thought how frightened we would have been if we had been the only store downtown *not* boycotted."

"Freedom Cap"

During the historic 1965 civil rights protest march from Selma to Montgomery, Alabama, a contingent of marching Reform rabbis noted that priests and ministers were wearing their respective ministerial insignia, which made them recognizable as clergy. The rabbis, on the other hand, were dressed in ordinary street clothes and realized that they were therefore unrecognized as representatives of Judaism in the demonstration. A Rabbi Braude of Providence, Rhode Island, suggested the rabbis put on yarmulkes, which they proceeded to do. The idea soon swept the crowd and many Jews and non-Jews followed suit, dubbing the yarmulke "the Freedom Cap."

The Golden Plans

The Southern Jew, usually sympathetic with the black struggle for equality yet chronically insecure as a "foreign" minority himself, fearful of alienating the white majority and becoming himself the target of the mob, walked a cautious line.

A traditional Jewish weapon in their ambiguous position was humor. During the 1950s, when racial segregation was first frontally attacked in the South and became a major national issue, Harry Golden, editor of *The Carolina Israelite*, proposed his "Golden plans" for "reasonable" resolutions of the racial crisis that could leave everyone happy. While Golden was in fact a strong civil rights movement supporter, the tone of his proposals often seemed to parody the earnest wish for "reasonable" compromise, for avoidance of conflict, that characterized the position of the typical Southern Jew.

Southern whites, Golden argued, for example had long accepted "vertical" integration. Black people were already free to shop at the same supermarket counters and hand their money over to the same bank tellers. Nobody even suggested segregating the races vertically. It was only when blacks wanted to *sit down* next to whites that any problem arose.

In order to comply with the 1954 Supreme Court decision integrating public schools yet maintain the Southern tradition of "sitting-down" segregation, Golden urged the North Carolina Legislature to pass a state constitutional amendment taking seats out of all public school class-rooms. This would, Golden argued, eliminate the danger Southerners perceived to their way of life while also saving millions in tax dollars. New desks would be made to be used standing up, like old-fashioned bookkeeping desks. Since no one in the South was bothered as long as blacks were standing up, this would eliminate the integration problem. Since students weren't learning to read sitting down anyway, Golden argued, standing might well spur them on.

The Golden Carry-the-Books Plan

Golden noted that the white South had not only accepted "vertical" (standing) integration but also "45-degree-angle" integration, as when blacks worked as servants or domestic workers. Golden proposed that black male students arrange to meet white classmates at designated street corners a block from their schools, and that the black students ritually carry the white students' books into the school building. Black female students would be asked to wear miniature aprons to school over their street dresses. Golden realized these compromise proposals would ask a lot from the emerging black consciousness. But in the tradition of "cooler heads prevailing" he argued, in his best-selling book *Only in America*: "This would settle the matter even for the most outspoken white supremacists."

The Golden White Baby Plan

In the 1950s, the only way blacks could get into Southern "whites-only" theaters and other such public places was to enter with a white child, presumably as the latter's sitter. To at once allow blacks into the movies while simultaneously aiding white working mothers, Golden proposed whites set up neighborhood pooling points where they would leave their children. Any time a black person wanted to go to the movies, she or he could just pick up a white child and go. With time, Golden foresaw, blacks would set up factories where they would manufacture their own ersatz white babies. Whenever blacks wanted to attend a film, concert or opera, they would just bring along their white dolls. The dolls, Golden advised, should be made with blue eyes and blond curls, which, he predicted, would give black couples priority for the best seats in the house.

The Golden "Out-of-Order" Plan

This plan, to integrate public drinking fountains with the acquiescence of white segregationist sentiment, was so daring Golden proposed it only after a successful pilot test. In place of the discredited "separate but equal" doctrine, Golden proposed a new face-saving regime of "separate but out-of-order." Stores would shut off their "whites-only" drinking fountains, placing "out-of-order" signs on them. After the first couple of days, experiments in a test location demonstrated, whites would gingerly start using the "colored" fountain. By the end of three weeks, everyone freely drank the still "segregated" water. Whites, Golden argued, could accept integration if assured the facilities were still separate, albeit out-of-order. The signs, he proposed, should be kept up for at least two years.

"We must do this thing gradually," he cautioned.

Prayers on the Bus

More recently, in 1971, Golden came up with a daring plan to resolve
controversies over busing and school prayer in one fell swoop with a
constitutional amendment allowing prayers in school buses but not
classrooms. There would be praying buses and non-praying buses. This
way, Golden argued, prayer would stay out of the classrooms, the
churches would be happy, and anti-busing parents would go along
because their children would get more chance to pray. His plan, Golden
assserted, "is not only gradual enough to satisfy Southerners, but it will
reinvigorate the parishes."

The "Nineteen Messiahs"

Few stories better capture the tension between segments of the national
Jewish community around the 1960s black civil rights movement than
the tale of those whom Birmingham, Alabama, Jews sarcastically dubbed
the "nineteen messiahs." These were nineteen Conservative rabbis who
left their 1963 annual convention to head south to that city, where the
forces of Bull Connor and "Southern justice" were facing off against
Martin Luther King Jr. and the civil rights movement.

King was leading a planned and massive series of marches and
nonviolent demonstrations in Birmingham, targeted as one of the
South's most oppressive cities for blacks. Meanwhile, large elements of
the Ku Klux Klan massed on the city's outskirts. Sheriff "Bull" Connor
promised to fill Birmingham's jails, which he more than did in May and
June 1963, arresting over 10,000 people, primarily young blacks, and
keeping them in makeshift detention centers.

On May 4, with King already in jail (for his first-ever defiance of a
court order), some 500 blacks demonstrated at a Birmingham park to
protest police brutality. When the crowd didn't break up promptly in
response to sheriff's orders, police dispersed the demonstrators with
dogs and billy clubs, followed by huge water gushes from high-pressure
fire hoses. "I want to see the dogs work," reporters quoted Connor
exulting, "Look at those niggers run!" Birmingham got full worldwide
press coverage; the pictures showed dogs ripping the clothes off fleeing

blacks and youths huddling together against the tremendous force of the fire hoses.

At their annual convention at Kiamesha Lake in upstate New York's Catskill Mountains, the Conservative movement's Rabbinical Assembly debated a resolution condemning the Birmingham violence. Faced with news of the latest outrages, some of the rabbis felt consumed with a sense their approach was inadequate to the demands of the moment. The time had come, they argued suddenly, for action. Nineteen of the rabbis volunteered to head immediately for Birmingham to lend their support to King's forces; the money for their trip was raised right in the convention hall.

When the rabbis' plane touched down in Birmingham, to their surprise, an anguished delegation of Birmingham Jews was there to meet them. Only two of the rabbis met with the community group. The rest, exhausted from their 2:15 A.M. arrival, headed for the night—to the local Jews' shock—to the black motel where King's entourage stayed. The delegation was further angered by the rabbis' evident disinterest in meeting with them and the need to intercede with a black welcoming party in order to get the rabbis' attention at all. The rabbis had, in fact, been discouraged by their Assembly from contacting the Birmingham Jewish community. In this way, it was felt, any adverse impact on local Jews from publicity over their visit would be minimized.

The Birmingham group argued that public participation by the rabbis in demonstrations would inflame anti-Semitic sentiment. The white segregationists, they pointed out, had long insisted the civil rights movement was "Jewish-Communist" inspired. Dynamite sticks had recently been found on the synagogue steps. A convention of the anti-Semitic National States' Rights Party was to begin in a few days.

Birmingham was not a liberal city.

Only a few years before, a proposed city ordinance to allow racially mixed baseball teams to play in Birmingham had lost nearly 3 to 1. They noted that whites staying at a black motel violated a city ordinance. They argued that Birmingham Jews were trying, behind the scenes, to improve race relations, by working with new moderate officials for the general repeal of segregation ordinances.

The rabbis were undeterred by the delegation's arguments. The local Jews had considerable success, however, in persuading the local press of their concerns; while the national media gave wide publicity to the rabbis' Southern journey, the Birmingham papers ignored it.

The rabbis spoke in black churches the next day and taught black students the Hebrew dance *"Hava Nagila."* That afternoon, the local Jewish Community Council met and agreed the rabbis must go. Word leaked out they planned to lead a protest march that Friday morning. After initial reluctance, fourteen of the rabbis agreed to another meeting that night at the offices of Birmingham lawyer and community leader Karl Freedman, who advised them: "You'll kill my wife and daughters."

One of the rabbis responded that Jews had been passive too long. "We know the risks," he said, "we may be shot at, but it is time."

A Birmingham woman told the rabbis, "You will go back on the plane heroes. . . . I hope your convictions are strong enough to carry the blood of my children on your hands."

One of the rabbis wrote later that what seemed to stun the Birmingham delegation most was that the rabbis came South "at the call" of the black leadership. "It appeared," he said, "to outrage the natural order of things."

The climax of the story failed to happen. By the time the rabbis arrived in Birmingham, a temporary truce was in fact being arranged in the ongoing confrontation and, as it turned out, the Friday morning march the rabbis expected to take part in was cancelled. The rabbis instead left town Friday morning in time to be home for *Shabbes.* The results of their trip were ambiguous. They had demonstrated solidarity with the civil rights movement without taking part in a public demonstration. They had outraged the local Jewish community while the larger white community remained relatively unaware of their presence. Shortly thereafter, Gaston's Motel, where they had stayed, was bombed; local Jews blamed the incident on the rabbis' visit, though the motel's being King's headquarters, it might seem, would have been enough.

BIBLIOGRAPHY

American Jewish Archives.

American Jewish History.

Ausubel, Nathan, ed. *A Treasury of Jewish Folklore.* New York: Crown, 1948.

————. *A Treasury of Jewish Humor.* Garden City, NY: Doubleday, 1951.

A Bentel Bref.

Berkow, Ira. *Maxwell Street.* Garden City, NY: Doubleday, 1977.

Berson, Lenora E. *The Negroes and the Jews.* New York: Random House, 1971.

B'nai B'rith International Jewish Monthly.

Botkin, Benjamin A., ed. *American Anecdotes.*

Brown, Claude. *Manchild in the Promised Land.* New York: NAL–Dutton, 1966.

Cohen, Sarah Blacher, ed. *From Hester Street to Hollywood.* Bloomington, IN: Indiana University Press.

Collier's Encyclopedia.

Cowan, L. M. *The Wit of the Jews.* Nashville, TN: Aurora Publishers, 1970.

Cowan, Robert E. *Forgotten Characters of Old San Francisco.* Ward-Ritchie Press, 1938.

Davidson, Sara. *Loose Change.* New York: Doubleday, 1976.

Dinnerstein, Leonard. *The Leo Frank Case.* Athens, GA: University of Georgia Press, 1987.

Donaldson, Norman, and Donaldson, Betty. *How They Died.* New York: St. Martin's, 1980.

Eichhorn, David Max. *Joys of Jewish Folklore.* Middle Village, NY: Jonathan David, 1981.

Elovitz, Mark H. *A Century of Jewish Life in Dixie: The Birmingham Experience.* University, AL: University of Alabama Press, 1974.

Encyclopedia Americana.

Encyclopedia Britannica.

Encyclopedia Judaica.

Evans, Eli. *The Provincials: A Personal History of Jews in the South.* New York: Atheneum, 1976.

Farnsworth, Marjorie. *The Ziegfeld Follies.*

Fein, Isaac M. *The Making of an American-Jewish Community: The History of Baltimore Jewry from 1773 to 1920.* Philadelphia: Jewish Publication Society, 1971.

Fried, Albert. *The Rise and Fall of the Jewish Gangster in America.* New York: Holt, Rinehart & Winston, 1980.

Friedman, Murray, ed. *Jewish Life in Philadelphia, 1830–1940.* Philadelphia: ISHI Publications, American Jewish Committee, 1983.

Gartner, Lloyd P. *History of the Jews of Cleveland.* Cleveland, OH: Western Reserve Historical Society & The Jewish Theological Seminary of America, 1978.

Glanz, Rudolf. *The Jew in Early American Wit and Graphic Humor.* New York: Ktav, 1973.

———. *The Jew in the Old American Folklore.* 1961

Gold, Michael. *Jews Without Money.* New York: Liveright, 1930.

Golden, Harry. *For Two Cents Plain.*

———. *Only in America.* Greenwood Press, 1950, 1973.

Hapgood, Hutchins. *The Spirit of the Ghetto.* New York: Funk & Wagnalls, 1902.

Hertzberg, Steven. *Strangers Within the Gate City: The Jews of Atlanta, 1845–1915.* Philadelphia: Jewish Publication Society, 1978.

Horwitt, Pink. *Jews in Berkshire County.* Williamstown, MA: DOR, 1972.

Howe, Irving. *World of Our Fathers.* New York: Simon & Schuster, 1976.

Howe, Irving, and Libo, Kenneth. *How We Lived.* New York: Richard Marek, 1979.

Hurvitz, Nathan. Collected papers and monographs.

Joselit, Jenna Weissman. *Our Gang: Jewish Crime and the New York Jewish Community, 1900–1940.* Bloomington, IN: Indiana University Press, 1983.

Kaganoff, Benzion C. *A Dictionary of Jewish Names and Their History.* New York: Schocken Books, 1977.

Karp, Abraham, ed. *Golden Door to America: The Jewish Immigrant Experience.* New York: Viking, 1976.

———. *The Jewish Experience in America: Selected Studies from the Publications of the American Jewish Historical Society.* New York: Ktav, 1969.

Koppman, Lionel, and Postal, Bernard. *American Jewish Landmarks*. (four volumes) New York: Fleet Press, 1977, 1979, 1984, 1986.

―――. *Guess Who's Jewish in American History*. New York: New American Library, 1978; Steimatzky/Shapolsky, 1986.

―――. *Jewish Landmarks of New York*. New York: Hill & Wang, 1964.

―――. *A Jewish Tourist's Guide to the United States*. Philadelphia: Jewish Publication Society, 1954.

Kramer, Sydelle, and Mason, Jenny, eds. *Jewish Grandmothers*. Boston: Beacon Press, 1970.

Krefetz, Gerald. *Jews and Money*. New Haven, CT: Ticknor & Fields, 1982.

Levinson, Robert E. *The Jews in the California Gold Rush*. New York: Ktav, 1978.

Levitan, Tina. *First Facts in American Jewish History*. Northvale, NJ: Jason Aronson, 1996.

Madison, Charles A. *Eminent American Jews*. New York: Frederick Ungar, 1970.

Manners, Ande. *Poor Cousins*. New York: Coward, McCann & Geoghegan, 1972.

Marcus, Jacob R. *The American Jewish Woman*. New York: Ktav, 1981.

―――. *Colonial American Jews, 1492–1776*. Detroit: Wayne State University Press, 1970.

―――. *Early American Jewry, 1649–1794*. Philadelphia: Jewish Publication Society, 1951.

―――. *An Introduction to Early American Jewish History*. American Jewish Historical Society, 1971.

―――. *Jews and the American Revolution: A Bicentennial Documentary*. New York: Ktav, 1976.

―――. *Memoirs of American Jews, 1775–1865*. New York: Ktav, 1974.

―――. *Studies in American Jewish History*. New York: Ktav, 1969.

Marinbach, Bernard. *Galveston: Ellis Island of the West*. Albany, NY: SUNY Press, 1983.

Mendelsohn, S. Felix. *Let Laughter Ring*. Philadelphia: Jewish Publication Society, 1941.

Moskowitz, Milton, et al., eds. *Everybody's Business: An Irreverent Guide to Corporate America*. New York: Harper & Row, 1980.

Narell, Irena. *Our City: The Jews of San Francisco*. San Diego: Howell-North Books, 1981.

Novak, William, and Waldoks, Moshe, eds. *The Big Book of Jewish Humor*. New York: Harper & Row, 1981.

Patai, Raphael, and Dorson, Richard M. *Studies in Biblical and Jewish Folklore*. Haskell, 1960, 1972.

Polner, Murray, ed. *American Jewish Biographies*. New York: Facts on File, 1982.

Rischin, Moses. *The Promised City: New York's Jews, 1870–1914*. Cambridge, MA: Harvard University Press, 1962.

Rose, Peter J. *Strangers in Their Midst: Small-town Jews and Their Neighbors*. Merrick, NY: Richwood Pub. Co., 1977.

Rosenbaum, Fred. *Free to Choose*. Berkeley: Judah Magnes Museum, 1976.

Rosten, Leo. *Hooray for Yiddish: A Book About English*. New York: Simon & Schuster, 1982.

Rudolph, B. G. *From a Minyan to a Community: A History of the Jews of Syracuse*. Syracuse, NY: Syracuse University Press, 1970.

Sanders, Ronald. *The Downtown Jews: Portraits of an Immigrant Generation*. New York: Harper & Row, 1969.

Selzer, Michael. *Kike!* World Publishing/Straight Arrow Press, 1972.

Sharfman, I. Harold. *Jews on the Frontier*. Chicago: H. Regnery, 1977.

———. *Nothing Left to Commemorate: The Story of the Pioneer Jews of Jackson, Amador County, California*. Glendale, CA: Arthur H. Clark, 1969.

Shepard, Richard, and Levi, Vicki Gold. *Live and Be Well: A Celebration of Yiddish Culture in America from the First Immigrants to the Second World War*. New York, Ballantine: 1982.

Siegel, Richard, and Rheins, Carl, eds. *The Jewish Almanac*. New York: Bantam, 1980.

Sifakis, Carl. *Encyclopedia of American Crime*. New York: Facts on File.

Slater, Robert. *Great Jews in Sports*. Middle Village, NY: Jonathan David, 1983.

Spalding, Henry. comp. *An Encyclopedia of Jewish Humor*. Middle Village, NY: Jonathan David, 1969.

———, ed. *A Treasure-Trove of Jewish Humor*. 1976

Swichkow, Louis J., and Gartner, Lloyd P. *The History of the Jews of Milwaukee*. Philadelphia: Jewish Publication Society, 1963.

Vorspan, Max, and Gartner, Lloyd P. *History of the Jews of Los Angeles*. San Marino, CA: Huntington Library, 1970.

Zarchin, Michael. *Glimpses of Jewish Life in San Francisco*. Oakland: Judah Magnes Museum, 1964.

Index